Tonys

M000316046

Best Wishes!

You rock!

Tony,

Best Wishes!

You rock!

(signature)

Veni! Vidi! Autism!

Essays and Reviews from
Alexander Frazier

Second Edition

SECOND EDITION

Published 2019   Autistic Reality Press   Washington, D.C.

All Rights Reserved
ISBN_978-0-578-47962-0

TABLE OF CONTENTS

ACADEMIC REVIEWS

MY PREVIOUS BOOK

DISABILITY ESSAYS

Reviews

AVATAR

For friends and family,
By blood and by spirit,
Near and far,
I owe to them any and all success.

INTRODUCTION

"I am the Senate!" I cackled as I stood in the midst of the Old Senate Chamber in the United States Capitol Building. I was delightfully engaging in one of my favorite fandoms, all with the support of my United States Senator's office. In fact, my Senator's staffer was filming me and photographing me performing as Emperor Sheev Palpatine from Star Wars.

But how did I get here? My story is not a short one and is most unconventional.

I was born in Boston, Massachusetts, in 1986. Almost immediately, my parents knew that I was not your average person. You see, I have autism, bipolar, obsessive compulsive disorder, sensory integration disorder, was born without hip joints, and have a number of other diagnoses. Life growing up was definitely not easy. I was often ostracized by both peers and adults. Nevertheless, I have been public schooling throughout my life, and would gladly repeat it. I am proud of the fact that my parents strove to give me a "normal" life, including my loving brother, Nick.

My parents have always been my biggest supporters, and Nick has always been one of my best friends. It didn't matter how bad things got with bullies or misguided or abusive adults; I always had my family. As I grew up, I had a more and more steady group of friends my own age. I understand completely that autistic individuals normally have a very tough time making friends our own ages (in fact, I cover that in one of the essays in this book).

In 1994, right after second grade, we moved to Boulder, Colorado, where I went to the rest of elementary school, middle school, and high school. I also took some college classes during high school, both at Colorado University and at Cornell University. In fifth grade, I gave my first speech to lieutenant governor of Colorado. In middle school, I became involved in disability rights politics for the first time, testifying twice before the state legislature to increase the budget for special education.

Nonetheless, things could still be tough, and after high school when we moved to Ithaca, New York, I was bullied horribly in community college. My support network, for whom I am very thankful, told me I had to get out of there, and I got my act together and graduated. I moved to Buffalo, New York, and went to the State University of New York at Buffalo as an undergraduate student in political science and a graduate student in disability studies.

During that time, I became involved in disability rights politics again, serving in the 2011 class of interns for the American Association of People with Disabilities (AAPD). Through that group, I got connected with a number of other wonderful programs and organizations, such as VSA — the international organization on arts and disability, the National Council on Independent Living (NCIL), the United States Business Leadership Network (USBLN), and more.

My time since then has been spent tirelessly advocating for the disability population, and humanity as a whole. I have given speeches, lobbied legislators, mentored others with and without disabilities, and helped provide guidance. In the midst of all this, I founded my own advocacy organization, Autistic Reality, and published my first booklet, Without Fear: The First Autistic Superhero.

Finally, after graduating with my masters in disability studies, I moved to the Washington, DC area. I have since been involved with disability rights on a national level, being privileged to work with such individuals and organizations as the Obama White House, Senator Chris Van Hollen, the Lights! Camera! Access! 2.0 disability and media symposium, the United States Department of Education, and many more. I have given speeches in front of the United States Capitol, written this new book, appeared at comicons, done business with Marvel Comics, hosted conferences and symposia, and started work for an international advertising firm.

I have collected a number of essays, reviews, and other thoughts. Some of them are a few years old, some of them are very, very recent. They are published in this book. My goal is to inspire you, and give you hope for the future. I can only hope that these essays inform you, and make you feel worthy.

Life can have its downsides at times. It can seem disheartening at moments. Yet everything has the potential to work out for an optimal outcome. You have to believe in yourself and find others who believe in you as well. You are capable of anything you put your mind to. My family motto is "Je suis prest", which means "I am ready". I am ready for what the future may bring. And, I hope that after reading this work you may be better prepared as well.

Warm regards,
Alec Frazier

ACADEMIC REVIEWS

A Hunger For Information

The President's House: A History by William Seale is considered by many to be the definitive go-to source on the social history of the White House, the home of America's presidents. Seale has made a career for himself as the historian for the White House Historical Association. He has authored a great number of books on the White House in addition to The President's House. What is telling of his regard in the matter of America's executive mansion is that almost all of his books are the official accounts of record.

Now, let us engage history!

William Seale is a graduate of two universities. He acquired a Bachelors of Arts at Southwestern University in 1961, acquired a Master of Arts from Duke University in 1964, and acquired a Doctorate from the same school in 1965. He has taught at a number of schools, including Lamar University, the University of Houston, the University of South Carolina, and Columbia

University. He was the curator of cultural history at the Smithsonian Institution from 1973 to 1974. All of this makes him incredibly qualified to write social histories and other works within his expertise. He has been writing books on historic American buildings and working on their restoration efforts since 1975. He is now the premier scholar for the White House Historical Association (WHHA), an organization founded in 1961 to manage the historical collection and document information pertaining to the White House. Arguably the highlight of Seale's career was in 1995, when he was invited by President Bill Clinton and First Lady Hillary Clinton to take part in a sweeping redecoration of the main ceremonial room in the White House, the Blue Room, using his expertise in history of that house to guide the artistic efforts.

William Seale's The President's House: A History is at its very heart a social history. It traces societal evolutions in the United States and to a limited degree the world and how they have been reflected by the history of the White House. Seale begins with the foundation of the United States of America, and reflects upon the search for a proper capital city in the home for the nation's new executive, the President of the United States. He then focuses on the construction of the executive mansion, its early occupants, and the horrible fire set by the British during the War of 1812. After this point, Seale demonstrates great skill in describing the first true decoration of the house by presidents such as James Monroe and Andrew Jackson. Seale uses his considerable talent in describing the 19th century in the White House, under a plethora of presidents. He attracts our interest when describing how Victorian attitudes contributed to, and occasionally detracted from, the declaration of the house. Upon describing the myriad of changes to the house in the 20th century, William Seale proves himself up to the task. He describes the sweeping renovations under Theodore Roosevelt, Franklin Roosevelt, and Harry Truman as if he were writing a great novel. He is also incredibly sensitive to the personal stories of the occupants of the White House, as well as those others who have left a great impact on this famous property. Seale takes great care to report the factual events, and presents opinions as points of view, not the definite truth. He describes the events in the lives of the presidents and how they had great impact on the social history of America's most famous home. Seale comes out with a new edition of The Presidents House every few years, taking time to report on the most recent caretakers of the White House. The President's House uses as its sources practically every piece of information about the White House under the sun. Seale uses a great variety of material for inspiration, including but not limited to books, correspondence, architectural drawings, inventories, official records, and other more informal records on the history of the house.

The White House: An Illustrated Architectural History by Patrick Phillips-Schrock is very much a fan endeavor. Phillips-Schrock is an extreme fan of White House history from Iowa who has joined many fan endeavors for discussing and critiquing the house in question. He especially focuses on the architectural and decorative history of the mansion, having acquired a great deal of input from other historians, both amateur and professional.

His methods in discussing the White House in his book focus entirely on architectural and decorative history, down to the placement of particular items of furniture. He employs a great number of illustrations in illustrating this. These illustrations include practically all kinds of architectural drawings, including but not limited to the floor plan, the elevation, the cross-section, among others. What is noteworthy is that Phillips-Schrock has made the vast majority of these renderings himself, with the aid of his research. With these illustrations, Phillips-Schrock tells of the impact on the social history of the house that the architecture of the same has had. He devotes chapters to each era in the history of the mansion, and also includes a number of appendices on specific architectural spaces or items of note. Phillips-Schrock uses a great variety of sources, including the works by William Seale himself. Other sources include period newspaper articles, government surveys, magazine articles, scholarly papers, books, and a seemingly unlimited supply of time and energy for investigating these resources.

Phillips-Schrock has told a story extremely strong in imagery, both metaphorical and visual, and focuses on architectural detail more than many would think possible. He tells the story of a home and an office that has grown to adapt to the social, diplomatic, and business needs demanded of it. On the downside, it seems as if Phillips-Schrock has provided more detail than the typical layman could understand. His book is, indeed, a specialty book that is well beloved, but by a very intensely curious portion of the population. Of course, the biggest issue with the book is that it is an architectural history first, and uses that architecture to tell the story of American society over the ages as exemplified by its elected leaders.

Phillips-Schrock does not hide his opinion on William Seale, calling him "the respected authority on the social history of the White House". (Phillips-Schrock, 4). In fact, he calls Seale's book The President's House "the definitive account of the White House". (Phillips-Schrock, 186). A great many of the architectural changes in the house over the years, and their relevance to American society, are covered in The President's House. Phillips-Schrock has taken Seale's account of these changes, and given the blow-by-blow report of them, along with illustrations. Of course, Seale is not Phillips-Schrock's only source, but he is by and large the one of seminal value.

Dream House: The White House as an American Home by Ulysses Grant Dietz and Sam Watters is a review of the life of America's executive mansion in the context of other American homes in the eras in which it has existed, and how its roles as a home and home office have changed it over time. The book smartly points out that the White House was quite large for the time in which it was constructed, but lost that role to opulent Gilded Age mansions around the turn of the 20th century. Dream House further points out that much of the decorating and refurbishing of the White House was and often still is carried out upon the personal initiative of its occupants, mostly the first lady although sometimes the president himself. The book does include a sizable number of architectural drawings, but that is not its primary focus. As a result, a great deal of the other illustrations are photographs, portraits, paintings, and other renderings of both people and locations. <u>Dream House</u> relies on many sources, including books, articles, and other written sources on the White House. It is interesting to note that it actually does not rely very much on records such as surveys, inventories, and letters.

The approach of studying the White House as an American home over time is a novel one, and is definitely a strong selling point. This book appeals to everyone's curiosity by treating the president and his family as Americans living their lives and analyzing them as such. One can easily follow their way through the book, learning about how the lives and work of the presidents have caused this famous home to evolve. The weakest point of <u>Dream House</u> is that it cannot seem to decide what it wants to be. Although it is best described as a social history, it does not describe itself as such. It is definitely not an architectural history, since it focuses more on the aforementioned social issues.

Dietz said Watters certainly have respect for William Seale, although their respect for him is not overreaching, but just stating the fact. In the notes portion of their book, they mention that <u>The President's House</u> is "an essential source of information on the White House". They also note that the used The President's House as a reference repeatedly throughout their own book, mainly for dates and specific details on interior decoration. So, while they do not rely on Seale as heavily as some, they do make known the invaluable contributions he has had on their book. (Dietz and Watters, 279)

Bette C Monkman has worked with the White House curator's office since 1967, during the Lyndon Johnson administration.

Although she is no longer formally employed by them, she continues to work very closely on exhibits, books, and the White House itself given that the White House is not only an office and residence, but a Museum of American history. The White House: It's Historic Furnishings & First Families is Monkman's most acclaimed book, and profiles the collections of the White House as a Museum of American history. Along the way, it profiles several of the historic personalities and events that have shaped this collection. The addition of each item to the collection tells the story not only of the item's various owners, but also of the presidents who purchased them. In addition, the trends in decorating the White House over the years often reflect the various individuals, styles of the time, and financial well-being of the nation over the years. In terms of sources, Monkman uses a great deal of correspondence such as letters, memos, and other personal writings to provide reference for her book. In addition to the correspondence, she uses a selected, limited amount of other writings such as books.

Historic Furnishings tells the powerful story of the nation's executive mansion as reflected through its furnishings. How one chooses to appoint their home tells a great deal about themselves and that abode. It is only fitting that valuable property is used to furnish the White House. Monkman hammers home the fact that our belongings may tell a story about us, but that the furnishings of the White House tell a story about the nation. The most obvious shortcoming about Historic Furnishings is that, although it tells a social history according to adornment by furniture, that social history is still very light. It is peppered with politics and social trends, but does not tell as much as it should about the people who have lived in America's most famous home.

Like many other White House authors, Monkman references William Seale and his writings. She goes on to call <u>The President's House</u> "definitive". She goes further to mention that The President's House is one of the standard historical studies of the White House. Monkman recognizes that Seale's work is arguably the most important chronicle of the White House, and mentions it in her preface. It could be said that Monkman is the second most prolific writer on the White House, so her recognition of Seale is of great importance. (Monkman, 16).

William Seale has written a great deal about the White House, so it should come as no surprise that <u>The President's House</u> is not his only book on the subject. In <u>An Artist Visits the White House Past</u>, Seale describes paintings by historic artist Peter Waddell from various periods of the history of the White House spanning from 1796 to 1902. Seale is only a natural choice as the author, because it is upon his descriptions that Waddell based his paintings of the White House past. Waddell's paintings and Seale's descriptions work together to tell a very historically minded story of the history of America's executive mansion. This book is particularly noteworthy because of its detailed illustrations, providing readers a chance to experience a world long past. William Seale uses himself and his decades-long research of the White House as a source.

It is a definite strength of <u>An Artist Visits the White House Past</u> that it relies upon Seale, the premier White House historian, in order to depict images of the White House past. As such, the general details of the views depicted in the book are extremely accurate. The general furnishing, decoration, and appointment of all the interior spaces is by and large very accurate, presenting us with an excellent view of spaces past. Nonetheless, there are several minor inaccuracies in the number of the renderings. They are small things like the number of panes that make up a mirror, or the size of the molding around a ceiling. However, small though they may be, these inaccuracies definitely detract from the overall majesty of Waddell's paintings and Seale's descriptions, especially because Seale of all people should know differently. In fact, he does, as illustrated by his narrative in The President's House. Therefore, we can only assume that the errors in the paintings are Waddell's, due to lack of direction on minor issues.

William Seale also authored the book, The White House: The History of an American Idea. This book is essentially a shorter, illustrated version of The President's House, except for the fact that it primarily focuses on architectural history instead of social history. History of an American Idea profiles in great detail how social changes have led to physical changes in the makeup of the White House. The book has a great deal of images, including but not limited to photographs, floor plans, architectural renderings, paintings, etchings, and other images. Unlike Phillips-Schrock's book, Seale's images all belong to various different historical periods. The book uses as sources a wide variety of other books, including Betty Monkman's The White House: It's Historic Furnishings & First Families. In addition, it uses a number of essays in journals and letters and other forms of correspondence in its research.

History of an American Idea is definitely a strong book. It uses historical research to arrive at basic and moderate truths about the architectural history of the White House, and how it has impacted, and been impacted by, the social life in that house. The only real possible downside is that it could come across as removed and academic compared to some of the other, more personable accounts. Seale has been in the world of research and writing for a very long time, and may have sacrificed some of the feeling in his works. Then again, there is generally not much feeling to be had in most architectural histories.

The President's House is a tremendously useful read for anybody interested in architectural history, or the social history of our nation's leaders. This book leaves no stone unturned when teaching us about the White House. It even focuses on small details, such as the second wedding of John Tyler or Booker T. Washington's dinner with Theodore Roosevelt, and then tells us of the far-reaching implications of those small details. In effect, no detail is too small to be covered. The President's House teaches us that in the White House, everything can potentially impact history. What we can learn from The President's House, is a possibly unlimited amount of information on the home of America's leaders. There is only one major downside of this book, and that is the fact that a two volume, comprehensive reading may not be in the cards for people who are short on attention span were tight on time.

The President's House is a must read account on how the microcosm of White House social history has impacted the macrocosm of US history. Seldom has there been a book more perfectly written about a single subject, and it is clear that other authors on the subject tend to agree. In fact, it is fair to say that as a book, <u>The Presidents House</u> has had a fair impact on history itself, since those with power over the White House's future tend to regard it as the go to source on America's premier home. This is truly a book for anyone with A Hunger for Information!

Epilogue

After graduating with my master's degree in disability studies, I moved to the Washington, DC area. Due to my interest in architecture, I stayed on the mailing list for the White House Historical Association (WHHA). One day I got an email saying that William Seale himself would be autographing books and holding discussion at their headquarters. I recognized that this was the opportunity of a lifetime. I dressed up spiffy and headed down there, and soon after, the man made himself known. I had discussion with him about my disability rights work, and he let me know that autistic advocacy is dear to him, since his nephew is autistic. I let him know about the theory that Thomas Jefferson was autistic, and how his lack of social graces almost caused war with Great Britain. I also got his autograph on my copy of The Presidents House and gave him an autographed copy of the paper you just read. I positively skipped all the way home, not imagining a better result from my scholarly dream could happen.

It did. A few weeks later, I received a pleasantly handwritten letter from Dr. Seale in the mail. The letter states, "Of course I am flattered by the well-written account, but also happy that you understand what I intended in the book." He also stated, "Your work sounds fascinating and worthy." This is the highest praise possible from my favorite scholar.

Never give up your studies! They pave the way to dreams come true!

Sources

Seale, William. The President's House. Washington, DC: White House Historical Association, 2008.

Secondary Sources

Dietz, Ulysses Grant and Sam Watters. Dream House: The White House as an American Home. New York City: Acanthus Press, 2009.

Monkman, Betty C. The Living White House. Washington, DC: White House Historical Association, 2007.

Monkman, Betty C. The White House: Its Historic Furnishings and First Families. New York City: Abbeville Press, 2000.

Phillips-Schrock, Patrick. The White House: An Illustrated Architectural History. Jefferson, North Carolina: MacFarland & Company, Inc., 2013.

Seale, William. The White House: The History of an American Idea. Washington, DC: White House Historical Association, 2001.

Seale, William. An Artist Visits the White House Past: Paintings by Peter Waddell. Washington, DC: White House Historical Association, 2011.

A Good Man

Since I was little, I have been fascinated by royalty, in particular the British monarchy. Coupled with that are my fascinations with history and politics. As such, <u>The Madness of George III</u> proves an extremely exciting work to review. At its heart are the changing viewpoints on the guilt and mental state of the King in question. Enjoy my review!

Alan Bennett's play, *The Madness of George III*, is a remarkably gripping tale of the year of madness of King George III from 1788 to 1789. It is imbued with a remarkable amount of realism, and proves what a remarkable man can become when in the grip of mental illness. Written by Alan Bennett in 1991, it provides a suspenseful, mostly accurate, entertaining tale of madness of the King in question from 1788 to 1789, its treatment, court intrigue, and political maneuvering of the time. The play was first performed in that same year by the National Theatre in London, with Nigel Hawthorne in the title role. It was later adapted into a feature film called *The Madness of King George* in 1994. Hawthorne reprised his role as the King in the film. Both the play and the film have won numerous awards, and although the play's original run has ended, it is being shown again as a revival with David Haig in the title role. Both Hawthorne and Haig have been praised for their portrayals of the King. Each actor who plays the King brings their own unique attributes to the role, and their own thoughts on how the monarch should be portrayed. Therefore, the role of the King is seen as a character study. This paper shall attempt to profile three sources on the King's madness. It shall then recount the King's year of madness according to these sources. Finally, it shall evaluate the play according to the profiled sources.

One of the best sources one can use to evaluate the play is America's Last King, written in 1941 by Manfred S. Guttmacher, M.D. The book is quite thorough in profiling the King's madness throughout his life, sometimes to the point of nausea. Two chapters profile the King's period of madness that is discussed in the play. At its end, the book reaches some rather shocking conclusions. The book claims that King George III was actually seriously bipolar throughout his life, and that the bipolar disorder simply flared up from time to time. This view has since been largely discredited by another one of our sources, the first chapter of Porphyria — A Royal Malady entitled "The 'Insanity' of King George III: A Classic Case of Porphyria", published by Ida Macalpine M.D. and Richard Hunter M.D. in the British

Medical Journal on January 8, 1966. It was this revolutionary paper which first put forth the idea that the madness of George III was, indeed, porphyria, and not traditional madness. The book also goes on to discuss how porphyria was hereditary in the King's dynasty, and the historical implications of this hereditary disease. Finally, a chapter in <u>Kew Palace: The Official Illustrated History</u> by Suzanne Groom and Lee Prosser entitled "The Shadow of 'Madness'" provides basic details on the King's condition, court dynamic during recovery, and provision for his care.. This book is the official history of Kew Palace for the public released by Historic Royal Palaces, the British entity which manages a number of old royal properties. Given that the King's period of recovery was spent at Kew, this book goes into detail about the basics of his madness.

One of the first signs that something was amiss was when the King complained of bilious attack in letter to his son Augustus who was in Göttingen on written June 17, 1788. (Groom and Prosser 2006, 89) This was accompanied by abdominal pain, and was diagnosed as "biliary Concretions in the Gall Duct." (Macalpine and Hunter 1966, 5) From the very early stages of the King's illness, officials encouraged King to take care of himself. (Guttmacher 1941, 189) The King went to take the water cure at Cheltenham, and seems to have swallowed far more mineral water than was advisable. His doctors also try to treat him with bowel purging. (Guttmacher 1941, 191) The King was quite excitable in July and August. (Macalpine and Hunter 1966, 5) The King displayed highly uncharacteristic violent attachment to the Lady Elizabeth Pembroke. Guttmacher remarks that,

"This display of affection was so totally out of character that it betrayed an abnormal mental condition, in which the King's powers of inhibition had been diminished." The King engaged in odd behaviors as well, such as running a race with a horse, asking individuals about supposed infidelity, pretending to play the fiddle, having a house moved by thirty men for a one night stay and increasing the speed of his already rapid eating. (Guttmacher 1941, 192)

Politicians, ministers, and members of Parliament were kept in the dark about the King's condition. It is true that the King was almost always active while ill, and he often flagrantly violated the doctors' advice to rest. Hives began to manifest themselves on the King's body, most notably his arms and legs. (Guttmacher 1941, 193) The King also showed various signs of what were initially diagnosed as "rheumatism" and "gout", with colic, aches, muscular weakness, and stiffness. His legs were most notably affected. (Macalpine and Hunter 1966, 5) The Prime Minister, William Pitt, held emergency meetings with the King during his brief moments of lucidity, as depicted in the play. The idea was to acquaint him on the stands of the ministers at cabinet while the King was well enough to receive the news, so that Pitt could act on his own while the King was most ill, all the while having the best of faith that he was acting in the King's best interest. During the Kings moments of lucidity, he remarked upon how his diagnosis was giving doubt to Pitt's ability to reasonably believe His Majesty's opinions. The King also clearly recognized his own madness. (Guttmacher 1941, 194-195)

At this point, the King was being treated by another doctor as well, Dr. Richard Warren. Warren was the last person the King should have had treating him, as he was the personal physician to the King's son, George, Prince of Wales, who was eager to gain the King's powers and obtain a Regency. George was quite eager to take the throne, and war and was also a sympathizer with the Whig Party, which opposed the King and Parliament. (Macalpine and Hunter 1966, 7) Upon meeting with Warren on November 6, 1788, the King refused to cooperate, and stated "You may come here as an acquaintance, but not as my physician, no man can serve two masters, you are the Prince of Wales' physician, you cannot be mine." That night, the King wandered about the castle, riddled with insomnia. At about 1:00 AM, he found the Prince of Wales and the Duke of York along with the physicians and the gentleman of the Royal household. He went to his son Frederick, the Duke of York, and burst into tears. Fully grasping the gravity of his madness, he stated, "Oh my boy, I wish to God I might die, for I am going to be mad. The King's physician, Sir George Baker then tried to lead the monarch back to bed, only to be pinned in the corner, grabbed about the throat, and insulted. (Guttmacher 1941, 200) On November 7, 1788, Dr. Warren stated: "The King's life is in danger. The seizures upon his brain are so violent that if he lives his intellect will not be restored." (Guttmacher 1941, 201) Warren insisted on November 8, 1788 "Rex noster insanity; nulla adsunt febris signa; nulla mortis venturae indicia". This is Latin, and translates to "our King is mad; there are no signs of fever; no danger to life". A diagnosis of madness would greatly help the Prince of Wales achieve a Regency. (Macalpine and Hunter 1966, 7) The King's illness was by then known to the general populace, and the *Morning Chronicle* of November 28, 1788 assured the public that "Although the disorder has deranged the head, it is not, as was once dreaded, a mental incapacity called Insanity, for that calamity will not admit of a sudden and effectual cure." (Macalpine and Hunter 1966, 6)

At this point, the decision was taken to move him to Kew because of the lack of privacy at Windsor. He lived at the White House at Kew, where every single room was aired for occupation. The Queen and princesses came first. The Queen in particular was disturbed by the lack of a consistent medical diagnosis, as well as the illness itself. The King spent the time from November, 1788 to March, 1789 at the White House at Kew. It was the longest visit to Kew in his entire reign. It was the Prince of Wales who had ordered that the King moved to the White House. He was given ground-floor rooms fronting the gardens. His accommodations included a bed and a water closet, as well as a wing for his doctors and servants. The rooms over his apartments were kept empty so that no one could disturb or overhear him. The Queen and Princess Augusta took other rooms on the first floor, and shared a bed chamber. The second floor contained bed chambers for ladies, surgeons, and equerries. The rooms for the maids off of the long dark passage were described as being "like little cells of a convent". The mansion house which is today referred to as Kew Palace was used for the Groom of the King's Bedchamber, who is responsible for all issues relating to the King's personal maintenance. Kew Palace also provided overflow accommodation. (Groom and Prosser 2006, 89)

The Queen was greatly displeased with the King's physicians, as was the King during has moments of lucidity. He had been tricked into going to Kew upon the pretext of being reunited with his family, only to be locked away from them. The King blamed his wife to some amount. On December 3, Frederick, the Duke of York (1763-1827) wrote to his brother Augustus (1773-1843) that the King was afflicted with "a total loss of all rationality". On December 5, Dr. Francis Willis, the so-called "'mad' doctor" arrived at Kew. The King commented to his page that with the Mad Doctor's arrival, he could "nevermore shew his face again in this country and that he would leave it for ever and retire to Hanover". This seems to imply that the King was utterly ashamed of his madness, and that he did not feel worthy of ruling his country any longer. Although the King continued to be lucid at times, they were constantly interspersed with periods of madness. The King had no control over this madness, and he realized it. (Groom and Prosser 2006, 89-90)

It was around this time that the King's symptoms were first described as similar to those of a manic disorder, what we now know as bipolar disorder. When the King encountered his family at this point in his illness, he was subject to hysteric fits. (Guttmacher 1941, 196) His sleep remained very poor, with insomnia. Up until this point, the King's treatment had included not much more than blistering upon the head, which he kept shaved under his wig, as well as the treatment of medicines that made him void himself and purge his system. (Guttmacher 1941, 197) In late December 1788, Sir George Baker wrote in the official bulletin the word "better". For this, he was seriously taken to task. He apologized frequently for this, claiming that his age and his own illnesses were to blame. Baker was indeed quite afraid, as Queen Charlotte was quite angry with him. (Groom and Prosser 2006, 90) By this point, manifestation of the King's disease was accompanied by a great deal of bodily agitation and talking. The King also showed great concern about his wife, Queen Charlotte, as he had been separated from her upon his move to Kew, although she resided in a different location in the Kew Palace complex. (Guttmacher 1941, 199)

Dr. Francis Willis was a former minister who is trained as a minister at Oxford University. He had a large build, and a firm gaze. At his house in Gretford, he had nearly 800 patients who were all paid at least four guineas a week for their work in rehabilitation, although some were paid up to fifty guineas a week. Dr. Willis was recommended by Gen. Harcourt's wife, who testified that Willis had cured her mother of madness. Upon entering the King's bedchamber at Kew, the King remarked "Sir, your dress and appearance bespeaks you of the Church, do you belong to it?" "I did formerly, but lately I have attended chiefly to the physick," Willis remarked. George went on to say that he greatly appreciated the profession of minister, and had always detested the profession of doctor. (Guttmacher 1941, 217-218) Dr. Willis treated the King with new methods that were considered rehabilitation at the time. These methods included restraining the King in a straitjacket, and surrounding the King only with his own men. (Groom and Prosser 2006, 90)

Parliament, as eager as always to hear of the King's condition, required regular bulletins. Nonetheless, these bulletins were continuously disputed by various factions which are developed amongst the King's doctors. As always, regency was a regular topic of discussion. (Groom and Prosser 2006, 90) Dr. Willis became the first physician to be called to testify before a committee of the House of Lords on December 8, 1788. (Guttmacher 1941, 219) He described the King thusly:

"If it was any common person, I should scarce doubt of his recovery; I have great hopes of His Majesty's recovery; but I am afraid it may be retarded by his recollection of his present indisposition. ... His Majesty's disorder is attended the symptoms of violence and acuteness. Another species of this indisposition is attended with lowness of spirits and despair; the latter of which is the most difficult to cure." (Guttmacher 1941, 219)

The King's condition began to improve in the first week after Willis's arrival. (Guttmacher 1941, 225) His methods, although not rehabilitation by today's standards, helped motivate the King. Willis was tough at times, at one point ordering pages to stuff a handkerchief in the King's mouth when the King shouted him down. The King's behavior was physically, mentally, emotionally, and verbally outrageous, and he often had to be held back by a straitjacket and other restraints. His legs were tied, as well as his arms to his chest. This was not entirely for the protection of others, as the King risked hurting himself as well. (Guttmacher 1941, 226) At last, the King's health began to improve in the New Year, although quite slowly. It was due to this improvement that the King and princesses started visiting him for short durations. (Groom and Prosser 2006, 90)

Dr. Willis was also able to practice his famed farming rehabilitation upon the King at about this time, when the monarch took a fascination with the flock of sheep at Kew, and became responsible for their upkeep. This was, after all, in keeping with the established practices of Dr. Willis, who liked to keep his patients busy with farming and other work. However, the King's recovery came in fits and starts, which allowed the Prince of Wales to continue to seek a regency, while the government was running out of ways to excuse the King's absence from affairs of state. (Groom and Prosser 2006, 90) Many of the King's behaviors were still very erratic. Kew Gardens, which are open today, provided the venue these behaviors of the King, such as the time that he threw a fit when not allowed into the pagoda, or that the doctor should be packed up in a basket, or the time when he kissed English novelist, diarist and playwright Fanny Burney (1752-1840) with no provocation. (Groom and Prosser 2006, 90-91) Towards the end of his recovery, the King read Shakespeare, including King Lear, which could have been construed as situationally inappropriate. He also played music with the Queen, she on harpsichord and he on flute. (Groom and Prosser 2006, 91) The King had always been fond of exclamations such as "What! What! What!" and "Hey! Hey!" It was during a visit with the Queen and Princess Amelia (1783-1810) that the King blurted out "What! What! What!" which gave Dr. Willis great hope for his recovery, as he had not engaged in his regular exclamations throughout the duration of his madness. (Groom and Prosser 2006, 91-92)

Regency was seen as unavoidable by January 1789, and had passed the House of Commons. It was on its way through the House of Lords when the King began to recover, much against the odds and expectations of everyone in government. Due to his recovery, "a progressive state of amendment" was announced on February 12, 1789. (Macalpine and Hunter 1966, 5) The King had a partial, tearful reconciliation with the Prince of Wales on February 23, as 1789, whom he had not seen since the beginning of his madness. (Groom and Prosser 2006, 92) On February 26, "the cessation" of the illness was announced. At about this time, thanksgiving prayers were offered. (Macalpine and Hunter 1966, 5) On March 7, the remainder of Willis's men left Kew. The King successfully delivered a speech in Westminster on March 10, 1789, signaling the end of his madness and returning to government. (Groom and Prosser 2006, 92) on April 23, 1789, services were held offering thanksgiving for "delivering our most Gracious Sovereign from the severe illness with which He hath been afflicted". Thus ends the historical madness of King George of 1788 through 1789. (Macalpine and Hunter 1966, 5)

The reality of the King's illness is not that far off from the play, although there are some key differences, as well as a number of minor ones. The play heavily follows the King's court life, with endless salacious stories and gossip being told about the King behind his back. This is actually quite unlike the reality, because as mentioned, people tended not to gossip about the issue within the King's court. A great deal of the play focuses on the King's equerries, as well as his pages. This is completely accurate, as in reality, these members of his staff followed the King everywhere. Rather conspicuous, however, is the complete absence of English playwright Fanny Burney, who spent a great deal of time at court, and interacted with the King quite regularly.

The King's relationship with William Pitt, his Prime Minister at the time of the madness of 1788-1789, is quite well depicted in the play, with Pitt doing or at least attempting to do business with His Majesty upon his rare moments of lucidity. At one point in the play, the King mentions William Pitt's drinking, but that is all that is made of it. This is rather remarkable, considering that Pitt was a notorious drunk. In fact, Pitt is portrayed in the play as a capable, efficient minister who lives and works only to serve the crown. However, this is not at all inaccurate, as Pitt's sensibilities did not allow for the least bit of inefficiency or disloyalty while on the job. Indeed, although he did drink, it did not affect his ability to do his work.

Her Majesty Queen Charlotte is featured heavily in the play, as well as the film based on the play. In fact, it is to Queen Charlotte that King George III admits that he may be going mad in the play, not the Duke of York. However, both fail to focus on the attentiveness and constant company that the royal princesses provided to the King while he was at Kew. It is true that they could not always visit him, especially early in the treatment of his madness, but Princess Amelia and the Queen were definitely there for his recovery, especially the pivotal moment when he remarked, "What! What! What!" Signaling his recovery. In the play and film, it is the King's doctor and equerries who are present for this momentous occasion. What is true is that the Prince of Wales, the future George IV, was adamant about obtaining a regency. He was very fond of spending money, building many great houses, estates, and other follies with money he just did not have. An increase to Regent, and then to King, would have also increased his funds greatly. However, George III ended up living a very long life, and reigned longer than any English monarch aside from Queen Elizabeth II and Queen Victoria. Nonetheless, a regency finally was established in 1811 as the King slipped irrevocably into madness. Nonetheless, it should be no surprise that by the time King George IV died and King William IV took power, the country was heavily in debt.

Kew in itself is a quite noteworthy estate, having once been home to a sprawling palace complex, which is all but gone now, replaced by the Royal Botanical Gardens. Although the play does not purport to accurately depict historic sites, the film does. It shows a great deal of the King's recovery taking place at an empty manor house of neoclassical, Georgian style, un-surrounded by any other structures, alone in the countryside. The White House at Kew was neoclassical, but predated the Georgian style, and was more Palladian. It was also certainly not on its own, being surrounded by a village of other palace buildings, including the brick manor house which is now called Kew Palace. That manor house was in turn surrounded by a massive park of royal grounds, with many features to delight and interest the visiting Royals, including the aforementioned pagoda. Even in the times of King George III, Royal Botanist Sir Joseph Banks was advising the King on plant collections and managing the gardens at Kew. King George III had always been a fond collector, and it was from his efforts with Sir Joseph Banks that the Royal Botanical Garden at Kew was born.

The King's doctors, including his private physician, Sir George Baker, are depicted in the play as a group of yes-men, whose only wish is to please His Majesty, even if it involves quackery or malpractice. This is, in fact, a quite accurate depiction of the man, as he only wanted to please the King. Displeasing the King could have resulted in his termination or even his imprisonment. Dr. Richard Warren only interacts with the King briefly in the play, although he is seen as condescending and eager to cause the King the most hardship possible. Given that he belonged to the opposing political party, and was a servant to the Prince of Wales who wish to be placed quickly upon the throne, this, too, is completely accurate. We have seen that Warren was a complete opponent of the King's political power, insisting that the King was mad in order to either remove him from the throne, or grant the Prince of Wales a regency. This is completely in keeping with the play and the film. Dr. Francis Willis is portrayed quite realistically. His propensity to use rehabilitative treatment, however primitive it was at the time, is thoroughly integrated into the play and the film. In the film, we even see his farm where he employed inmates as workers.

George III is still hated in the United States of America, although that hatred is almost certainly unwarranted. King George III was widely seen as the father of his people, and duty-bound. Dr. Francis Willis restrains the King in the play, insisting that he is a patient rather than a monarch. Eventually, the King gains a Pavlovian reaction and starts heading for the restraint chair once he realizes he is about to be chastised for misbehaving. It would seem that when the King was of sound mind, he was a consensual inmate. It would seem that the King, when sane, was willing to put up with almost any treatment, including but we would today call torture, in order to better serve his people. This makes King George III a benevolent leader, and a good man.

Sources

Bennett, Alan. <u>The Madness of George III</u>. London: Faber and Faber Limited, 1995.

Secondary Sources

Macalpine, Ida, and Richard Hunter. "The 'Insanity' of King George III: A Classic Case of Porphyria". British Medical Journal, (January 8, 1966): 1-16.

Guttmacher, Manfred. <u>America's Last King: An Interpretation of the Madness of George III</u>. New York: Charles Scribner's Sons, 1941.

Groom, Suzanne, and Lee Prosser. <u>Kew Palace: The Official Illustrated History</u>. London: Merrill Publishers Limited, 2006.

A Measure Of A Man

*Autism was first diagnosed by Dr. Leo Kanner, with stud-
ies shortly thereafter by Dr. Hans Asperger. Later interpretations
were made of Asperger's work by Dr. Lorna Wing. One of the most
reputable current autistic sociologists is journalist Steve Silberman.
What if Kanner, Asperger, and Wing had evaluated Silberman?
Here is a study in that matter.*

Steve Silberman is an established expert on autism. In his
book Neurotribes as well as his TED talk, "The Forgotten History of Autism", he traces the history of autism. But what do
seminal figures in the history of the autism diagnosis have to say
about Silberman? The answers may surprise you.

In his TED talk, "The Forgotten History of Autism", and book
<u>NeuroTribes: The Legacy of Autism and the Future of Neurodi-
versity</u>, Steve Silberman investigates the history of the diagnosis
of autism, and the future of the neurodiversity movement, going

into great detail about the initial diagnosis and studies of autism by Dr. Leo Kanner. He talks about the impact that Kanner's initial theories on autism had on society's perception of the diagnosis. Later, Silberman discusses work contemporary with Kanner's by a Dr. Hans Asperger based out of Austria. Asperger's work was not followed very heavily in the United States at the time, due to the fact that we were not listening to much of the opinion of that part of the world during World War II. Later, a British doctor named Lorna Wing popularized Asperger's definition of autism, while clarifying several diagnostic traits. But what of Mr. Silberman? He, too, is diagnosed as autistic. Since Mr. Silberman goes into great depth and detail in researching Kanner, Asperger, and Wing, we find it is only fitting to evaluate him by their standards. In this paper, we shall use "Autistic disturbances of affective contact" by Leo Kanner, "Autistic Psychopaths" by Hans Asperger, and "Asperger syndrome: a clinical account" by Lorna Wing to evaluate and shed light on the life and research of Steve Silberman. We shall use Silberman's TED talk as well as his book NeuroTribes in order to glean the proper information about him. We do not seek to deny his autism diagnosis, but rather to clarify the original research by Kanner, Asperger, and Wing, using Silberman as an example.

To become familiar with the neurodiversity movement, one must be familiar with the medical and social models of disability. The medical model of disability states the disability is a completely clinical, medical issue. This has continuously led disability to be viewed as a problem. For the majority of history, the medical model was followed. Disability rights advocates and activists have traditionally not agreed, however. It was only in the 1970s that a different model, the social model arose. The social model of disability postulates that disability is a difference with great social impact and is active and fluid in the social spectrum. In the early 1990s, autistic advocates online started using the term neurodiversity. Neurodiversity is the theory that differences in forms of mind such as depression, autism, ADD, schizophrenia, and others are naturally occurring forms of diversity, rather than being medical problems. In truth, the whole world can be regarded as being neurodiverse. Everyone's form of mind is different from one another.

Leo Kanner mentions that, when speaking, the autistic individuals he studied were repetitive, said little, and almost had a mocking content in their messages. Their sentences were short, as were their words. Often, they did not speak at all. (Kanner, 219). This is a stark contrast to Silberman, who has no problem speaking to a large audience, and into a camera that will display his visage to millions of people. In stark contrast to Kanner, Hans Asperger mentions that autistic individuals speak in quite complex and elaborate arrangements, often stating their thoughts in full sentences. He also mentions that autistic individuals speak as if they were much older than their actual age. (Asperger, 325.) Asperger says of the speech patterns of the autistic individual:

What draws attention is his look: in most cases, when she does not display a malicious glare, he turns into the void, does not dive into the look one who is before him, which establishes the unity of the dialogue; his glance only seems to go quickly, "peripherally", by people and objects. IT IS as if "you were not present." We have the same impression of his voice, it is thin and sharp, it seems to come from afar. He lacks normal melody of words, the natural flow of speech. In most cases he speaks very slowly, speaks a few words isolated especially entrained medium; modulation is high, its speech is a psalmody. (Asperger, 327.)

It is clear that Silberman has an awkward time talking in his TED talk, although he is perfectly understandable. He quite obviously wants to get his point across, although he is a bit apprehensive in front of the cameras. This is a completely accurate description of Silberman's address to the TED talk crowd. He comes across as very well prepared and knowing what he is going to say long before he says it. He describes everything with complete adequacy, and even mastery. Wing states, "The content of speech is abnormal, tending to be pedantic and often consisting of lengthy disquisitions on favourite subjects (No.2). Sometimes a word or phrase is repeated over and over again in a stereotyped fashion. The child or adult may invent some words. Subtle verbal jokes are not understood, though simple verbal humour may be appreciated." (Wing, 2.) Silberman also has a blank face, deep in thought, instead of a face that directly engages the audience. His tone is a bit out of sync with the typical tone of a public speaker. He stands, and delivers, and he delivers properly, but without the typical engagement of a public speaker. This is right in par with Wing's writings, as she also mentions that, "Nonverbal aspects of communication are also affected. There may be little facial expression except with strong emotions such as anger or misery. Vocal intonation tends to be monotonous and droning, or exaggerated. Gestures are limited, or else large and

clumsy and inappropriate for the accompanying speech (No. 2)."
(Wing, 2.) In addition to issues in speech are issues in motor coordination. Silberman appears to be of slightly awkward posture,
and possibly not the best at physical skill. Asperger mentions
that motor control often comes late to those with an autism diagnosis. (Asperger, 325.) Wing mentions that, "Gross motor movements are clumsy and illcoordinated. Posture and gait appear
odd (No.1)." She further states that "Stereotyped movements of
the body and limbs are also mentioned by Asperger." (Wing, 3.)
In fact, Silberman remains still and rigid during his entire TED
talk.

In terms of social interaction, Kanner states that his research
subjects avoided all contact with other human beings, instead
heading directly for objects which they found to their interest.
They often treated human body parts as intruding objects, and
not parts of people. Of one, Donald, Kanner states that, "he gave
no heed to the presence of other children but went about his
favorite past times, walking off from the children if they were
so bold as to join him." Kanner even states that, if a child took a
toy from him, he passively permitted it." By Kanner's definition,
autism involved almost a complete avoidance of all other people.
(Kanner, 220.) However, Asperger mentions the highly talkative
nature of autistic individuals in his care. (Asperger, 318.) Silberman is, indeed, very emphatic about his favorite topics, hence his
excellence at delivering an entire TED talk on the history of the
autism diagnosis. Asperger also states that when understanding
a person, "The mood of a person reveals his whole personality and only by can the personality as a whole be understood."

(Asperger, 319.) Watching Silberman give his TED talk allows one almost to gaze into his mind and see the wonderful works within. We can see that he is apprehensive, yet eager to impart wonderful information. Furthermore, Asperger mentions that, while unique, human beings have much more in common than we have that sets us apart. (Asperger, 322.) Silberman's book, and indeed, his life's work, strive to bring people together, instead of separating us. Wing mentions the commonly known fact that the social skills of those with Asperger's syndrome are "outside the normal range." She mentions that the behavior of autistic individuals in social settings is "naïve and peculiar". Although we would be rushing to judgment and possibly incorrect to call Steve Silberman naïve, his actions and interactions certainly are peculiar according to normal standards. She also mentions that Asperger syndrome constantly affects "speech, gesture, posture, movement, eye contact, choice of clothing, proximity to others, and many other aspects of behaviour." From viewing the TED talk, it is readily apparent that Silberman is affected in all of these ways, and possibly more. Wing, like Asperger, tunes relationships of an intimate level are certainly difficult for the autistic population. She describes them as "relations with the opposite sex," which is noteworthy, for reasons that will soon become apparent. (Wing, 2-3.) Wing also mentions that autistic individuals may "he may solve the problem [of social interaction] by becoming solitary and withdrawn." In NeuroTribes, Silberman mentions that he whiles away a great deal of his time in libraries, particularly those of the University of California. (Silberman, 6.)

Kanner states that this same patient, Donald, did not display much intelligence in his actions, but rather that he behaved erratically. This is a constant theme throughout Kanner's studies. His artistic research subjects would rather spend their times spinning, flapping, and rocking than actually interacting with people or performing tasks. In fact, many of his subjects were disruptive, throwing items and otherwise acting out physically. (Kanner, 219.) After observing his subjects, Asperger poses the following question: "How different, for example, is the typical intelligence of boys and typical intelligence of girls, and qualitative difference from the success of the dysphoric inventor that the pedantic inventor; the 'integrated' primitive autistic-original?" Thus, Asperger notes the difference between non-autistic individuals who are routinely focused on myriad tasks, versus autistic individuals who are hyper focused on specific topics. Wing mentions that individuals with Asperger's syndrome "have excellent rote memories and become intensely interested in one or two subjects, such as astronomy, geology, the history of the steam train, the genealogy of royalty, bus timetables, prehistoric monsters, or the characters in a television serial, to the exclusion of all else. They absorb every available fact concerning their chosen field and talk about it at length, whether or not the listener is interested, but have little grasp of the meaning of the facts they learn." (Wing, 3.) It should also be mentioned that Wing takes a key difference of opinion with Asperger on the skills of autistic individuals. Whereas Asperger claims that this skill level involves capability of originality and creativity, wing mentions that it is probably more due to a logical, literal, narrow thought process on the parts of the autistic individuals. (Wing, 4.) Steve

Silberman has made excellent use of his remarkable ability to retain knowledge, working for Wired magazine and writings at least two books and several other articles. It is very apparent that he does in fact care about his audience, and that they learn what he has to speak about. However, because it is not appropriate to speak at unwilling audiences, he has become a master of writing and speaking in sources in events which people can voluntarily buy or where people can voluntarily show up. This hints that Asperger was probably correct, and Wing is most likely incorrect with regards to her difference in opinion.

There is one other key way in which Kanner's, Asperger's, and Wing's accounts dramatically reflect Steven Silberman's life. Kanner concludes one of his papers with a terrific fallacy: "We must, then, assume that these children have come into the world with innate inability to form the usual, biologically provided effective contact with people, just as other children come into the world with innate physical or intellectual handcaps." Thus, Leo Kanner discounts any ability of autistic individuals to form strong connections and relationships. (Kanner, 250.) However, Hans Asperger makes an interesting observation. He states that, in the case of a boy named Harro, "His willful and reckless activity proves to be a little way sinister in serious sexual games with other children; true homosexual acts occur, [even] intercourse attempts! (Asperger, 520.) Asperger may be onto something. Lorna Wing mentions that, "A young man with Asperger syndrome observes that most of his contemporaries have girl friends and eventually marry and have children. He wishes to be normal in this respect, but has no idea how to indicate his interest and attract a partner in a socially acceptable fashion." Therefore, Wing postulates that it is difficult, and even unlikely. As it turns out, Silberman is homosexual, married to a man, and even moved to San Francisco due to its famous tolerance of the lesbian, gay, bisexual, transgendered, and queer community. In this case, Kanner is dead wrong, Wing is still mostly wrong, and Asperger is the only one who hints at anything remotely near the truth, even though this could be a primal tendency, rather than seeking true relationship.

In conclusion, we see that Dr. Leo Kanner was clearly very limited in his interpretation of autism. Back in his day, the diagnosis had begun as "childhood schizophrenia". He dealt in mostly nonverbal children and pictured the diagnosis as quite rare. He could not imagine any of his patients ever having a chance in interacting in the larger world. Dr. Hans Asperger had a much different approach, and saw many bright, talkative. Individuals, once again mostly children with the diagnosis. Asperger actively interacted with his patients, and treated them like fellow human beings, rather than as research subjects. He openly expresses a great deal of wonder in dealing with his "little professors". Although it could be said that Dr. Lorna Wing simply clarified Asperger's stances, she put the diagnosis in clear-cut definitions. She took Asperger's rambling German language paper and brought it to a modern, English-speaking audience. However, she also took it back to a colder, more clinical approach. When evaluating these three individuals and how they reflect the actual, modern-day autism of Steve Silberman, we must discount Kanner completely. What we're left with is a mixture of Asperger and Wing. Between the two of them, we are left with a mostly accurate insight into the diagnostics of Mr. Silberman. However, they are mostly incorrect in their suppositions that autistic individuals such as Mr. Silberman cannot have strong interpersonal relationships. Autistic individuals can, and do make wonderful, powerful friendships and relationships. The diagnostics of autism have come a very long way since the beginning. One can only imagine where they shall go from here!

Sources

[A note: the primary source, Steven Silberman's TED talk "The Forgotten sHistory of Autism", is not cited at each individual mention, since it is mentioned constantly throughout the paper.]

Primary Sources

Silberman, Steven. "The Forgotten History of Autism." Filmed March 2015. TED video, 13: 48. Accessed April 2016. https://www.ted.com/talks/steve_silberman_the_forgotten_history_of_autism.

Secondary Sources

Asperger, Hans. "Die "Autistischen Psychopathen" im Kindesalter [Autistic psychopaths in childhood]." Latin American Magazine of Fundamental Psychopathology, 18 (2), 314-338, Jun. 2015. Trans. Alec Frazier.

Asperger, Hans. "Die "Autistischen Psychopathen" im Kindesalter [Autistic psychopaths in childhood]." Latin American Magazine of Fundamental Psychopathology, 18 (3), 519-539, Sept. 2015. Trans. Alec Frazier.

Asperger, Hans. "Die "Autistischen Psychopathen" im Kindesalter [Autistic psychopaths in childhood]." Latin American Magazine of Fundamental Psychopathology, 18 (4), 704-727 Dec. 2015. Trans. Alec Frazier.

Kanner, Leo. "Autistic disturbances of affective contact." Nerv Child 2 (1943): 217–50.

Silberman, Steven. NeuroTribes: The Legacy of Autism and the Future of Neurodiversity. (New York: Penguin Random House 2015).

Wing, Lorna. "Asperger's syndrome: a clinical account." Psychol Med, 11 (1) (1981): 115-29.

Chronicle of a Catastrophe

One of the worst lies in medical history is the hoax that vaccines cause autism. This hoax has claimed the lives of many and perpetuates the absolutely false myth that autism is a problem, and not a natural difference. This literature review contains my viewpoint on the matter. By learning from the mistakes of the past, we can improve the future.

In 1998, British scientist Andrew Wakefield published a paper on how the measles, mumps, and rubella (MMR) vaccine caused autism. Wakefield was lying. Yet this lie caused one of the worst clinical crises in history. This paper evaluates how Paul A. Offit chronicles this crisis in his book, <u>Autism's False Prophets, Bad Science, Risky Medicine, and the Search for a Cure</u>.

Initially, the diagnosis of autism was quite rare. The condition was initially proposed by Leo Kanner, an Austrian born clinician in the United States, and, independently from him,

Hans Asperger, a researcher in Austria. Although a British doctor, Lorna Wing, helped expose Asperger's work in the 1970s, it still remained In the 1990s, the number of children diagnosed with autism ballooned to enormous levels, growing so large that one in one hundred and fifty were diagnosed on average. This was difficult to understand, and many believed that a great disease or plague was taking their children from them. Therefore, they were thankful for a 1998 paper by British scientist Andrew Wakefield which proposed that the measles, mumps, and rubella vaccine had a heavy rate of causation for autism. Many parents, activists, other medical professionals, and even autistic individuals jumped on the opportunity for something to blame for autism. However, Wakefield had conducted shoddy work and research, and had many of outstanding interests which caused his research to reflect a great bias. However, the damage was done. Thousands and thousands of people continue to believe the lie that vaccines cause autism. Wakefield's work, its fallout, and the great myth that vaccines cause autism are covered in the book <u>Autism's False Prophets, Bad Science, Risky Medicine, and the Search for a Cure</u> by clinician Paul A. Offit. In this paper, we will use sources to judge the accuracy and content of Offit's evaluation of Andrew Wakefield's disastrous study, and its consequences. The first few chapters of Offit's book discuss Andrew Wakefield's unfortunate study, the middle discusses reaction to that study, and the last chapter discusses the actual causes of autism.

Andrew Wakefield's study came out in the United Kingdom's most esteemed medical Journal, the Lancet, in 1998, and profiled twelve children It suggested a link between the measles, mumps, and rubella (MMR) vaccine, gastrointestinal symptoms, and autism. (Wakefield, et al., 637) Since then, 20 much more thorough studies have failed to show such a link. In addition, separate study profiling more than 500,000 children for an average of four years also failed to show such a connection. What's more, another study of 1294 autistic children and 4469 non-autistic children also failed to show such a link. Analyses of the effects over time have also shown no such association between autism and vaccination and the Canadian study also shows no link between them. (Allan.)

Offit does not mention much of the research that Wakefield had done. In fact, it seems that Wakefield, a relative newcomer to the medical profession, had done very little research. We now know that the twelve children in Wakefield's study were selected very carefully, and that many of their parents already believed that the MMR vaccine was the cause of their autism. (Allan.) Offit often remarks on the absolute amount of confidence that Wakefield exuded in his report and his efforts. In fact, Offit mentions that Wakefield personally led efforts to boycott the MMR vaccine. It should come as no surprise, then, that Wakefield had taken a great deal of money from lawyers involved in lawsuits against immunization. In addition, he was applying for a new vaccine patent. This is a clear conflict of interest, one that Wakefield did not disclose. (Allan.) Offit also covers the eventual downfall of Wakefield, and the protests that ensued as many took up arms against Wakefield's indictment. Eventually, Wakefield was put on trial and sentenced to prison for negligence. In 2004, a number of the supporters of Wakefield's studies retracted their support. Britain's General Medical Council eventually found Wakefield guilty of dishonesty and irresponsibility. Finally, in 2010, the Lancet completely retracted the Wakefield study. In layman's terms, Wakefield was a liar, and there is no link between autism and vaccination, whether for measles, mumps, and rubella or any other kind. (Allan.)

Nevertheless, many, many people still believe that vaccines cause autism, or at least have some causal relationship. Offit fills the majority of his book chronicling these individuals and groups. But what are they thinking? Let's profile one and find out. One of these individuals is Michael Snyder, an attorney who dabbles in amateur medical studies. Right off the bat, the fact that he is an attorney makes Snyder a beacon for conflict of interest. In addition, the fact that he dabbles in amateur medical studies does not mean that he is a certified medical scientist. In his paper, "Vaccines Cause Autism", Snyder takes note of the exploding number of autistic children. He never once mentions autistic adults. In addition, he does not take into account the fact that the broadening of the diagnosis over the last half-century has caused almost all of these increased figures. Instead, Snyder blames the "mainstream media" and "'experts'" Snyder puts quotes around the term "expert", as if to question their credibility. Furthermore, Snyder quotes a number of sources including a number of sympathetic books and articles. The most credible source he quotes is an editorial in the Huffington Post. Every other source seems tailor-made to serve his cause and the cause of the other anti-vaccination advocates. Snyder also goes into the argument that vaccines can cause brain damage, although not quite autism, in adults, as well as malnutrition and gastrointestinal disorders. The source this, Snyder quotes a doctor sympathetic to his cause. Doctors sympathetic to the anti-vaccination cause do exist, although a great deal of them have been disbarred. Snyder spends a significant amount of time talking about the harm of Mercury, and how amounts of it are found in children after vaccinations. This is been shown to be almost completely a fabrication, with most children having normal amounts of mercury. After all, vaccinations that do contain it have such a tiny amount that it doesn't have any impact at all. One source that Snyder cites is a 1977 Russian study. Almost all scientific studies from the former Soviet Union must be discounted without significant revision, as they were conceived by the political apparatus to make points of propaganda, rather than actually imparting scientific knowledge. (Snyder.) By the way, that Huffington Post article that Snyder cites thoroughly dismantles the anti-vaccine argument within its text, making it dangerously hypocritical that Snyder would turn it into a key source.

In the last chapter of <u>Autism's False Prophets</u>, Chapter 11, "A Place for Autism", Offit discusses the actual cause of autism. Offit mentions that autism is genetic, because "genes contained in chromosomes in the nuclei of cells provide a blueprint for cell function." He further mentions that studies of twins have shown that autism is genetic. In studies of identical twins where one has autism, the probability of the second twin having autism is higher than ninety percent, whereas if the twins are fraternal, the probability of the second twin having autism is less than ten percent. This can be can explained because identical twins share the same genes and fraternal twins don't, thus providing substantial proof that autism is in great part genetic. (Offit, 217.) Offit also mentions the 2007 Autism Genome Project, a collection of research groups for more than 50 institutions which discovered that abnormal proteins in the area between nerve cells or synapses tend to play a key role. The particular proteins involved appear to be neurexin and neuroligin. Furthermore, he mentions that the symptoms and timing of autism are widely varied and diverse. (Offit, 219.)

Research and medical literature has more to say in the matter. Offit is correct that evidence shows that autism is extremely genetic in nature. In addition to studies on twins, other studies have shown that if there is a first child with autism, the risk of a second child having the diagnosis is twenty to fifty times higher than the base rate of the population. In addition, parents and siblings may show mild manifestations of autism that don't quite classify as a disability diagnosis. These manifestations may include delayed language, difficulties with social aspects of language, delayed social development, absence of close friendships, and a perfectionist or widget personality style. In addition, the causes of autism are multifaceted, and in addition to genetics may include environmental factors. It is key to understand that these environmental factors do not refer to their being "something in the water" or some such other paranoid notion. Instead, the environmental factors mean that there is a chemical component to autism which may kickstart an already existing genetic condition. What's more, psychological experience such as stress and other tension may also kickstart the autistic genetic tendencies. (Levy,

Mandell, Schultz, 1632.)

Of course, the anti-vaccination movement is nothing new. The vaccine, the idea that one could inject a small, weaker part of the disease and render themselves immune to the disease overall, was discovered by Edward Jenner. Jenner published his findings in 1798, and by the year 1820, millions had already been vaccinated in the United Kingdom, Europe, and the United States. A few people objected to vaccinations on religious grounds or economic reasons, or simply because they felt ill at ease. In the 1850s and 1860s, the British Parliament passed the Compulsory Vaccination Acts. The first one, in 1853, compelled parents to vaccinate their children on penalty of fines and imprisonment. There had been a particularly bad smallpox epidemic in England the year before, so these laws were widely accepted at first. In 1867, a harsher compulsory vaccination law was passed. The first organized anti-vaccination efforts were launched in opposition to this law, and by 1900, there were approximately two hundred such groups in the United Kingdom. In the United States, people began to take notice and form similar groups in the 1870s. In 1898, it became legal for conscientious objectors to refuse to be vaccinated in the United Kingdom. In the United States, there has never been mandatory vaccination, for better or for worse. (Brotherton, 798.)

Nonetheless, Wakefield's study just generated a great deal of publicity. Offit covers this public circus in great detail in his epilogue, "'Next, on Oprah'". This paper shall conclude with a story from that epilogue, and lessons from that story. Offit mentions Jenny McCarthy. In the United States, McCarthy, a woman who had grown famous in the pornography industry, is most famous proponent of the lie that vaccines cause autism. She had a young son with autism or at least autistic tendencies and claimed that the MMR vaccine had caused her child's autism. At one point, Oprah Winfrey asked McCarthy what she thought had triggered her son's autism. McCarthy stated that she believed that vaccines caused autism, and that she felt very alone. Oprah then asked McCarthy how she was made to feel alone. McCarthy replied:

> *"Because right before my son got the MMR shot I said to the doctor, "I have a very bad feeling about this shot. This is the autism shot isn't it?" And he said, no! That is ridiculous. It is a mother's desperate attempt to blame something on autism." And he swore at me. And then the nurse gave [my son] that shot. And I remember going, "Oh, God, no!" And soon thereafter I noticed a change. The soul was gone from his eyes."*

When Oprah asked McCarthy to give a basis for her theory, she said that it comes from "mommy instinct". McCarthy has rallied a great deal of the American public into believing that the measles, mumps, and rubella vaccine was evil, and could take your child from you. Nowadays, she downplays this effort, but she has invested significant efforts into popularizing the belief that vaccines cause autism. She even runs a foundation called Generation Rescue, which attempts to prevent children from getting autism, on the basis that it is an evil scourge upon humanity. (Offit, 235.) As a researcher and a scientific scholar, let us state that what McCarthy calls "mommy instinct" is pure, unbridled hogwash. It is the old-fashioned patronizing paternalism that we as disability studies scholars are trying to eliminate.

In Autism's False Prophets, Bad Science, Risky Medicine, and the Search for a Cure, author Paul A. Offit makes sure that we are aware of the extreme fallacy and fallout of Andrew Wakefield's falsified research paper. The number one problem behind Andrew Wakefield and the followers of his false paper stating that vaccines cause autism is that they believe that autism is a fault, a problem, a plague upon society. Wakefield outright fabricated his research in order to push a paternalist agenda. Autism is not a problem. We are reminded of our very first research paper for this degree, in which we cited Marc Wheeler, who concluded that, "there is no psychological, neurological or genetic evidence to contest the fact that AS [Asperger's Syndrome] is a difference, not a deficit." (Wheeler, 848) And although persons with other forms of autism may have trouble in the world that those without do not, truth remains that autism is a difference, not a deficit. That is the whole basis of the neurodiversity movement, in which we tolerate and accept diversity in forms of minds, instead of viewing them as problems to be corrected. Similarly, the very problem behind Jenny McCarthy, Andrew Wakefield, and many of the parents, doctors, caregivers and others who follow them is that they believe that something wrong must have happened to cause the autism. As we have shown, autism is naturally occurring, and is not caused by any problem. Those who worry or believe that vaccines cause autism should stop worrying and stop believing this fallacy. People with autism come in all shapes and sizes. There are kids with autism, and adults with autism.

Yet most of the individuals who believe that vaccines cause autism are worrying about children. To them, we say, your child is different, yes, and may have challenges that others do not have, but there autism is not a problem, and what should stop seeking something to blame for the condition. Instead, be tolerant, be accepting, and, as necessary, be accommodating those with autism. Everyone is human, no matter of our differences. We all deserve a fair, equal opportunity in life.

Primary Sources

Offit, Paul A. <u>Autism's False Prophets, Bad Science, Risky Medicine, and the Search for a Cure</u>. (New York: Columbia University Press, 2010.) Kindle edition.

Secondary Sources

Allan, Michael and Noah Ivers. "The autism-vaccine story: fiction and deception?" Canadian Family Physician. 2010; Volume 56: 1013, October 2010.

Brotherton, Rob. Suspicious Minds: Why We Believe Conspiracy Theories. (Bloomsbury Sigma, November 19, 2015.) Kindle edition.*

Levy, Susan E, David S Mandell, and Robert T Schultz. "Autism." Lancet 2009; 374:1627-1638, 314-338, October 12, 2009.

Mnookin, Seth. "The Autism Vaccine Controversy and Responsible Science Journalism," Huffington Post, March 5, 2012, accessed May 5, 2016, http://www.huffingtonpost.com/seth-mnookin/need-for-reliable-science-journalism_b_1183429.html.

Snyder, Michael. "Vaccines Cause Autism." Behavioral Disorders. Ed. Roman Espejo. (Farmington Hills, MI: Greenhaven Press, 2014.) Opposing

Viewpoints. Rpt. From "Vaccines and Autism: The Secret That You Are Not Supposed To Know." The American Dream. 2012. Opposing Viewpoints in Context. Web. May 10, 2016.

Wakefield, Andrew, Murch S, Anthony A; et al. (1998). "Ileal-lymphoid-nodular hyperplasia, non-specific colitis, and pervasive developmental disorder in children". Lancet 351 (9103): 637–41. RETRACTED.

Wheeler, Marc. (2011). Syndrome or difference: A critical review of medical conceptualizations of Asperger's syndrome. Disability & Society, 26(7), 839- 851.

My Previous Book

Without Fear:
The First Autistic Superhero

All my life, I have been a huge comic book nerd. Of course, I have also always been into disability rights. When I took my Disability Studies Master's degree at the State University of New York at Buffalo, many of my final projects were in the form of literature reviews. My favorite hero has always been Daredevil, due to his nature as the first big-name disabled superhero. When I was searching for topics of my literature review for my first-ever Master's class, I was delighted to find that a Daredevil character holds the honor of being the first properly rendered autistic super-hero. Here is his story.

Daredevil is widely regarded as the premier disabled super-hero. Created by writer Stan Lee and artist Bill Everett with key design features by comics' legend Jack Kirby, Daredevil premiered in <u>Daredevil #1</u> in April 1964. His secret identity is Matthew Michael Murdock, or Matt Murdock for short. Matt's father, Jack, raised him as a single parent and tried to instill in him a strong sense of morals. Jack was a poor boxing prize-fighter who went by the nickname "The Devil", and wanted a better life without conflict for his son. Matt stayed out of trouble, and was bullied for avoiding fights. The bullies mockingly called him "Daredevil". One day, he was blinded by a radioactive isotope while jumping to rescue an old man who was crossing the street. He eventually came to realize that although he was blinded, his other senses had increased exponentially. He had also gained a sense that was much like radar. Meanwhile, his father was killed after refusing to throw a fight, because he wanted to stay an honest man in front of his son. To honor his promise to his father, Matt became a lawyer by day, while adopting the mantle of Daredevil in order to fight for the underprivileged. (Marvel Universe Wiki RSS)

Timmy Lange, introduced in <u>Daredevil: Wake Up</u>, is the autistic (Marvel Universe Wiki RSS) son of Buford and Allison Lange. Buford is a criminal who has adopted the villainous identity of Leapfrog. He has been mostly engaged in petty thefts around the Hell's Kitchen neighborhood of New York City. Allison has been left the responsibility of raising Timmy. Buford physically abuses Timmy, and child protective services has already been called once, but they never followed up. Timmy is a very emotional child, and seems to be going through sensory overload following an incident where he saved the above-mentioned superhero Daredevil from his father. After this incident, Timmy has become non-communicative, and his father has gone missing. Timmy has been placed into a care unit, with a nurse present. (Bendis)

Much of Timmy's behavior during this part of his life has been explained by educational psychologist Tom Billington:

> hypersensitive to incoming stimuli from their environment
> ... their feelings may often be of an intense and overwhelm-
> ing nature — leading them to avoid interactions with others
> by a process of 'shutting down' or shutting out. On this view,
> unresponsiveness can be construed not as a lack of thinking
> or feeling, but as an indication of very intensity of these
> states. (Billington 2006)

Timmy had suffered from trauma inflicted by his father and the event with Daredevil. It is clear that he was undergoing sensory overload. His system subconsciously decided to shut down for a while, so that he could deal with the stress.

Many people with autism also have a condition known as Sensory Processing Disorder (SPD). Formerly known as Sensory Integration Dysfunction, Sensory Processing Disorder entails having higher than average awareness of input from one's senses. Sounds are louder. Smells are stronger. Tastes are more acute. Textures are more noticeable. Visuals are more detailed. People with Sensory Processing Disorder are often also much more susceptible to sudden sensory input. This can make life distracting to say the least, and very difficult in extreme cases. To many, this means that extremely large crowds can be troublesome. Although some are able to be amidst in large crowds of almost 500 people, if those people were partying and making a lot of noise it would be difficult. Flickering fluorescent lights and other sudden stimuli are also often a problem for the people with SPD, as is sudden touching.

Upon Timmy's placement in care in the first book, he starts to make sense of his world, mostly through making drawings of an evil frog creature, symbolizing his father, battling the superhero Daredevil. "Play therapy is an intervention often used by occupational therapists when working with a child diagnosed with ASD. Children are more apt to express themselves through play as it is a way professionals can enter the children's world. Play allows these children to problem solve by using toys as well as express any fears, anxieties, fantasies and guilt through objects." (Hartmann, 22) The reporter Ben Urich starts attempting to communicate with Timmy, believing that there is an important story to be told. Urich is aware of Daredevil's secret identity, and communicates with Matt Murdock on a regular basis.

Part of the reason why Timmy Lange's parents may have had significant stress dealing with his autism is that it was recognized and treatments devised relatively recently, whereas many other forms of neurodiversity such as Down syndrome (DS) were recognized much earlier. This has had a great impact on the amount of stress caused by coping with a child with the disorder in question. Indeed, "Mothers and fathers reported more stress when having a child diagnosed with autism as opposed to parents who have children with Down Syndrome and parents of typically developing children (Meadan et al., 2010)." Part of this can be attributed to the earlier recognition of Down syndrome compared to autism. Due to this earlier recognition, people believed they know what to expect from a child with Down syndrome, whereas autism is still, in many cases, a mystery. Of course, autism is also a much more emotionally variable form of neurodiversity, which is to say that children and adults with autism may in certain cases be subject to a wide variety of different emotions, whereas this is not the case with many other forms of neurodiversity including Down syndrome.

Children who are diagnosed with ASD are very interested in friendships but lack the social skills to develop these relationships and are unable to relate to peers. The population often displays atypical sensory related behaviors such as excessive rocking, spinning and twirling in order to self-stimulate. Another aspect of the autism diagnosis can be sound sensitivity. (Schaaf, Toth-Cohen, Johnson, Outten, & Benevides, 2011).

Certainly, life is not easy for the Lange family when it comes to taking responsibility in caring for Timmy. "With the causes of autism still unknown, parents experience blame for their child's autism. Some fathers may blame the autism on their wives" (Barnes, Hall, Roberts, & Graff, 2011). This would at least partially explain why Buford Lange has had failure to cope with caring for his son. What is unfortunate is that he has turned to a life of crime as a way of dealing with his stress. Also fitting this model is the fact that Timmy's mother is the one left taking care of him. She has great concern for his well-being, but cannot properly take care of him herself.

Some other adults who interface with Timmy are also very concerned for his well-being. His teacher, Ms. Andreyko, has noticed the bruises on Timmy's skin caused by his abusive father, and reports them to Ben Urich, finally resulting in intervention by the law. It is then that Timmy is allowed to personally meet Daredevil for the first time. Daredevil displays a great deal of trust in him, even going so far as to unmask in front of him. Timmy is then fostered and eventually adopted by Urich's family.

Daredevil: End of Days takes place ten years in the future. Daredevil's arch nemesis, Bullseye, kills him in broad daylight in the center of New York City. Before he dies, Daredevil utters one word: Mapone. This one word causes Bullseye to go mad and eventually commit suicide. Ben Urich is assigned to cover the story for the last headline article of The Daily Bugle, which is going under and will then cease publication. In the course of trying to figure out the meaning of "Mapone", Urich deals with many unsavory characters and organizations, and ends up raising more questions than answers. He often interacts with his stepson, Tim Urich, who is sixteen years of age at the time of this book. The whole while, he is being followed by, and protected by, a new Daredevil, who has taken over for the one killed in the beginning of the book.

Hannah Rosqvist had interesting findings in her study with an autistic youth subject named Mikael:

Mikael also stresses the importance of differentiating between important and less important training. He relates how his parents have decided that certain things are "essential, so that you can live an independent life," such as showering every day. He and his parents have tried other things, such as learning to ride a bike, but have given up and concluded that they are not "necessary." Here, the parents are described as people who are able both to adapt to Mikael (the Asperger) and to distinguish between important training and training that is not essential for Mikael's (the Asperger's) wellbeing. (Rosqvist, 5)

This very well describes the older Tim Urich's upbringing as an autistic young man growing up in the Urich household. The 16-year-old Tim speaks very often about wide and varied topics, some of which seem irrelevant at the time. He is very emotional when dealing with his father, but mostly sticks to himself when he is on his own. There is a scene towards the book End of Days where he is successfully living by himself, albeit in a rough lifestyle, in the gym where Matt Murdock's father trained. This dichotomy between his conversation tactics, which are rough, but mostly nonessential in his life and his living on his own, which is also rough, but essential, shows that he has been successfully taught which skills are essential, and which skills can be put on the back burner.

Also cited above from the Rosqvist study is the ability of a parent or set of parents to adapt successfully to living with an autistic individual. It should be noted that this was one of the key failures of Tim Urich's birth parents in the first book, Wake Up. Their inability to properly interact with him and focus on his strengths had led to his institutionalization in that book. Reporter Ben Urich recognizes that his son is neurodiverse, and has different tendencies as a result, but focuses on the pressing matters with Tim amidst his busy work life, rather than abusing him as Buford did or being incapable of properly caring for him, as Allison was. Like all disabled individuals, Tim Urich is depicted as "fully human and capable of all major life activities," and is an individual with autism "empowered by constructions of [his] identity that [is] individualized, affirming of difference, reinforcing of personal dignity, and dynamically interpreted in the context of everyday living situations. (Bumiller, 971)

In the penultimate issue of the book, Ben Urich finds his story, but is killed as a result, just as it is revealed to him that his stepson Tim is the new Daredevil. It should be noted that while Daredevil: End of Days does not focus exclusively or even mostly on Tim Urich, this is the first time an autistic individual has been portrayed as a superhero in comics. Plainly stated, the bottom panel of page twenty of Daredevil: End of Days #7 features the reveal of the first autistic superhero in history. (Bendis)

Just because Tim Urich is autistic does not prevent him from being a superhero. Traditionally, superheroes have been defined by their differences rather than their deficits. Take the original Daredevil for instance. It is not his perceived deficit of being blind which makes him a superhero, but rather his highly acute sensory perception. In End of Days, Tim Urich is viewed as different rather than defective. After all, Marc Wheeler concludes that, "there is no psychological, neurological or genetic evidence to contest the fact that AS [Asperger's Syndrome] is a difference, not a deficit." (Wheeler, 848)

At the end of <u>End of Days</u>, Tim puts on his Daredevil costume while seated at a bar, with many criminal witnesses. Given the very recent passing of the original Daredevil, many of the witnesses believe that they are seeing a natural copycat incident. Of course, they are still beaten senseless. While it is unrealistic in this world to see a superhero, it certainly does make sense that an untrained new superhero with autism would commit the faux pas of suiting up in public:

The insistence that autistic citizens must modify harmless idiosyncrasies for the comfort of others is unreasonable and oppressive. Such idiosyncrasies often serve a productive purpose for the autistic person. Placing the burden of adaptation on autistic citizens only serves the purpose of enabling others to avoid the discomfort of confronting their own fears, their vulnerability, and their destructive attitudes towards difference. We are living in a time when many adults have recognized their own autism. Concurrent with this expanded awareness, the Internet has offered autistic citizens unprecedented opportunities to communicate and to establish relationships in a manner suited to them. (Seidel 2005)

This highlights that proper behavior in social settings is not a strong suit for those with autism, which can be considered, among other things, a social disability. Making genuine friends is very difficult, as is conversing and using appropriate manners. Indeed:

As a group whose identity is based on their failure to conform to social norms, people with autism are likely targets of social discrimination, and resistance to this discrimination is essential for participation in society. The existence of a neurodiversity movement, in itself, is evidence of the desire of autistics to reframe their social challenges in political terms. While for many autistics the social realm is explored reluctantly and viewed as treacherous territory where conventions, attachments, and mores present obstacles for self-expression, the impetus to engage in the public realm, to act politically, is perhaps motivated by a desire to create the conditions where they have greater freedom to express their individuality. (Bumiller, 980)

Of course, Tim Urich is not the only one beating up the criminals in this setting. Helping him is a girl named Mapone Romanova, who is the reincarnation of Stick, the sensei who trained Matt Murdock to be the original Daredevil. In meeting her, Tim Urich finally finds the answer that his father died to uncover. He finds out that Mapone is the name of an illegitimate daughter of the Murdock by a female superhero and former spy, the Black Widow, Natasha Romanova. She becomes Tim Urich's first genuine friend, as well as his sensei, demonstrating his ability to have a social life, and starting him on his path to being a hero. According to Hannah Rosqvist's studies:

NTs are described as people who cannot understand Aspergers. However, the participants distinguish between NTs who understand that they do not understand, or who try to understand, and those who are neither aware of this nor make any attempt to understand. The first are described as people who try to adapt to Aspergers and the latter as people who simply demand that Aspergers adapt to NT norms. (Rosqvist, 9)

Conclusion

The depiction of Tim Urich is reflective of society's view of the autistic population. He begins as an uncommunicative and abused child, needing help to express himself, but eventually becoming a fully-fledged member of society, as well as the first autistic superhero. Initially, society viewed autistic individuals as pitiable and helpless, as Tim was with the Langes. But with the new self-advocacy movement, autistics are becoming as free and empowered as Tim Urich. It Tim's autism is not presented in the comics as an obstacle or a gift.

Tim Urich's autism has been confirmed by Marvel in their online authoritative encyclopedia. It is not mentioned by any of the characters or references in the comics. After all, autism should not define the autistic individual. In our primary identity we are all human, with the wondrous shared experience of living in this reality. Our secondary identity is that of the individual, the unique person that we all are within the same reality. Any other identity is tertiary to the human reality and the individual reality. For those of us with autism, those of us like Tim Urich, Albert Einstein, Bill Gates, Leonardo Da Vinci, Thomas Jefferson, and Nikola Tesla, our lives are the Autistic Reality.

Sources

Comic Books

Bendis, Brian Michael (w.) with Mack, David W. (a.). "Daredevil: Wake Up." Daredevil: The Man without Fear! V2 #16-19 (May 2001 - Aug. 2001), Marvel Comics.

Bendis, Brian Michael (w.) with Mack, David W. (w,a.) and with Janson, Klaus and Maleev, Alex (a.). "Daredevil: End of Days." Daredevil: End of Days v1 #1-8 (Oct. 2012 - May. 2013), Marvel Comics.

Scholarly Journals

Billington, T. (2006). Working with autistic children and young people: Sense, experience and the challenges for services, policies and practices. Disability & Society 21, no. 1:1-13.

Bumiller, Kristin. (Summer 2008) "Quirky Citizens: Autism, Gender, and Reimagining Disability" Signs, Vol. 33, No. 4, pp. 967-991

Hartmann, Ashley, "Autism and its Impact on Families" (2012). Master of Social Work Clinical Research Papers. Paper 35.

Meadan, H., Halle, J. W., & Ebata, A. T. (2010). Families with children who have autism spectrum disorders: Stress and support. Exceptional Children, 77(1), 7-36.

Rosqvist, Hannah B. (2010). Practice, practice - notions of adaptation and normality among adults with Asperger Syndrome. Disability Studies Quarterly, 32(2), 1-12.

Schaff, R. C., Toth-Cohen, S., Johnson, S. L., Outten, G., & Benevides, T. W. (2011). The everyday routines of families of children with autism: Examining the impact of sensory processing difficulties on the family. Autism: The International Journal of Research and Practice, 15(3), 373-389. doi: 10.1177/1362361310386505

Seidel, Kathleen. 2005. "The Autistic Distinction." NeurodiversityWeblog, August 20. http://neurodiversity.com/weblog/article/34/autistic-distinction/.

Wheeler, Marc. (2011). Syndrome or difference: A critical review of medical conceptualizations of Asperger's syndrome. Disability & Society, 26(7), 839- 851.

Websites

"Daredevil (Matthew Murdock) - Marvel Universe Wiki: The Definitive Online Source for Marvel Super Hero Bios." Marvel Universe Wiki RSS. N.p., n.d. Web. 13 Dec. 2013.

"Urich, Ben - Marvel Universe Wiki: The Definitive Online Source for Marvel Super Hero Bios." Marvel Universe Wiki RSS. N.p., n.d. Web. 13 Dec. 2013.

The Essay On The
Publication Of The Above

After I released <u>Without Fear: The First Autistic Superhero</u>, (which you have just read), I found it in high demand. I spoke at comic book conventions, classes, and academic symposia. I was soon out of copies and decided to publish a second edition. I wrote a new essay on the first edition's publication for this follow-up and included it in the second. This essay is of particular interest to independent publishers and authors. Here is the essay.

In this portion of the book, new to the second edition, I shall profile my journey in producing the first edition of this book, <u>Without Fear: The First Autistic Superhero</u>. <u>Without Fear</u> is my first book.

In my first semester in UB's Master's program in disability studies, one of the classes I took was Introduction to Disability Studies. For the final presentation in that class, I was required to do a literature review on some work of literature that related to disability. One of my favorite comic books is Daredevil: The Man without Fear. I will not spoil the literature review, but I will point out that it has a great deal to do with autism.

After I was done with my paper and my first semester as a grad student, I asked my advisor, Michael Rembis, whether he would know of any way to get the book published. He pointed out that as it was my first literature review for my Master's, it would be difficult to get it published in a professional journal. He stated that there may be fan journals to publish it in, but that I would know more about that he would, as I am the comic book fan.

I have been a fan of comics since I was at least two years old reading Scrooge McDuck. At four, I got my first issue of Spider-Man. When I was living in Ithaca, New York, I was a member of the Comic Book Club of Ithaca, the oldest continuously active comic book club in the nation, and perhaps the world. In Buffalo, New York, where I currently live, I'm a founding member of the current incarnation of Visions Comic Art Group.

One of my very good friends, Emil Novak, Sr., is the editor-in-chief of Visions. I asked him if it would be possible to put my story in the next Visions Anthology. He informed me that unfortunately it was not the kind of work that would fit in with the rest of the work in the anthology. The work was originally a literature review, and it will stay that way. I was not expecting a physical publication; these days, it is far more likely to be published online. Nevertheless, I received a phone call a few days later saying that Emil had decided to give me my own book.

It was this offer on his part that showed me what a wonderful friendship I had cultivated.

Initially, my assumption was that Emil would pay for the production of the book. However, he said that copyright considerations had made him wary of completely financing the production of my work. After checking with a legal expert, I was able to assure him that copyright would not be an issue. Nonetheless, he stated that I would have to pay production of the book. That was perfectly fine with me.

One of the next steps was to commission artwork for the book. Emil promised to get some artwork for the book from some of his many artistically inclined contacts. The idea was to have four or five drawings. I stopped in one week, and asked whether or not he had drawings yet. He told me that we may have to go with stock drawings. In other words, he said we may have to go with drawings that had already been made for other purposes. I pointed out that I would much rather not have the book published if it could not have original art. I spent the next several hours rushing around looking for drawings from many of my artistic contacts.

One artist wanted to do an elaborate watercolor for $100 or more. I respectfully declined, because it was not what I was looking for. I asked Aaron O'Brian to do one of the drawings, of Daredevil in a heroic pose, and he agreed. In the middle of this, I received a message from Emil asking for short, immediate answers as to which drawings I needed done. It turns out that, without me asking for his help, he was going ahead and commissioning drawings for me. I would still have to pay for them of course, but I was ecstatic that he was able to pull favors with his contacts in the art world. In the end, we got Aaron O'Brian to do the drawing for part one of the book, of Tim Urich as a kid, we got Jeff Perdziak to do the part two drawing of Daredevil in a heroic pose, and we got artist Darius Johnson to do the cover. The deadline was tight, but they managed very well. I also asked Emil to make a PDF copy of the book, so that it could be made accessible to people with disabilities.

While the artists were finishing their work, I worked on layout, formatting, and overall arrangement of the book. I rewrote the ending a little bit, did spell check again, added an acknowledgments section, and added my list of resources for the disability community, not all in that specific order. When the cover drawing came in, I mocked up a layout of the front cover. I also mocked up a layout of the back cover with a synopsis and my biographical information. The last change I made before submitting the book to Emil for publication was that I moved the biographical information including a photograph of myself to the last page of the book, instead of the back cover, thereby giving it more room.

Now the book has been turned in for publication. I have yet to pay for the publication and see the final product, but I am very confident that it will turn out well. I am very grateful to my wonderful friends in the comic art business for helping me get this book done. It by far surpasses my wildest dreams.

Update!
I have been informed by Emil that there is space for four

illustrations, as I have planned. What is news to me, however, is that all four of the illustrations have to be on the cover: one on the front cover, one on the inside front cover, when on the inside back cover, and one on the back cover. I have since edited my mock-up accordingly, and sent it back to my editor, Emil Novak, Sr.

Update 2.0!
Emil Novak, Sr. has come up with a logo for me, and has put it on the cover of the book. He is currently busy working on layout of the interior of the book to send it to the publisher.

Update 3.0!
Emil Novak, Sr. came up with pricing options for me today, March 26, 2014:

1. For 100 Books the total cost would be $225 for all printing and bookletting.

2. For 250 books the total cost would be $517.50 for all printing and bookletting.

3. For 500 books the total cost would be $995 for all printing and bookletting.

I asked him if 150 books was an option, to which he said it was and he would come up with a price for me. He got back to me and said that printing and book letting for 150 books would be $337.50, and that print turn around would only be one day. I stated that I would go with 150, and for each book I would levy a suggested donation of five dollars, except for students for whom it would be three dollars. The money I would make off of selling the books would go towards making back the money spent on publication and getting my business, Autistic Reality, registered with the proper authorities. I also requested that Emil put on the front cover the wheelchair logo and a notification that accessible format copies would be available upon request. The book is now in the phase where it can no longer be edited on a whim, and will shortly be presented to the publisher for printing. Emil should get the invoice for the publishing on Monday, at which point I will pay him the $337.50 cost for publication. I thanked him for making my dreams a reality, and he said, "All I know is, you're one of Prof Xavier's gifted mutants," which has to be one of the biggest compliments I have ever received!

An Ideal Experience With Disability In Comics At ComicCon

I would like to talk you about a wonderful experience I had that ideally reflects disability in comics being promoted at comic book conventions. This is not about accessibility at conventions, but rather on successful promotion of comics and other creations involving disability, as exemplified by my experience.

The convention in question is RocCon in Rochester, New York. I had already been friends with its manager, Alicia Lurye, for some years now. This was my second year guesting at her show, but it was also my first year guesting for the entire three day convention weekend, which includes Friday, Saturday, and Sunday. I was staying with a friend who is a local advocate for people with traumatic brain injuries. At the convention itself, I was representing my firm, *Autistic Reality*, and selling my book, <u>Without Fear: The First Autistic Superhero</u>, as well as the first anthology for Visions Comic Art Group, for which I am the publicist.

After I got to the show, Alicia easily found me a table that was right in the middle of passenger traffic, but still off to the side of the room so that I would get little breathers here and there. Countless other creators were there, including my friend Liz Prichard, who has also created autism-related work.

Later in the day on Friday, I chose to get the autographs of two of the main guests while the lines were still short. I am a lifelong fan of Star Trek, so I went to get their autographs. I am in possession of the 40th anniversary book for Star Trek. In this book I got the autographs of two key Star Trek actresses. The first is Nichelle Nichols, who played Communications Officer Uhura on the original series of Star Trek. More on her later. The second is Marina Sirtis, who played Counselor Troi on Star Trek: The Next Generation. I grew up watching her in the late 80s and early 90s.

I was scheduled to give a talk the next day, Saturday, so I arrived in costume as the character from my book, Tim Urich, the second Daredevil. My version of the costume was based off of the recent costume of the first Daredevil, Matt Murdock, who had taken to fighting without a mask in a very elegant suit, plus his trademark billy club. It is the most kick ass costume I have ever seen! Before my speech, an autistic couple posed for photos with me, which I gave them for free. It should be noted that most convention guests charge a fee for an autograph or a photo. During my talk, I showed a presentation that I had developed for Syracuse University on how the comics reflect autism, the making of the book, and an encouraging message for autistic people. After that, it was back to my table, where I sold a great many books!

I was also dealt a swift blow by a super villain…and saved by one of my all-time favorite superheroes! The gentleman in the Batman costume was autistic, and was going on the reasonable assumption that Bruce Wayne must be autistic as well, due to his inventive nature and perseverance on good deeds. After all, Bill Gates is much the same, and he is autistic!

Back to Nichelle Nichols, who played Communications Officer Uhura on the original series of Star Trek. I mentioned while getting her autograph the previous day that I was promoting the autistic advocacy cause. Her agent said that she is all for that cause, and that I should stop back to see her on Saturday and pose for a photo with her! This photo will also be used for public city purposes by both of us. Meeting Ms. Nichols and getting her photo and autograph has been a dream for me for more than a decade! You see, she is more than an actress. She is a civil rights hero from its heyday back in the 1960s. If there is any celebrity who I idolize the most as both a fan and the person, it is Nichelle Nichols! She even took part in the first interracial kiss on TV!

The next day, Sunday, was slower than Saturday, but not as slow as Friday. It was an ideal day to explore the convention! This girl showed up in a Totoro costume that was so cute and cuddly that I had to get a photo of me hugging her! One of the vendors even had Pusheen dolls! I am a firm lover of cats, and Pusheen is just the cutest!

Before the convention ended, someone asked me for an autograph and presented a blank page, so I decided to do some artwork, provided that they could pay five dollars. This will be standard at other conventions in the future. I drew a grinning face with a domino mask typical of many heroes such as Green Lantern and the Spirit. I also drew a tie, because the tie is very important in my character's costume. I added the logo for autistic reality, my autograph, and my character's autograph.

I hope that the day will come when all conventions are friendly to disabled vendors and creators!

The Wonders of FanExpo Canada 2016

After the success of two editions of <u>Without Fear: The First Autistic Superhero</u>, I tried repeatedly to get in touch with Marvel Entertainment. Unfortunately, I did not get a response, but I realized that I could simply go to them! I did so at FanExpo Canada 2016!

FanExpo is a convention that focuses on pop culture, but especially comics, fantasy, science fiction, gaming, and geek culture. It is held annually in Toronto in Ontario, Canada. The full event lasts for four days: Thursday, Friday, Saturday, and Sunday. It has merchants, creators, gamers, various celebrities, cosplayers, panel discussions, photo opportunities, autograph sessions, parties, and more. It takes up both gigantic buildings of the Metro Toronto Convention Center in the heart of downtown.

I got an early admission along with my premium admission, so I explored the merchants' stalls in the North Building. I was amazed by the variety of products available! There was everything from Pokémon to clothing to novels to jewelry and much more. They also sold to the adult market and various niche markets. In addition, there were a number of stalls for creators to sit at during their signing sessions, and an area for photo ops.

Afterwards, I went to the South Building and bought my autograph ticket for Stan "The Man" Lee. Stan Lee is the most influential person in comic book history, having created or cocreated a seemingly infinite number of titles including but not limited to Spider-Man, Daredevil, the Hulk, the Avengers, the Fantastic Four, the X-Men, and much, much, much, more. All of his work has been for my favorite brand, Marvel Comics. I have been trying to meet Stan Lee all my life. This was his last show ever, as he has worked in the field of comics and creativity since the 1930s, and is ninety-three years old. I also bought a photo opportunity with him ahead of time. Nonetheless, the lines to see him are infamously long. In fact, legendary cartoonist Fred Hembeck once even did an award-winning comic about the lengthy line to meet Stan Lee!

The next day, Friday, I spent most of my day in the South Building. I repeatedly went to the line for Stan Lee's autographs, only to be told that it was too long, and that I should come back later. Later on, I had a private autograph session with Joe Quesada. Whereas Stan Lee is the most influential person in the history of comics, Joe Quesada most likely has the most decision-making power in the current world of comic books and related media. He is an artist and a writer for Marvel Comics who was their editor-in-chief for fifteen years. He has both written and illustrated a number of Daredevil comics, and before I went to his autograph session, I bought a packaged action figure for him to autograph. When I met him, I raised the point that I had done a book on the first autistic superhero from the Daredevil comics. For those of you who do not know, the book is called Without Fear:The First Autistic Superhero, and it is copyrighted with the Library of Congress. I mentioned this to Quesada, and gave him a copy. He asked if I had been in touch with the character's creator, Brian Michael Bendis, or the current editor of the Daredevil comics, Sana Amanat. I mentioned that I had tried, but that I hadn't managed to get in touch with them. Quesada said that he would make sure they get in touch with me, and asked for my info. He said that Marvel was interested in working with me about the character I profile in my book. My heart soared! I had never in my wildest dreams expected an answer that good!

After my autograph session with Joe Quesada on Friday, I went back to the Stan Lee line one last time. I was told that he had finished autographing for the day, and I knew how busy he would be on Saturday, and that it would be nearly impossible to get an autograph. I negotiated with The Man's handlers, until I was allowed backstage to see him. The spry nonagenarian greeted me, and I told him, "You mean the world to me." He said, "I'd better!" It was totally awesome to see that, despite his advanced age, his wit has survived. I shook his hand, he signed his autograph, and I gave him a copy of my book. He promised to read it when he gets home! This is a very big deal for me!

The next day, Saturday, was the busiest day at the show. People were packed wall-to-wall, and the crowds were so intense that it was in large part physically impossible to truly admire creators, art, or merchants. I am amazed that anyone got any business done! There was a booth for Showcase, which is what the Canadians call Showtime, the pay-per-view media channel with a great deal of interesting content. That booth was set up to resemble a dining scene from the show *Outlander*, a historical fiction/fantasy based on the lives of Scottish Highlanders in the 1700s. What is extremely noteworthy about *Outlander* is that the books and show are about my family, the Clan Fraser of Lovat. I took several photos of their set up, although it was difficult because of the massive crowds.

Later on, I went to a question and answer session with Joe Quesada and asked him about a comic he illustrated and wrote for Daredevil entitled <u>Daredevil: Father</u>. Much to my surprise, Quesada teared up as I asked him about his inspiration and influences for Father. It turns out that he wrote the entire comic as he was staying with his dying father in the hospital. A few days later, his father passed away. There is a scene in <u>Daredevil: Father</u> in which Battlin' Jack Murdock hugs his son, the young Matt Murdock. This was meant to be a symbol of affection between Joe Quesada and his daughter, showing that the love of the generations continues. That night, I went to dinner with some fellow *Outlander* fans and made some new friends!

On Sunday, I had my photo taken with Charlie Cox, the actor who plays Matt Murdock/Daredevil in the Netflix series about that hero. He is such a nice man, and asked my name. Because he is British, Alec is a much more common name for him to understand. I then had a photo taken with Stan Lee. The machine that scanned the tickets broke down, and he went to the restroom. When he came back, I was ready for my photo, and he said, "Let the WONDER commence!" The emphasis was his, and I was extremely gleeful to see that the sense of fun and enjoyment that The Man shows about his celebrity and his work is completely genuine. I told him I enjoy his work tremendously, and he said, "That's wonderful!" and you could tell that he was also completely genuine about that statement! Afterwards, I went to have Charlie Cox sign his autograph, and he continued being an absolute gentleman. I told him that his work meant a lot to me, because I work in disability rights advocacy. He said, "You do wonderful work. God bless you."

It should be noted that my favorite comic is Daredevil due to its strong disability themes. Daredevil's alter ego, Matt Murdock, is a blind lawyer whose senses were heightened in the same accident that took his sight. In addition, the person who became daredevil after Matt Murdock passed away, Tim Urich, is the first properly rendered autistic superhero in history. As I have mentioned, I have done a copyrighted book about Tim's disability, and how it reflects the evolution of common conceptions of autism. At the 2016 spring show of Buffalo Comicon, I bought a painting of Daredevil by Tyler Wrobel of Under the Hood Artists based out of Buffalo, New York. The painting is based on the opening to the Netflix show, and is done in red oil paint. Tyler signed the work in the bottom right corner, also in red oil paint. At FanExpo, I got three additional signatures on the work of art. The top right corner is signed by Stan Lee, the creator of Daredevil and most of the other successful comics media that exist today. The top left corner is signed by Charlie Cox, the actor who plays Daredevil in the current show on Netflix. The bottom left corner is signed by Joe Quesada, who is a writer and artist who has done a great deal of work on the Daredevil comics. Quesada was the Editor-in-Chief of Marvel Comics for fifteen years, and is currently the Chief Creative Officer of Marvel Entertainment, overseeing a vast body of work in comics, movies, television, music, games, and more. Lee, Cox, and Quesada signed in black permanent marker. Having this work of art with these autographs in my collection means the world to me, and I am incredibly grateful to Tyler Wrobel, Under the Hood Artists, FanExpo Canada 2016, Charlie Cox, Joe Quesada, and Stan Lee for helping my dreams come true!

Our Meeting with
MARVEL Entertainment

Ever since the release of my first book, Without Fear: The First Autistic Superhero, which reviews the character of Tim Urich, the second Daredevil and first successfully rendered autistic superhero, I have been trying to arrange a meeting with Marvel Entertainment. Thanks to my boss and client, Jd Michaels, Executive Vice President of BBDO New York, a large advertising firm, this dream has become a reality.!

We were met at Marvel by Jon Ennis, the Director of Business Development for Marvel Entertainment. He escorted us through the halls filled with original art, and into the Spider-Man Conference Room, which contains two life-sized figures of Spider-Man, and several large figurines of his supporting cast and villains. We were joined by Darren Sanchez, the editor of Marvel responsible for custom content.

For a while, we shot the breeze about what we liked about Marvel's work, and how we got into it. After a while, I brought up the review I mentioned earlier, and Jon and Darren mentioned that they had read it. I pointed out that the autistic population is the fastest-growing disability, and one of the largest. We also mentioned that the disability population is the largest minority in the world, a fact that many people do not realize. We also pointed out some of the other successful work that Marvel has done with disabilities in the past, such as Matt Murdock, the first Daredevil, Professor X, and even Hawkeye. I also pointed out that having an autistic character in the Netflix show Daredevil for the hero to mentor would be a wonderful idea. At one point, Jd even brought out my book, and insisted that I have great qualities as a writer. This is a rough draft of the book Veni! Vidi! Autism! In which this essay appears. I had never seen a physical copy of the book yet, and we were all very impressed to hold it in our hands.

Our key mission was to make Marvel Entertainment aware of this large market. Darren mentioned that he had created some characters with disabilities as part of his projects in the past, and often worked with disability rights advocates. At that point, I mentioned my firm, Autistic Reality, and what we do, including but not limited to public speaking, lobbying, consulting, and peer advocacy. I also warned against working with radical organizations on either side of the spectrum such as Autism Speaks and the Autistic Self Advocacy Network, both of whom tend to do more harm than good.

Darren and Jon appreciated all of this information, and definitely agreed that there are stories to be told, as well as an untapped market. In particular, they agreed with me that having a character around Tim Urich's age, between 15 and 25, would be amazing as they could show personal development and growth in the character as an autistic individual. All of us agreed that identity politics have the potential to tear us apart, and that autism is incidental to identity, and not the absolute primary focus, just as I had pointed out in Without Fear.

At the end of the meeting, we agreed to be in touch, and my boss and I were allowed to take some photos for publicity. Having a meeting with Marvel Entertainment, whom I have adored and appreciated since the age of five, is already beyond my wildest dreams. I get the distinct feeling that something will come of this meeting, although we do not quite know what. This is already a dream come true, and I already know that it will lead to furtherance of disability visibility in the media!

An Addendum on Stan Lee

When great creator Stan Lee passed away, I made the following statement via my personal Facebook profile, as well as professional statements for this book, Veni! Vidi! Autism! as well as my firm, Autistic Reality.

What follows is a slightly amended version of that post.

Stan Lee

1922 – 2018

Creative Veteran of the Second World War. Writer of Captain America. Creator of Fantastic Four, Spider-Man, Daredevil, the X-Men, the Hulk, the Avengers, the Punisher, and the entire Marvel universe. Movie star. Author. Award winner extraordinaire. Pioneer of comic book culture. Unprecedented creator without equal in human history.

I met him about two and half years ago and told him he

meant the world to me. He told me that he'd better. He signed an original oil painting of Daredevil for me, also signed by Daredevil actor Charlie Cox and Marvel Entertainment creative head Joe Quesada. I also had my photo taken with him. I also gave him my first copyrighted booklet on the first autistic superhero from his Daredevil titles. A few moments after his death was made public, I learned that shortly before he died, Stan "The Man" Lee got a personalized copy of this book, Veni! Vidi! Autism!.

He got my book.

That is an immense point of pride to me. Stan has always been a pioneer of equality and civil and human rights. He created superheroes without regard to differences. It didn't matter if they were black, white, disabled, not disabled, gay, straight, or anything in between. Stan always fought for humanity as a whole.

I am extremely honored to have met this man, and immensely thankful for the better world he has left us with, and on his birthday, December 28, my brother and I celebrated his life wearing shirts commemorating his rich contributions to society. There never will be another man like him, but we can all strive to contribute great works to the common good!

EXCELSIOR!!

Disability Essays

My Coming Out Story

Pride is the contentment and wonder that results from the exciting, amazing ability everyone has to be who they truly are.

My brother and I have been known to tussle. One time when I was about 19 years old, one of these tussles ended with me bleeding out my ear. My mother and I went to the hospital and as I lay in the emergency room, I told her that I was bisexual. She asked what had brought that about, and I said, "Well mom, I saw Troy..." We discussed it further, and I admitted that I had been that way from the get-go. There was a short time of me telling people, none of whom reacted negatively at all. My father was fine with it, my brother was fine with it, my friends were fine with it.

Shortly after this time, I had my first sexual encounter with a male, and it was much more fulfilling than the sex I had had with a female earlier. My brother had at one point said, "Come on Alec, we all know you're actually gay." So, I admitted to myself after this encounter that I was gay. My mother was great with it, saying she had known from the moment I was born. My brother was awesome with it, as were all of his friends except for Carl Sagan's youngest son, who ran from the house and would not come back in. He later admitted that I had just caught him by surprise. My father was also great with it, and asked me "technical" questions that I had no problem filling him in on. My relatives were all okay with it, except for my grandmother, whose only reservation was that she did not support gay marriage. I said that was okay, since I do not support the current framework that is used for marriages in today's society. My employers have all been very accepting of my sexuality.

Being gay has been socially beneficial in many ways, such as the time that I put on a briefing on "Gays in Comics" for the oldest comic book club in the United States, the Comic Book Club of Ithaca (CBCI). I later gave the same presentation at UBCon at the University of Buffalo. I have also gone to the 20th annual Gay Days in Orlando and Walt Disney World, where the main day in the Magic Kingdom was home to the biggest gathering of gay people in history. I also joined the gay group at my school, the University of Buffalo's LGBTA.

All of this said, that was part of my time of "Newly-Born Queerdom". After I was out of my period of Newly-Born Queerdom, I came to many gradual realizations. For example, I realized that the University of Buffalo's LGBTA was not an advocacy group, but rather a social club, most of whose members were much younger than I and had many different interests than myself. I also realized that I was probably not completely gay. In terms of relationships, I consider myself to be gay in that I would much rather have a meaningful relationship with a man or men. However, there are a few women—not most, but a few—who sexually entice me. I currently consider myself to be Homoflexible. I am also perfectly fine with sex with or relationships with more than one person, although I have no experience with either as of yet.

In my life, I have only been gay bashed once, over a course of months by a group of roommates at Tompkins Cortland Community College (TC3). I got out of that situation, although not as quickly as I had hoped. I have never been physically harmed because I am gay, but I have been called very horrible things by the aforementioned roommates. Even so, that was not the worst part of that situation. I have since realized that I am incredibly lucky compared to many people who receive or have received anti-gay bullying on a regular basis.

So now you have my coming out story.

Questions for Alec, an Interview on Living Life with Autism

The following is an interview I did with author D.A. Charles at Making an Impact. Although it is a little bit dated, it still provides a fantastic, in-depth look at my viewpoints on disability rights, education, recreation, and more!

D.A. Charles:

Hello Everyone. It's my pleasure to introduce my friend, Alec Frazier. Hello Alec, thanks for taking the time out of your schedule to sit down with us today.

Alec Frazier:

Hello everyone! It's great to speak with you! Thank you, Denise, for interviewing me!

D.A. Charles: As I mentioned on my Facebook post, Alec is autistic and has a number of other diagnoses as well. My career experiences have exposed me to a wealth of disability related information, but I'll be the first to admit that my experience with conditions on the autism spectrum is very limited. I had questions for Alec and thought you might too, and he's graciously agreed to answer them.

Alec Frazier: I have the following diagnoses, which shape my life a great deal:

Hereditary Hemorrhagic Telangiectasia (HHT)

This is a disorder of the blood vessels, which gives me higher risk of stroke, nosebleed, hemorrhage, and other related difficulties. It also means that I am more susceptible to infection. HHT used to be called Osler Weber Rendu Syndrome. It is usually hereditary, through the female line in the family, and my mother has it as does her aunt. I found out that I had it after I got a stroke. I was rushed to the hospital, where they caught it on time, and have since altered my life accordingly. It was found that I had three lesions in my brain, and one in my lung. I have had brain surgery to glue one of the lesions that this is left on my brain. This actually took only about an hour, in which the doctors inserted a catheter into my groin, sending it up through a blood vessel and into my brain. I actually felt the catheter moving in my brain and asked them if that was what it was. They said, "Yes, now shut up!" I know that I will need additional surgeries to correct the other lesions. For the remaining lesions in my brain, they will not risk gluing again. Instead, they will use gamma radiation.

Hip Dysplasia

I was born in a breach birth, with my bottom coming out first in my head last. This caused, or at least contributed to my having Hip Dysplasia. What this meant for me is that the pelvic material was there, but the ball and socket joint was not formed. Prior to my birth, this would have meant youth in a wheelchair with later life being spent with successive artificial hip transplants. However, in the month prior to my birth, two Japanese babies had successfully had a new procedure done. Others were not so lucky, and died. I was the first person in North America to have the procedure done successfully. The new procedure entailed having several operations and other procedures done to electrostatically stimulate bone growth into forming the ball and socket joints. I then spent a year in a full body cast, and another year in traction. It is safe to say, that if I were born any earlier or at a different hospital I would not have the ability to walk today.

Sensory Processing Disorder (SPD)

Formerly known as Sensory Integration Dysfunction, many people have it, especially people on the autism spectrum, but few know that it has a name. Sensory Processing Disorder entails having higher than average awareness of input from one's senses. Sounds are louder. Smells are stronger. Tastes are more acute. Textures are more noticeable. Visuals are more detailed. People with Sensory Processing Disorder are often also much more susceptible to sudden sensory input. This can make life distracting to say the least, and very difficult in extreme cases. To me, this means that extremely large crowds can be troublesome. Although I am able to sit in large classes of almost 500 people, if those people were partying and making a lot of noise it would be difficult. Flickering fluorescent lights are a problem for me, as is sudden touching. Make no mistake though, I love to give and receive hugs!

Attention Deficit Disorder (ADD)

People with ADD are very easily distracted, with our attentions drawn elsewhere. Sudden occurrences or interesting objects can easily distract us from previous involvements. One ramification this has for me is that reading is extremely difficult, since I am so easily distracted. As a result, I get my school books in digital format, so they can be read to me while I am also doing a secondary task to occupy my mind. There are many teachers and professors will tell you that a student who is doing work on a computer in class is easily distracted from their lecture. Because of my ADD, being on a computer in class actually helps me to pay attention by focusing my loose attentions elsewhere.

Dysgraphia and Digital Atonia

Dysgraphia is to writing as dyslexia is to reading. Whereas dyslexia is a disorder hampering understanding of the ordering of letters and words, dysgraphia is a disorder hampering the proper placement of letters and words while writing. Many people believe improper placement when writing is a symptom of dyslexia, when in fact it is dysgraphia. This is because dysgraphia is not nearly as well-known as dyslexia. Digital Atonia is a lack of muscle development in the hands leading to poor eye-brain-hand coordination. To counter my dysgraphia and digital atonia, I dictate papers on Dragon NaturallySpeaking software provided by the Nuance Corporation. I am able to train it to recognize my voice, and I am able to speak to it naturally, while it transcribes my speech on various programs such as Microsoft Word or Facebook.

Bipolar Disorder

Bipolar disorder used to be called manic depression. It is not called that anymore, but unfortunately many people do not recognize this fact. Bipolar disorder entails having periods of high, happy feelings, and periods of low, unhappy feelings. People have a right not to take medication, and I am against radical amounts of medication. But for me, moderate amounts of medication have helped with a number of my diagnoses, including the high-low swings of bipolar disorder.

Obsessive-Compulsive Disorder (OCD)

Obsessive-Compulsive Disorder or OCD is about exactly that: obsessions with particular topics and compulsions to do specific things. There is a misconception that OCD is almost completely about the compulsion part. This is not true. For me, my obsessions involve focusing in detail on various topics, such as architecture, government, photography, and Star Trek. You'll notice that these obsessions are also hobbies. In my world, if I am going to have obsessions, then they might as well be fun! For me, compulsions have been about such things as straightening out the cricks in my neck and doing things favoring the right side of my body.

Asperger's Syndrome

Asperger's Syndrome, which is a form of Autism, is not a disorder but a form of neurodiversity. Neurodiversity is a recognized form of diversity, entailing diversity of the forms of the mind. It is as natural as diversity of skin color and sexual orientation. It is also inherent as is gender and religious affiliation. Asperger's Syndrome is a form of autism which is no longer officially recognized by the diagnostic index, but it should be. Instead, all formerly recognized forms of autism are lumped together under the title Autism Spectrum Disorder (ASD). In reality, there are vast differences between various types of autism. Asperger's Syndrome has traditionally been called a high functioning form of autism. Those of us in the autistic rights movements are trying to reject the terms high and low functioning as those terms have their origins in the institutional setting where they were used to discriminate against various types of patients. Instead of using the terms high and low functioning, people should just describe the person in question. Like people with all forms of autism, people with Asperger's Syndrome, I have a tough time interacting socially, and can have mood swings and a degree of emotional variation from time to time. Over the 28 years of my life, I had become to a large degree able to socialize with other people in a structured setting. Therefore, I have a tendency to find friends in clubs and organizations of like-minded people. Interpersonal relationships between myself and other individuals tend to be more difficult. I do get pretty emotional at times, but I do my best to keep this in check on a social level.

D.A. Charles: I made Alec's acquaintance through a common bond. We were both readers of "Little Green and Easy Bella," a Twilight Fanfiction story written by our mutual friend, Betti Gefecht.

Alec Frazier: I adore "Little Green," he's an endearing character with multiple layers, one of those layers being autism. When I read the story I felt like I was seeing the world through his eyes, the story is a sensory experience for me that I don't often discover reading fiction. I can't describe it other than to say it is just so much more...

D.A. Charles: Alec, what drew you to Little Green?

Alec Frazier: I was drawn to Little Green for a number of reasons. Betti lives in Germany, a nation that I adore in part because my mother is from that land. I also enjoy that country because of its liberal political, economic, and social tradition, as well as all of the wonderful culture and history in that nation. Betti is also very creative, quite artistically inclined, and very loving. She is also very crazy, in a good way! After all, you have to be crazy to live on this planet! When I started reading her fiction, Betti said that she had never met a person with autism, but had heard a great deal about it. This is interesting, because I am sure that a majority of the Western human population would say this. It is doubly interesting because I am sure that a majority of the Western human population has actually met and is even friends with an autistic person. Those of us on the higher end of the spectrum tend to slip by is just odd or quirky.

I then proceeded to befriend Betti and tell her a little bit about what it is like living with autism. She was very eager and willing to learn! Many autistic activists believe that only a person with autism should be able to write about a person with autism. I think that that is just silly! Many men write about women! Many African-Americans write about white people! In fact, the best of writers proves their mettle by writing very well about people whom they have nothing in common with. I do believe that autistic writers should be more prevalent, but I also do not believe that autistic writers who write poorly should be coddled.

I went to visit Betti at her wonderful home in Bützfleth, outside of Stade, in the Lower Saxon land of Germany. Her home has been built by her husband, Liber Freeman, and she has designed much of the decoration. It even has a giant sign outside saying that it is her house! Betti used to be a quite popular musician, and has also made paintings, dolls, and other artwork. Freeman currently produces music and makes the most beautiful guitars on the planet. I spent fifteen minutes with him, and my autdar (like gaydar, but for autistic people) was going crazy. I do believe that he is autistic, and that that is part of why he is such a multi-talented creator! So, although Betti had claimed that she had never met somebody with autism, it turns out that she has actually been living most of her life in a very loving relationship with an autistic genius. The two of them have an absolutely wonderful world together! Everybody should be as lucky in life as they have been! I have since adopted them as my Aunt and Uncle.

D.A. Charles: The Edwards in the Fanfiction fandom come in many incarnations. While Betti's Edward is autistic, mine has a spinal cord injury. Do you have a favorite "fic" that features a Twi-character whose circumstances help bring awareness to others about a specific issue?

Alec Frazier: I am certainly a proponent of the way that Little Green and Easybella promotes autism awareness. Your own fiction was phenomenal in its promotion of people with various disabilities. I am also a fan of various fictions promoting successful character development for people who have formerly been bullied. I like high school reunion fictions, and fictions where someone has come back from a long time living somewhere else after redefining themselves. I was bullied quite a bit as a kid, and have now made quite a name for myself in my field. See-ing fictions where people are able to prove successfully that they have gone somewhere in life is a true wonder to behold. I myself have accomplished just that; I recently went to my high school's ten-year reunion, and many people told me that they were thor-oughly impressed with how far I have gotten since then! I also like slash fiction, since I am gay and like reading about positive gay role models. So, in short, my favorite fiction that helps bring awareness to something is Betti's Little Green and Easybella.

D.A. Charles: You recently endorsed Amber Johnson's book, Puddle Jumping which was recently released, as you're doing with my story, Impact. What does that endorsement mean for potential readers?

Alec Frazier: My endorsement of Puddle Jumping should be read as twofold. First of all, it is a reaffirmation on the part of an autistic advocate and self-advocate that the book in question is indeed representative of the real life and world of an autistic per-son. Please bear in mind that a number of more radical people in the autistic activism world had attacked Amber Johnson for her portrayal of Colton Neely as an autistic individual. They claimed that they were not like Colton, and therefore the story was hog-wash. I disagree, and would like to cite the fact that autism is a spectrum disorder with a great variety of people in it. One of those people could very well be Colton Neely.

The second factor in my endorsement, which plays a part in any endorsement that I make, is the fact that I am someone with disabilities representing the disabled population, and the advoca-cy movement of that population, giving my full-hearted approval to a book that deserves notice. I do not claim to speak for the whole disabled population, or even the whole autistic population. I do, however, claim to speak as a person with a disability, which happens to be autism who appreciates the said book, and its endeavors to represent those populations. The endorsement says that I would recommend it to others with an interest in disability, autism, advocacy, and a realistic portrayal of those things. I cannot make the entire disabled or autistic population appreciate something, because that is up to the individuals themselves. Nonetheless, I can encourage it. That is what Amber or anyone gets out of my endorsement. What I get out of the endorsement is increased name recognition for my firm, Autistic Reality, as well as a recognition that these endeavors are the kinds of things I look favorably upon.

D.A. Charles: You've done some writing of your own. Would you mind telling my readers about your literary review and why this is a project so close to your heart?

Alec Frazier: My literary review profiles the first positively, realistically portrayed autistic superhero, Tim Urich as the Daredevil of the future as written by Brian Michael Bendis for Marvel Comics. Urich's appearances take place in two comic book story arcs, Daredevil: Wake Up, and Daredevil: End of Days. I have done the literary review from a disability studies point of view. It has been for sale at a number of comic book conventions and conferences, including Ithacon in Ithaca, New York, Cripping the Comicon in Syracuse, New York, and Free Comic Book Day in Buffalo, New York. I have also given copies to some of my favorite comic book creators, including the legendary writer

Roger Stern, and prolific animator Warren Greenwood. I will be giving a copy to the legendary Stan Lee next year. The book is so important to me because it profiles a perfect example of my philosophy of Autistic Reality. The character in the books is shown as living his life with autism, not living an autistic life. A key philosophical point of view of Autistic Reality is that autism should not have to define the individual. Autism is not the main feature of the character in the books, nor should it be. Instead, the books show how the character is living a productive life as an individual, who just so happens to be autistic. In this way, the character is human first, themselves second, and the other identity, autism, is incidental to that.

D.A. Charles: You are a super hero expert. Who's your favorite super hero and why? What's your most memorable super hero moment? You do public Relations for Visions Comic Art Group, can you tell us a little about that?

Alec Frazier: A bit of background first. I have been reading comic books of some form or another since I was at least four years old. I started off with Scrooge McDuck comics, and have been reading mainstream superhero comics since shortly thereafter. I have a number of favorite superheroes for different reasons. I like the regular Daredevil, Matt Murdock, because he is the original disabled superhero, being blind and yet extremely powerful with his extra senses and his success in life. I also like Wiccan and Hulkling of the Young Avengers because they are young guys who are gay, madly in love, and save the world on a regular basis. Lastly, I like the original Wildstorm Comics team The Authority, because they actually get stuff done. Imagine a team of superheroes who are not afraid to overthrow governments, kill people, and even take over the United States in order to create a better world. It's kind of messed up, but it makes for a very interesting read. Please keep in mind that that title is not fit for children.

I have two most memorable superhero moments. The first one took place back in 1992, when the superhero Northstar said the words "I am gay!" becoming the first ever superhero to come out of the closet as homosexual. This was courageous, as only a few years earlier it was illegal to do this. There have since been a number of superheroes who have come out as homosexual, bisexual, transsexual, and many other sexual orientations. Northstar himself has gotten married in the meantime.

The second moment was in *Daredevil: End of Days #7,* which premiered on April 17, 2013. In it, the Daredevil of the future takes off his mask, revealing that he is the autistic Tim Urich. It is a watershed moment in comics. In the 1980s, there was an autistic character named Dehman Doosha, also known as Jonny Do, in a team called Psi-Force put out by Marvel Comics. However, the character's autism was not portrayed correctly at all, and it can be argued therefore that he did not have autism at all. Tim Urich is the very first character to be properly and positively portrayed with autism.

As I mentioned, I have always been involved with comics. In 2004 or 2005, I joined the oldest continuously active comic book club in the country, and possibly the world, the Comic Book Club of Ithaca (CBCI), in Ithaca, New York. I started cohosting a number of their conventions, and when I moved to Buffalo,

I started cohosting Buffalo Comicon. I also take a number of photos at those conventions. There is a multitalented genius of a businessman in Buffalo, New York named Emil Novak, Sr. He runs Queen City Bookstore, the local comic book store, and he also runs Buffalo Comicon. In the 1980s, he started a group called Visions Comic Art Group, a group of local artists, writers, and other artistic talent to create comics right here in Buffalo. He recently restarted the group in its current incarnation. I have been privileged to be their official publicist and photographer from the beginning of the current incarnation. We have since put out an anthology over one hundred pages long, and will be coming out with another one in October. They have also helped me with the printing of my book. I owe a lot to Emil Novak, Sr. for mentoring me through the creative process.

D.A. Charles: Patti has asked- If your life was a movie, what actor would portray you and why?

Alec Frazier: I would probably go with having Jude Law play me. His hair is naturally similar to mine, although he often wears a hairpiece for his roles. He is also not averse to packing on the pounds for a role. If he could do that the same way that Christian Bale did for American Hustle, that would be great. Jude Law is also known for intellectual roles, of which my life certainly would fit the bill. Yes, he is over a decade older me, but I would want the majority of my movie to be set ten years from now, when I am more established. He also does very well with glasses. In fact, he played Karenin in Anna Karenina, which if you subtract the beard, resembles an older me quite well. However, I am not only intellectual, but also a very fun person with a great sense of humor and a number of quirks. If the movie were to take place about thirty years down the road, I would have preferred for the late James Gandolfini to have the role. Although Jude Law best embodies me as an intellectual, Gandolfini would be best playing me as a fun guy. Overall, I would probably want Christopher Heyerdahl to narrate the story of my life in the voice of Marcus of the Volturi from Twilight. The life he would be narrating would probably not fit that voice, but there is so much authority in Marcus's tone that I demand it!

D.A. Charles: I've heard that you're quite the globe trotter. Do you have a favorite place you'd go to again and again if you could? Someplace you've never been but would love to see? Is there someplace you've visited that would be an ideal travel destination for a family who has a member that is autistic?

Alec Frazier: I would love to go to Walt Disney World over and over again! I have already been there four times. They keep on adding new things, and soon they will have a land dedicated to James Cameron's Avatar, which I am looking forward to a great deal! I would love to go back to Rome, London, Paris, Berlin, Florence, Venice, and a number of other places now that I have a proper camera. In terms of places I have not gone before in my life, I would like to go to Vienna and Prague. There are a number of other places that I would be interested in, such as Bavaria, St. Petersburg, Russia, and Moscow, Russia. I am not going to go to Russia until they rescind their horrible laws against homosexuality. I would also like to go to Amsterdam and The Hague, as well as Madrid. When I travel somewhere, I go to take photographs, as well as enjoy the beautiful architecture. Landscaping is also something I enjoy tremendously. I also collect capital buildings, and would love to visit more of them!

For a family with an autistic individual, I would suggest that they visit a number of the sites in Washington, DC and New York City, as they are known for being very accessible to people with disabilities. For example, the Capitol Building and Library of Congress in Washington, DC are reasonably quiet compared to many other tourist attractions, and that is easy for someone with sensory difficulties. Government buildings tend to be very beautiful, as they are built to showcase the prestige of the populations they represent. I would also recommend a lot of other beautiful churches, other places of worship, and government buildings for the same reasons that I recommend government buildings. These government buildings and places of worship also have wide open spaces, which is important for people with autism, as we sometimes feel like our personal space is being encroached upon. It is also good to visit universities and places on their campuses because people are often trying to study, and they keep quiet. Overseas, and occasionally in the US, there are a number of monastic environments such as missions and abbeys were people have even taken vows of silence, and that is very easy on the ears.

The Smithsonian Institution in Washington, DC and the major museums in New York City are extremely accessible because they are used to large numbers of people, and the larger the numbers of people, the more people with accessibility needs are expected to attend. The Smithsonian Institution is free, which is really quite awesome! I would recommend visiting monuments and memorials everywhere, as those tend to be quieter environments, and in the United States of America they also tend to be pretty accessible. A hallmark of disability design can be found in the Franklin Delano Roosevelt Memorial in Washington, DC, which features a statue of the president in a wheelchair, and a message on disability in braille in the main entrance. It should be noted that the disability community had to fight like hell for these features to be included. It is also very sensory friendly Memorial, with a lot of peacefully running water and tactile spaces. It should also be noted that people with fears of enclosed spaces should stay away from the interior of the Washington Monument and the dome climbs on many buildings, as these can be quite cramped. Museum buildings tend to be some of the more accessible places wherever you go in this country, with the more public ones like art museums, science museums, and museums run by national, state, and local governments being among the most accessible. If you are ever in Buffalo, New York, don't forget to stop by the world's only Museum of disABILITY History on Main Street!

In Western Europe, many tourist sites tend to be very accessible, often more so than in the United States since they have improved on the ADA to a degree that we have not. I very highly recommend the Hagenbeck Zoo in Hamburg, Germany. It has spaces that are very accessible to people with mobility and sensory impairments. Keep in mind though that a lot of cute, friendly animals are allowed to roam free in that zoo. There is plenty to cuddle with! In Eastern Europe, however, accessibility still has a lot of catching up to do. I would also stay away from smaller castles and medieval buildings, because although the authorities that be try to retrofit those buildings, they are not always very successful. I have to admit that I have not traveled to Latin America, Africa, or Asia, but it should be noted that those places have a pretty poor record of accessibility for people with disabilities.

D.A. Charles: You recently shared your experiences using various modes of transportation during your trip to California, it sounds like you had a very enjoyable trip and navigated the transportation system well. Do you have any pointers for readers who are autistic or who might be traveling with an autistic child? Perhaps you have ideas to help lessen the sensory overload of navigating a crowded airport or being stuck on a long flight?

Alec Frazier: The key for all autistic people who wish to deal better with hectic public situations is to compartmentalize. You should view yourself as one unit, and the world around yourself as another unit. Then, and this can be kind of tricky, pick and choose the appropriate times and methods to deal with the world around yourself. Of course, this leads to temptation to shut yourself off completely from the world. Never do this! Be a part of the world, but establish healthy boundaries. This is the mental part of my tip. As for physical stimuli, I have noticed a number of autistic people using sound canceling headphones, and that might be a good idea. If someone takes issue with it, tell them that it is a disability accommodation. When traveling on an airplane, it is often very tempting to take the window seat. This actually squeezes you in with very limited means to maneuver. Take the aisle seat! That way, you have the most possible room during the majority of the flight, except when the flight attendants are serving. Bringing a book along is also a wonderful idea, but cassette tapes or something else to listen to will do just as well. For family members of autistic children and adults, please keep in mind that you have to be patient.

Alec Frazier: I will not lie. Once, airport police were called on me because I was overwhelmed. This was when I was already an adult, so I calmly told them that I was autistic and having sensory overload. They told me that they understood, and were just concerned about my safety. In the case of a child, it would be very useful to have a calm, collected guardian who can tell authorities the same thing. Also, airports often provide staff members to guide underaged minors through the process. Having one of these staff members accompany an autistic minor is a wonderful idea. Many autistic people, although not all, will eventually be able to navigate airports on their own.

D.A. Charles: And on the fun side of travel, because travel should be enjoyable... You don't travel alone, your friend Millard has gone on a number of adventures with you. It appears this might be a family tradition. You're not the only member of your family who travels with a companion are you? Scotch Tapir is quite the globetrotter as well. Could you tell us a little bit about this tradition? How did it start and who initiated it? I've got to admit, I've got a travel companion of my own. There are a number of pictures someplace on the internet that feature myself, my daughter Patti, our friend Debbie Powell and a sharp dressed guy with shades by the name of Pocket Edward. Good times, in Chicago... Maine...

Alec Frazier: Ha! Yes, I bought Millard the Buffalo at the gift shop in the student center of my university, the State University of New York at Buffalo. He has since gone a number of places, some mundane, and some very interesting. In the United States, he has gone around Buffalo, Ithaca, Southern California, New York City, and Colorado. In Europe, he has gone around Germany including Frankfurt, Hamburg, Cologne, and Stade. Some of the more exciting places he has been include Griffith Park Observatory, the San Diego Zoo, the Morgan Library and Museum, the Römer (seat of the Holy Roman Empire for at least 600 years), and the tomb of the three Magi in Cologne Cathedral. Some of the more intriguing places he has been include on top of a lily pad in the Denver Botanic Gardens, on a scale in a gas station in Batavia, New York, on an original staircase from the long since demolished Penn Station in New York City, on the praying hands of Father Junipero Sera at the Mission in San Diego, and even with an eight-foot-tall flower! Of course, I cannot begin to explain all of the crazy situations he has found himself in! I intend on taking him to every new land where I travel and take photos of him with many of the sites!

Since this interview, I have met Denise, who gave me a hedgehog named Abby, who has taken over Millard's role as my travel mascot.

When my father was a child, he had a little stuffed dog named Pinky. Through a series of unfortunate events, that dog was lost a few years ago. I offered to buy him a new stuffed friend. When we went to the gift shop at the Denver Zoo, we selected a small stuffed tapir. I named her Scotch is a joke. You get it? Scotch Tapir? The idea was that he would have something small, yet cuddly when he travels. He took it to the extreme, taking Scotch all over the world, especially Southeast Asia, and taking photos of her everywhere! Buddhist temples! On elephant-back! At fortresses! Even on a lily pad—you can see where I got that idea! So, when I bought Millard, I decided that he embodied something unique about me. Buffaloes are rugged and tough, yet often playful. I named him after one of the founders of my university, Millard Fillmore. While he was the first Chancellor of my university, Fillmore also held a very important job out of town. He was president of the United States! My dad's girlfriend also has a stuffed rabbit named Wasz, which is short for Wazskawy Wabbit. Wasz's trips have been significantly more limited.

It should be noted that everyone in my immediate family has a totem animal which they best embody and is best embodies them. I am playful, curious, and cuddly, so I am a wombat. My father is happy, loving, and also very playful, so he is a yellow lab. My brother has odd habits, is very rambunctious, and, you guessed it, playful, so he is an otter. My mother is multitalented, also loves to cuddle, and of course, playful, so she is a cuttlefish. Each of us has a stuffed animal version of our totem animal. My wombat is named Lucy, my mother's cuttlefish is named Magic Fingers, I'm not sure what my brother named his otter, or if he still has it even (he lives a very wild life), and my father's yellow lab is named Joyful. I have also given fellow fan fiction writer Betti Gefecht a lemur, which she has named Fulton, and which plays with her cat quite regularly! My home is also called The Wombatorium, and has its own Facebook page!

D.A. Charles: I see you as a very strong, self-directed young man who has embraced life. It sounds like you had a unique experience growing up. In a day when many kids who learned differently were segregated into "special" classrooms, your parents refused to do that. Can you tell my readers how that impacted your learning experience? Children can be cruel. Someone in my life was diagnosed at a very early age with a learning disability. Prior to being identified as a person with a disability this person was a social butterfly, being moved to a non-inclusive classroom created a stigma that lasted through out school and with that, socialization took a huge nosedive. How did being mainstreamed impact your social interactions? Do you feel your fellow students treated you like everyone else in a mainstreamed environment?

Alec Frazier: In the short run, my learning experience in the mainstream population was both positive and negative. In the long run, it has been completely positive. As for the positives, I got to experience how everybody interacts with one another, I got to eventually make friends with other students, I got to experience the same learning and class lessons that everyone else did, and although at I frequently did not feel like everyone else, I was definitely treated like everyone else. In addition to that, I had caseworkers in the Special Education department who were very devoted in making sure that my cause was advanced throughout the school. My parents were, as you said, instrumental in making sure that I was treated with the respect that every human being deserves. They went above and beyond the call of duty, and made sure that by the time I was eighteen, I was ready to live on my own and support myself with a bank account, traveling on my own, an apartment, and control over my own finances.

Students did not always treat me as an equal. There was frequent bullying in public school, although the worst bullying came in community college. There is a piece of advice that people tell you which seems like a cliché, but it is very useful. You are better than the bullies. You are always better than the bullies! Gay rights advocate Dan Savage started a whole campaign telling people one simple message: It Gets Better. That is true, not just for the gay population, but for the disabled population as well. As a child, I was often frightened and did not get along well with others. Now, I am an empowered disability rights advocate who has gotten a standing ovation from JFK's sister, passed two pieces of legislation, established his own advocacy firm, and even better, I have tons and tons of friends! It should be noted that my friends are almost all people without disabilities. After all, most of the human population does not have disabilities, so the same is true for my friends. No matter how much the bullying or pressure hurts, never give up. You will have a wonderful future!

D.A. Charles: Mary is having issues advocating for her daughter's educational needs and asks how to overcome when a school fights you for giving a student what she needs? The IEP is a very important tool in a child's educational plan. Can you provide other tips that might help Mary advocate for what her daughter needs?

Alec Frazier: The IEP is indeed very important! In fact, mine is still important in college. When my university was looking for proper accommodations to give me, they asked me for my IEP as a basis upon which to formulate accommodations. In addition to going to school, doing my independent advocacy work, and hanging out with friends, I also volunteer at the local Independent Living Center. The Rehabilitation Act of 1973 specifies that Centers for Independent Living, or CILs as they are also called, shall serve to benefit the disabled population all over the United States. Mary's independent living center should probably have an educational advocate, or at least caseworkers who can help her. I know this because the center where I work has an educational advocate, but it also has a number of caseworkers assigned to individuals. However, CILs are only obligated to serve people as far as is mandated by law, and although some of them serve people beyond the requirements of the law, that is up to their discretion. If Mary is having an issue with not getting adequate services from her local CIL, there is always a grievance process to follow at that center. I hope that this advice helps a little bit.

D.A. Charles: Socialization is important for anyone, but even more so for someone who is autistic. It appears, if one were judging by your social networking sites, that you're a very social person, yet you've stated that you've only really had a few close friends, and that occurred fairly recently. Would you share with us how you achieved and continue to work to maintain your social life?

Alec Frazier: Until relatively recently in my life, I did not have much of a social life. I did go to common interest groups such as comic book clubs in order to socialize with people. The massive wealth of friends I have right now started with four people. I first met them at a comic book club, Visions Comic Art Group in Buffalo, New York. By now, we're so close that we are like siblings. Sebastiano is quirky like me, but in a different fashion.

He is a genius and I love him like a brother. Megan gets business done, and is very supportive. Amanda is cute and fun-loving. Marcus is always happy and great with technology. These friends are, by now, also my family. The key was making these friends. I met them through a common interest group, as mentioned, and the next step was to actually ask them if I could hang out with them. For myself and other autistic individuals, that takes a great deal of courage. Draw from within yourself, and find that courage to ask people if you can spend time with them. You'll be glad you did!

D.A. Charles: I spend a lot of time sharing information on disability etiquette. In my head, these things should be common sense, but not everyone realizes that what they are saying or doing is condescending or negative. One of those things is the "Isn't he Inspiring" mindset people have when viewing an individual with a disability. While the knee jerk reaction to someone with a disability doing something the general public might see as monumental based on their perception of the person, that kind of reaction can be hurtful to the person with a disability. Can you tell my readers why it's important for you to just be seen as "Alec" and not as an inspirational super-hero who makes huge accomplishments, despite his limitations?

Alec Frazier: I have a relatively simple answer for that. Ironically, it is that I am not "just Alec". Everybody on the planet, myself included, is three things. We are all human. We share the wonderful, awesome experience of living in this existence. That is our primary identity. Secondly, we are all ourselves. We are all unique individuals who, although all human, have wonderful individual characteristics. Tertiary to any of that is any other identity, such as being gay, or disabled, or black, or Roman Catholic, or basically anything else. Remember this: We are human first, ourselves second, and any other identity is incidental to that.

D.A. Charles: What kind of accommodations do you use in dealing with your disabilities? Do you require anything specific in your working or learning environment that might be beneficial for others to learn about? Is there a special piece of software or a special assistive device that is really important for you?

Alec Frazier: These days, I use a few accommodations, but not as many as you may think. Crucial to doing anything is writing. However, as I have mentioned, I have two writing disabilities. As a result, I use dictation software to speak into a voice-activated system which renders my speech as text on the computer. The current software I use is Dragon NaturallySpeaking Premium 13. In addition to working with a word processor, it also works with emails, Facebook, the Internet, and just about anything I do on the computer. Another accommodation, one I use at school, and occasionally elsewhere, is having notes provided to me by someone else. That is because of the writing disabilities. I also have time and a half and a quiet, secluded location for tests at the school. Often this goes hand-in-hand with use the voice-activated software. One accommodation that I have on paper is the right to have electronic textbooks provided for me. These e-texts are then fed into a reading software that reads it back to me. However, I have also become quite adept at speed reading, which is been sufficient for the last couple years. Believe it or not, that is all the accommodation that I have at the moment.

D.A. Charles: What are the greatest barriers for you as a person who is autistic? These differ greatly from the physical barriers we often associate with someone who has a disability.

Alec Frazier: The greatest barriers for myself and several other autistic individuals is that we do not perform socially the same way that others do. This entails a wide variety of behaviors. Sometimes we do not understand things, and often make fun of them for existing, making us seem like the bullies. What I mean by making fun of people for existing is that we often find simple things silly, such as people's names, or the way they dress. I am not trying to say that an autistic person's lack of social finesse is their fault, but rather that we end up perceiving things differently than the rest of the population, and this can cause difficulties. It is this difference in perception and the ensuing troubles that is one of the greatest barriers for an autistic person. Of course, we also do not make friends as well as most people do, as was mentioned earlier. Therefore, when many accommodations with disabilities would include a ramp or an automatic door, for an autistic person, they would include patience and a willingness to understand.

D.A. Charles: Tiffany would like to know how much of a change you have seen from when you were a child to now, about the way people handle the news of their child having autism or a disability. You and I have talked about later in life diagnoses of people on the autism spectrum and even misdiagnoses of other neurodiverse conditions that are later attributed to autism. Can you tell us what you've learned about how social, sensory and stress factors that didn't formerly exist are now causing individuals whose behaviors might have been seen as odd twenty years ago to receive an autism diagnosis?

Alec Frazier: What I have to say on this matter will be very comforting to parents of younger autistic children. I have seen dramatic, almost unbelievable improvement since I was a child. For example, I used to be almost completely incapable of understanding social cues, and the ramifications could often be quite severe. Nowadays, I not only get social cues, but I help people understand them and generate several myself! In addition, I used to throw temper tantrums quite often. Nowadays, that never happens. The last time I was physically violent towards someone was in self-defense almost ten years ago. Nowadays, I believe that belligerent violence is never the answer. Parents need to be able to educate their children on proper social cues, proper behavior, and other important matters. Sometimes it helps if the autistic child believes that they have discovered the proper method of behaving by themselves. Having autistic children talk about their problems with their peers as equals is always important. It is also most important never to condescend to your child or in any way make them feel like they are less than you. Be a fun parent! Do activities with them! Always tell them that you love them! It also doesn't hurt to tell them that they are not alone in the world of autistic people, and that they share their beautiful minds with people such as Thomas Jefferson, Albert Einstein, Nikola Tesla, Bill Gates, Leonardo da Vinci, and many others who have been quite successful in life!

Remember that being autistic is not a fault, and no one is to blame for the child's condition. Remember that the condition is genetic, and staying away from various substances or vaccinations would not have prevented it. Also remember that you can empower your child to live a more productive life! Just because someone is a nonverbal autistic person does not mean that they are stupid. I have met many nonverbal autistic people who are quite articulate, just in different ways.

Many people believe that autism is caused by vaccinations or something in the water, or something else environmental. That is complete hogwash. The rates of autism have not gone up. Instead, a convergence of factors has made it seem more frequent. For one thing, there are more people on the planet than ever before, which of course means more autistic people. In addition, various stress factors that exist in today's society and formerly did not cause autistic tendencies to manifest themselves more frequently. Social media alone can be a nightmare for people with autism. Due to our sensory difficulties, living in a modern, urban environment often brings out more stress. Due to the fact that the development of modern urbanity has only happened in the last fifty years, this makes autism seem much more prevalent. When you add that a lot of the other stimuli provided by modern technology and way of life, it is easy to see why there appear to be more autistic people. In reality, the percentages have not changed.

Let me explain two words that everybody on the planet should know and use. Neurotypical is a word used to describe people without mental variations. Neurodiverese is a word used to describe people with mental variations. Autism, depression,

ADD, obsessive-compulsive disorder, and Down's Syndrome can all be seen as forms of neurodiversity. This concept was conceived by an autistic sociologist in the 1990s as an alternative to thinking of these mental variations as illnesses or problems. For this reason, I frown upon the term "mental illness", because the word "illness" treats the mental conditions at hand as if they are problems. With proper accommodation and work, they do not have to be problems. I also frown upon the term "handicapped". This is because of the origin of the word. Back in the day, people with disabilities would hold out a cap in their hand begging for money. Using the term handicapped is demeaning and speaks to a very negative stereotype. The idea of thinking of disability as a form of diversity, instead of a problem, is called the social model of disability, as opposed to the old method of thinking of it as a problem, which is called the medical model. Once you learn to accept disability as a form of diversity instead of a problem, much of the stigma goes away.

D.A. Charles: You've posted a collage on your Facebook describing the way other people see a person with autism vs how your life really is… When people hear someone is autistic, they automatically think of someone who is locked inside their own mind, unable to interact with the world, or they see Rain Man. While I love Dustin Hoffman as an actor, I suspect that the Hollywood version of Autism is sort of like going to one of those Americanized Chinese Buffets where everything is served up to meet people's expectations of what it they think it should be versus the authentic version.

Alec Frazier: The upper left image is of a number of my friends at a creative meeting, at least three of whom I would guess are autistic. The upper middle image is of a helpless child, embodying how Autism Speaks sees the autistic population. The upper right image is of a bunch of protesters—political hell-raisers—which is what the Autistic Self Advocacy Network (ASAN) wishes to make of us. The middle right image is of a woman being confronted by an absolutely crazy creature clearly about to disrupt her life by throwing a pie in her face, which explains how many neurotypical people may sometimes view the neurodiverse. The middle center image is of a poster for the film "Rain Man", which, as you mention, has come to embody the iconic stereotypical pop culture view of autistic people. The middle right image is of the cover to the children's book The Little Engine That Could, which features the train engine that overcomes tremendous obstacles, representing how the parents of autistic people often see them. The bottom left image is of me with a lot of my friends at my birthday party at the Buffalo Zoo, to illustrate how autistic people actually are with their friends. The bottom center image is of me hugging my mother and enjoying a tender moment, to illustrate how autistic people actually are with family. Finally, the bottom right image is of me giving a keynote address to over a hundred people in Auburn, New York, illustrating how autistic people actually are at work.

D.A. Charles: I've read that individuals with autism are more likely to have an interaction at some point in their lives compared to the general public. This is a frightening statistic. The Justice Department released a comment in July that it is working on a curriculum to educate local officers about interacting with citizens who have cognitive disorders. It seems the state of California has become forward thinking in this aspect as they have begun offering seminars for individuals with autism to be able to interact with law enforcement officers so both groups have better understanding. What advice can you offer a parent with a child who is autistic in preparing their child for a possible interaction with authority figures? We teach our children to go to the police if they are lost or in danger, but it's a confusing situation when those same children must be warned that the officers who are supposed to be protecting them can cause them potential harm, how does one find a proper balance where their child is educated but not fearful?

Alec Frazier: The main piece of advice I would give to an autistic person dealing with authority figures is something they should excel at. Provide the authority figures with their diagnosis, and what that entails. That means that if they are having a stressful moment, they will need to calm down first. Nonetheless, this should be pretty easy since we can compartmentalize so easily. Autistic people love dealing in facts and volumes of information. Conveniently, this is something the law enforcement and other authorities also require to do their jobs. Failing that, make sure that the autistic child is well-versed in the parts of the Bill of Rights to the Constitution which protect them from any abuses by law enforcement. Mind you, the advice that I just gave you is best suited for autistic children on the higher end of the spectrum, who can talk and interact with law enforcement. Another good tool for an autistic person to deal with authorities is a card explaining their situation that can be put in their wallet, something like the following:

In order for a child to be educated, not fearful, let me speak to the parents of autistic children for a moment. Parents, if there is one lesson for you, it is to push your kids. Push them, even if they resist tremendously. Mainstream your kids in education. Make sure that they know how to use public transit. Try to make sure that they know how to fly on their own. Help them navigate public spaces. Encourage them to go out on their own, so that when they reach a certain age, they are doing things by themselves, instead of always having a parent do everything for them. I know that most of these lessons are good only for someone on the higher end of the spectrum, but if you are on the lower end and have an aid, go out with your aid and try to navigate the world with their help, and not with a parent. My parents often created incentives for me to go out and do things on my own. I understand that children are precious, but they should not be coddled. In terms of dealing with law enforcement, make sure that your child knows their rights, and that they know to stay calm in any situation involving law enforcement. I do understand that law enforcement sometimes has very low patience, but it will reflect positively upon the autistic person in question if they are not the ones at fault.

D.A. Charles: Many families who have a member whose diagnosis falls under the category of neuro-diversity, be it Alzheimer's, autism, a cognitive functioning difference; worry about that person wandering off and being harmed or worse. A few years ago, a little boy in my community wandered off at Christmas. His father had recently passed away, it was a very stressful and frightening time for the family. The little boy was never found in time and unfortunately, he succumbed to the frigid weather conditions. His disappearance inspired a huge grant program funding tracking devices for individuals at risk of wandering off and not being able to find their way home. This is a controversial subject, many caregivers see it as a Godsend, many individuals with disabilities see it as a huge invasion of privacy. Your thoughts?

Alec Frazier: Whoa boy. This is a tricky issue. I definitely prefer not to have tracking devices of any kind on people. The idea is, that if you are a good parent or a good caretaker, these tracking devices are completely unnecessary. Let me draw a parallel. I know somebody who got a talking ball from a pet store, and gave it to their autistic child. They recorded it with their voice, and let their child take it everywhere, including school. This idea is completely idiotic, because it makes our children completely dependent on their parents, and uses a ball—I repeat a ball, you know one of those round things that is supposed to sit there until you throw it—to do the parents' job, and do the teacher's job. The relevant point is that parents and teachers and caregivers should do their job, instead of relying upon technology to do it for them. I actually feel rather strongly about this.

D.A. Charles: And last, but certainly not least, you've recently become the director of your own company, Autistic Reality. How did that all come about? What made you decide to start your own business and what types of services do you offer to the public?

Alec Frazier: I have realized that I have a rather unique philosophy in life. I am more liberal than Autism Speaks, who view the autistic population as helpless victims, but I am more realistic than the Autistic Self Advocacy Network (ASAN), who view us as revolutionaries who must fight like hell, almost to the point of open revolt. I believe that life is a person with autism should be governed by realistic expectations for the world around you, and realistic behavior, embracing such customs as slang, clapping during presentations, and other social behavior. Believe it or not, ASAN believes that these customs are inappropriate. Most of the people in that crowd call themselves advocates but are actually activists. I do find the difference between them in that advocates work within the system by having talks, meetings, and trying to cooperate with people, while activists throw protests, rallies, vigils and tend to sue people before they try to work with them. Therefore, with this realistic philosophy towards life, I decided to name my new firm Autistic Reality. It has recently been legally incorporated as a sole proprietorship consultancy firm.

As for what the firm does, after a wonderful life of learning how to advocate for myself and others, I realized that I had services to provide. I discovered that I am a wonderful public speaker, have a knack for photography, can put on some awesome events, can do promotional work, but most importantly, that I can advocate on behalf of myself and others. I have been through the corridors of power advocating for changes in disability policy. When I was in middle school, I got a state constitutional amendment passed to raise funding for education. What I consider my legacy up to this point in my life is the establishment of the Community Living Administration, a federal agency. Since the late 1960s, the Independent Living movement has been trying to establish a federal agency to promote their interests. One day, I and approximately eight other people spoke to a staffer for Sen. Chuck Schumer, urging him to promote the creation of said agency. What happened next was completely unexpected. The very next day, he went into the Senate chambers, and proposed a bill creating that agency. Even more unexpected, the bill passed and the agency was created. I know that I can enact change in this world, and the big lesson for everyone else is that they can too!

D.A. Charles: If you'd like more information on Alec's business, Autistic Reality you can find him at http://www.nothingaboutuswithoutus.net/

You can find Autistic Reality on Facebook at https://www.facebook.com/autisticreality

You can find Alec's books on Facebook at https://www.facebook.com/venividiautism

I'd like to extend a huge thank you to my readers for joining us and for posting questions for Alec; and Alec, I'd like to thank you for taking the time to answer and for being an integral part of my pre-publication team. Your time is greatly appreciated.

Alec Frazier: Thank you, Denise, for the questions, and all of the hard work that you do!

How to Make Friends when You Have Autism

This essay contains my personal experiences and tips in making friends if you have autism. I hope they help individuals with autism make new acquaintances and friends!

Throughout my youth, friends were freqently people around my age who were made for me by my parents. My odd social quirks frequently alienated people I spent time with regularly. As a result, classmates were very rarely my friends out of school. Frequently, my behavior was jarring and could also easily insult people. I often failed to recognize these facts, and that made things more difficult for me. My parents did their best for me, and frequently pushed and shoved me into social situations, even if I didn't want them. Things got so bad that I was actively looking for ways to stay away from people. There was no way that I wanted to hang out with other people my own age or other ages, although I did get along better with older people. It got to the point where my family would go out to do things, such as see concerts, movies, and meet people, and I would actively fight to stay home. At the very worst, I was skipping dinner with my family in order to do my own thing. This was clearly a low point in my life.

When my family moved to Ithaca, New York, I started turning over a new leaf. I had already been involved in social clubs during senior year of high school. When I moved to Ithaca, I became heavily involved in comic book club. Ithaca, New York, has the oldest continuously active comic book club in the nation, the Comic Book Club of Ithaca (CBCI). I started off slow with them, but after a while, I was giving talks to the club and helping them plan their annual conventions. When I moved to Buffalo, New York, I started attending a comic book creative group called Visions Comic Art Group. Through this group, I met some very wonderful people. Then one day I got the courage to do something I had never done before: I asked some of these people if I could hang out with them outside of the group setting. They said yes, and soon became my best friends. Through them, I met other wonderful people. I now see my life as an absolutely wonderful thing, filled with friends whom I love dearly.

As an autistic person, there are two steps you can take to ensure friendships. First, start hanging out with common interest groups! Second, have the courage, the audacity to ask people in these groups to hang out with you outside of the group setting. Do not be afraid to make friends with people who are not autistic or disabled in other ways. After all, the majority of the world does not identify as having a disability! I really do hope that these tips come in useful!

ADA 25 and an Autistic Advocate's Celebration of Disability!

What follows is a report I wrote on my attendance at the 2015 Conference of the National Council on Independent Living (NCIL), the 25th anniversary of the Americans with Disabilities Act (ADA), and other activities I took part in in Washington, DC during that time. I hope it provides an adequate point of view on the work of the growing, learning advocate that I was at the time. Enjoy!

I met with a number of really wonderful disability rights leaders while in Washington, DC. Yoshiko Dart, the Mother of the Americans with Disabilities Act remembered me quite fondly once I jogged her memory. We had an awesome time discussing advocacy, and I gave her a copy of my book. That afternoon, our region held a meeting to discuss advocacy and lobbying during the legislative day that was forthcoming. Clifton Perez, our region's coordinator, was made aware that I was representing Western New York Independent Living

(WNYIL), as well as my firm, Autistic Reality, at the conference. That night, we had a wonderful banquet to celebrate the 25th anniversary of the Americans with Disabilities Act. Practically every disability rights leader in the nation was at that banquet, and I met some wonderful folks. I also got to thank Joyce Bender for paying for my admission to the banquet.

The next day, Tuesday, we held our March to Capitol Hill. During the March, I walked with the rest of the New York delegation. At one point, the director of the Utica network of independent living centers, RCIL, offered me a paid speaking engagement, which would also include transportation, lodging, and per diem meals. This will be the second independent living network that has engaged the services of my firm, Autistic Reality, and the third speaking engagement I have had for a network of independent living centers. At the rally, a number of powerful, influential politicians spoke to us about the need to support the disability cause. They included Steny Hoyer, Tammy Duckworth, Bernie Sanders, and many others. Many advocates were also a part of that rally, such as Bruce Darling and other members of ADAPT. The Cortland, New York independent living center, Access to Independence, sent a whole bus full of people to advocate in DC.

As for the lobbying, on Capitol Hill, our main agenda was to get the Community Integration Act (CIA) passed. This act would create a new title for the Americans with Disabilities Act which would be aimed completely at getting people out of institutionalized living settings. We were aware of the unfortunate naming choice, but it was better than some other name choices such as the DEA! The legislators I spoke to included staffers for all three of the Congressman representing areas covered by Western New York Independent Living, as well as staffers New York's two senators. Just as a matter of record, the Congressmen are Chris Collins, Tom Reed, and Brian Higgins. The Senators are Charles Schumer and Kristin Gillibrand. I went to see the disability policy advisor for Congressman Brian Higgins, Leslie Brady, on my own. I pushed for the CIA to be passed. It should be noted that the Congressman's office was not aware of the Community Integration Act, but they said they given his record on other similar measures, he will most likely support it. He is also very much in favor of improving Buffalo's infrastructure, as well as employment opportunities, healthcare provision, housing opportunities, and more. In addition, I brought up the fact that many of Buffalo's new careers and publicity opportunities are in the arts, such as filmmaking, comic book art, museums, and the promotion of such. All but one of the remaining congresspeople and senators agreed completely with the CIA. One of the more rural congressmen proved harder to convince. Senator Schumer in particular agreed to promote the CIA heavily. Congresswoman Tammy Duckworth agreed to cosponsor the bill in the House of Representatives.

The next day, I attended the meetings of the United States Access Board, the federal government body that regulates accessibility issues for people with disabilities. In the morning, they were having an in-depth meeting to report findings on accessibility of rail travel, especially Amtrak. In the afternoon, they were having their general meeting. In between, I met with their finance chair, Mat McCullough. When I was an intern for the American Association of People with Disabilities (AAPD), they assigned Mat to me as a mentor. They were extremely astute, as he continues to be a mentor today. When he is not serving on the Access Board, he is the Executive Director of the Washington, DC Council on Developmental Disabilities. After I am done with my master's program in disability studies, I wish to move to Washington, DC to embark on my career as a disability rights advocate. Therefore, I asked Mat a number of questions about employment opportunities in the District of Columbia for people who wish to pursue my career path.

After the meetings of the Access Board, I headed over to the National Archives and Records Administration (NARA) to see the original ADA. In addition, I went to see the Articles of Confederation, Declaration of Independence, United States Constitution, and United States Bill of Rights. I also was able to see the Equal Rights Amendment (ERA). I continue to hope for its successful passage. The next morning, I went to the Smithsonian National Museum of American History (SI NMAH) Kenneth E. Behring Center to see the ADA exhibit. The exhibit included a replica of the original ADA, as well as the pen with which the original ADA was signed. While I was at the Kenneth E. Behring Center, I learned that Omar Sharif, Jr., a very prominent Muslim American actor and grandson of the iconic Omar Sharif, Sr., had become the first gay man in history to speak out about gay rights in the Arab world, on an Egyptian television show. I posted to my business Facebook page that this was a watershed moment in game rights in the Arab world, and it is. Posts to my businesses Facebook page automatically get sent from my twitter account. I then learned that NARA had retweeted a photo I had tweeted earlier of the original ADA, and that as a result, I had over a dozen new followers on twitter. Shortly afterwards, I learned that I will have full control over the disposition of charitable contributions generated by the profits of the film "Aiden's Walk", for which I am the disability consultant. Having this control humbles me. I vow to find proper recipients for these donations.

I then went to the legislative debriefing and closing plenary session of the NCIL conference. At the closing plenary, it was mentioned that all centers for independent living had been encouraged to send as many youths, members of the ADA Generation, to the NCIL conference as possible. The said youth were then invited up on stage, and given the opportunity to speak to the crowd. When it came my turn, I used my decades of experience as a public speaker to help close out the conference. I got at least five rounds of applause, including the time when I announced that I had been tweeting the entire conference, including every single last speaker we had had. I also introduced my travel mascot, Millard the Buffalo, whom I had been taking pictures of around Washington, DC. He was in good company, as one of the other members of the youth contingent had been bringing a dragon around wherever he had been going. Many staff members and attendees of the conference asked to have their picture taken with Millard! When I sat back down in my chair, I learned that Omar Sharif, Jr. had favorited my tweet about him. At that point, my time in Washington, DC became too positive for me to handle, and my mind exploded!

I am in the process of putting hundreds of photos from my time in Washington, DC on to my Flickr page and my business Facebook page. Before I conclude this blog entry, I would also like to note that I took the train to Washington, DC from Buffalo's Exchange Street Station, and I also went back to Buffalo the same way. I love the train so much! I would also like to recognize the Honorable Ambassador Steven Pifer, his extremely intelligent wife Marilyn, their charming daughter Christine, and their adorable cat Tina for being my hosts during my time in Washington, DC. I have so many wonderful friends, business contacts, and people who fill both of those roles! I am incredibly grateful for having been in Washington, DC during the historic 25th anniversary of the Americans with Disabilities Act! It was fun, informative, and a huge boon for my future career! Thanks to everyone who helped make it possible!

Autistic Reality's Trip to The Rebecca School in New York City

In this chapter, I chronicle my trip to the Rebecca School for developmentally disabled children in New York City. It was incredibly fun, and a wonderful learning experience for all of us!

I was in Rochester, New York in the fall of last year when I received an email from a gentleman named Zachary Freeman. Mr. Freeman said he represented the comic book club at the Rebecca School, a school for the developmentally disabled youth. I quickly did a Google search, and after looking at their information and some other search results, I decided that the school was a reputable business. I agreed to do business with Mr. Freeman. He asked what kinds of business I could do. I mentioned that I had a talk on my book, and that is comic book club might be interested in my talk. Over the next several months, he and I corresponded many times via email. The school agreed to pay my transportation by train, as well as my meals. I would be staying with a friend. The school also agreed to pay a $200 honorarium.

I got to the Rebecca School, and Mr. Freeman was summoned. He took me to the art classroom, where I set up my presentation. After about 20 minutes or half an hour, the students started to arrive. All in all, there were at least a dozen of them. A few of them had swim practice in a little while, so I talked with all of them first. Mr. Freeman introduced me, and then I reviewed more about what I do. I asked them about themselves, and tried to get to know them. The majority of the students I met were autistic, and all of them had developmental disabilities. All of them were verbal. Most of them belonged to the comic book club at the school, although a few other interested kids showed up. Their age ranges were mostly middle school and high school. They were very curious about me, and I shared information about myself freely.

I shared my presentation on the storyline in the Daredevil comics involving the first successfully rendered autistic super-hero. The kids were very bright, and super excited to hear my presentation. Then I talked with them some more. After that, I shared my It Gets Better video with them. For those of you who do not know, my It Gets Better video is all about encouraging socially awkward people and autistic youths that life will be really wonderful later on. It also gives some key strategies on making friends, as well as talking about support from loved ones. A couple of the kids said that the video moved them to tears.

In addition to comic book related matters, we discussed many other wonderful things. I encouraged them to be active in making decisions about their curricula. Afterwards, Mr. Freeman confirmed with me that the older children are allowed into the decision-making process. I also asked the kids whether or not they use public transportation, and gave them tips on that matter, such as planning logistics. I started talking about medication at one point, and one of the kids nervously mentioned his medication. I told him he had nothing to be ashamed of, and showed them all my medicine box. I also gave them tips on traveling by airline, and adjusting to situations which are tough on sensory disabilities. At some points during my presentation on my book, I used the book as a teaching point. One thing to note is that I never talked at or to the kids. I talked with the kids, including them equally in the conversation. At the end of my talk with the kids, I gave them each a copy of my card, and told every one of them that I am extremely proud of them.

Afterwards, Mr. Freeman and another staffer from the school gave me a complete tour of their facilities. The Rebecca School uses something called the Developmental Individual Difference Relationship-based or DIR model, which was developed by Dr. Stanley Greenspan. The DIR model relies heavily on building relationships, life skills development, and positive reinforcement. There is no punishment at the Rebecca School. Instead, good behavior is rewarded. The school is also dead set against behavioral modification, and instead works by finding the students' strong points. The ages of students vary from four years old to twenty-one years old, although they are considering raising the maximum age. There are social workers to help get the kids and their families oriented in life. They have a number of counselors who do one-on-one, couples, and family counseling. Although the school focuses on academics like any other, a special focus is given to teaching life skills. The school day lasts from 9 AM until 3 PM, except on Fridays, when the students leave at noon. The school is very centrally located, within walking distance of the Empire State Building, Madison Square Park, Grand Central Terminal, as well as Fifth Avenue.

The Rebecca school is an extremely sensory friendly facility, which makes sense given that many autistic and otherwise developmentally disabled people have sensory issues. They have a gymnasium which doubles as a venue for a number of conferences and other events they hold. Each month, a particular family presents on their child's development. The child will often be part of that presentation. In addition to the regular gymnasium, they have to sensory friendly gymnasiums, with swings, mats, giant beanbags, and more. These rooms have low lighting as well. They have a food lab where students learn how to cook and prepare meals. Their youngest student chef is four years old, and their oldest is an alumnus. They also have a facility called the Rebecca Café, which is their store for dietary friendly foods made by the students. There are a few quiet rooms throughout the facility. Kids are not sent here for punishment, but rather by mutual agreement that they need some downtime. The quiet rooms are filled with comfortable materials, and people are permitted to sleep there. The art room where I spoke has a number of murals drawn by the students, including a special one involving a number of superheroes. Mr. Freeman is the art teacher in addition to being the moderator of the comic book club. All of the classrooms are small, and definitely not overcrowded. These classrooms have equipment for doing lab activities, as well as for

stimulation, such as hooks for swings. On the roof of the building, there are two outdoor playgrounds. The one in the front is
rumored to have the best unimpeded view of the Empire State
Building in Manhattan.

Last but not least, our tour stopped at the computer lab. When
I was shown the computer lab, the staff worried that I would
disagree with their philosophy. Their philosophy is that students
should spend as little time as possible on the computer at school.
While I admit that University is quite different, students under
eighteen should definitely spend far less time on the computer.
In particular, the school's policy says that the time students spend
on recreation on the computer is currently a bit too high. I agree
with them completely. Except for the days when I am out of the
house, I always turn my computer off at 4:00 PM. The rest of
the day is spent reading and doing chores. I told Mr. Freeman
and my tour guide about this. I told them that I completely agree
with their stance on the overreliance of today's young students
on computers.

I was given my check for my honorarium and my meal ex-
penses, and I signed a copy of my book for display at the school,
as well as giving them one for circulation. I will also be sending
them an electronic copy for the visually impaired or other people who have difficulty reading. In addition, I signed a print for
them of the illustration from the back cover, made by the illus-
trator himself, Jeff Perdziak. It was a wonderful day! Although
I really wish that I had access to the many wonderful things in
this school when I was growing up, I am nonetheless glad that I
grew up the way I did and that I am who I am today.

Autistic Reality's Trip to the Ruderman Family Foundation and Special Olympics Massachusetts

This is a report on my business during a trip to Massachusetts on the dates of April 29, 2016 through May 4, 2016. The business actually took place on May 2 and 3, 2016. I had a wonderful time making new business contacts and interacting with old friends.

On Monday, May 2, 2016, I went to visit the Ruderman Family Foundation in Newton, Massachusetts. Specifically, my meeting was with Jay Ruderman, the leader of the foundation. The purpose of the meeting was to introduce him to my firm and my business outlook. I talked about some of the things I do, such as networking, public speaking, lobbying, peer advocacy, and other forms of advocacy. Mr. Ruderman then told me about what his foundation does. His foundation tries to promote diversity and inclusion in the United States and around the world, but specifically within the Jewish community. They fight for full or inclusion of the disabled in the workplace, policymaking, education, and elsewhere. The foundation also works with Israel significantly to promote peace, stability, and diversity in that country. Mr. Ruderman also introduced me to his family, including his wife and his sister. To him, the fact that he is running a family foundation means that each member of his family is very important. In the end, we agreed to be friends, and possibly work together. We also took photos together to promote our business relationship. It was a very good meeting, and an excellent introduction to one another.

The next day, Tuesday May 3, 2016, I went into Special Olympics Massachusetts in Marlborough, Massachusetts with Nick Savarese, their Vice President of Philanthropy. Nick and I go way back. When I was in seventh grade, he was the teacher's aide who followed me from class to class, assisting me, and making sure that things stayed on track. Speaking of networking, it is absolutely incredible that we are still in touch today. Facebook has aided in those efforts, and Nick even hosted me in his home during my trip to Massachusetts.

Special Olympics Massachusetts is one of the only Special Olympics state level offices that has its own headquarters, the Yawkey Sports Training Center. I got the full tour, and the training center contains a gym, a weight and exercise room, tons of storage, a lobby with commemorative exhibits and plaques, conference rooms, offices, and more. There is also a neat statue outside of three athletes holding a torch aloft, and this statue is great for photo ops and announcements. Special Olympics Massachusetts owns their own building, and has the right to expand it if needed in the future.

In the morning, I gave a talk to the staff of Special Olympics Massachusetts. I talked about my history with Special Olympics, how I knew Nick, what my educational background is in, and the various pieces of advocacy work that I have done. There was a question-and-answer session too, and some of the answers I gave regarded my philosophy on identities, and where I wish to go from here. I mentioned that everyone there was doing extremely admirable work, and gave everyone my business card. We also showed my It Gets Better video, and I talked about making friends when you have disabilities, including social disabilities.

Afterwards, Nick and I met with Charles Hirsch, the Communications and Marketing Manager, and I recorded an interview for the Play Unified podcast that Special Olympics Massachusetts sometimes puts out. I talked about everything I had mentioned in the speech I had given to the staff, as well as talking about bullying and giving encouragement to disabled youth. I also talked about my book, and my move to the Maryland/Washington DC area this summer. They are also going to be putting a link to my It Gets Better video in the podcast, as well as links for my website, my Facebook pages, and Twitter. Afterwards, Nick and I went to lunch.

That afternoon, I was hanging out in the conference room when Megan Hoffman, the Director of Community Development came in. She started apologizing profusely, and also noted that I seemed good at making up speeches on the fly. I told her yes, that I had not even had a rough version of my earlier speech that day in my head. She said that was good, and that she needed to teleconference with a class at Gordon College in Wenham,

Massachusetts. We got on Skype, and we both spoke to them. When I did my bit, I introduced myself, my experience with Special Olympics, and talked about the importance of internships. We finished shortly, and that was all the business for the trip.

At the number of points during this report, I talk about the benefits of being in Special Olympics. There are a great many of them, but one stood out to me. I was a student who had a great deal of trouble making friends and hanging out with people in casual settings. Special Olympics made me feel a great sense of belonging. Going to those events together with people, staying in hotel rooms and playing video games with them, watching movies, and taking part in humongous statewide festivals with the rest of the athletes was absolutely amazing. It was something I really needed at that point in my life, and I am extremely proud to have been a Special Olympics athlete.

I'm Glad I Don't Play: Pokemon GO and OCD

Sometimes, I help friends with school projects and university studies. Back when Pokémon Go was very popular, I avoided taking part, and my friend Sameer Zubin, who was doing a university study of the matter, interviewed me about it.

Sameer: Hello!

Me: Hello! Proud avoider of Pokey goings on, here!

Sameer So first things first: how come you do not play Pokemon GO?

Me: A few reasons. First off, I've never really been into Pokemon. I saw one or two of the movies and an episode or two, but to me, they were not very good and pretty forgettable. I'm almost never into fads. I'd consider Pokemon a fad. I do very much like the South Park episode that parodies Pokemon. Much more importantly, I have OCD. I try to avoid doing things that may become OCD issues. Pokemon Go is a classic example of this. In addition, I also have banned myself from ever going to Las Vegas for similar reasons. Finally, I am very busy. Even when I don't have a job, I have reports to do, agendas to organize, opinions to write, cases to study, and more. Add to that friends that I like to meet, parties to attend, and more.

Sameer: Wow I never realized Pokemon could be an OCD trigger. Thank you for sharing that info. So do you avoid the game entirely? I mean if you're out with friends who are playing would you ask them to stop or excuse yourself?

Me: No, I wouldn't ask them to stop. But if I play it myself, it could overwhelm me, and become both an obsession and a compulsion. I used to have similar problems when I was younger. For example, I once avoided my own birthday party to play on the computer. God, that really hurt me.

Sameer: I was close to being like that. So do you play video games these days?

Me: I wasn't playing video games back then. The only video game I play these days is Starcraft 2. Nothing to do with OCD. I just like the format, and other games tend to be too difficult.

Sameer: Gotcha. So how do you view video games? Positive/ Negative/Neutral factors in a person's life? Not just for yourself, but on the general scale.

Me: Wow. It really depends on how much people play. Video games are fun, entertaining, and interesting. They can also sometimes help develop skills and knowledge. HOWEVER!!! Over investing one's self in video games can ruin your life. It can destroy friendships and relationships, ruin your sense of self-esteem, and ruin your career and/or school. Always play in moderation. For example, I never play more than two or three levels at a time.

Sameer: Totally agree. That's why I avoided KOTOR and WoW.

Me: I also never do multiplayer. It's tough enough on my own. I actually have two motor disabilities that make it kind of difficult on me.

Sameer: Do you feel like you're missing out on special experiences video games can cause?

Me: Nah. My life is plenty of fun regardless.

Sameer: Awesome! Well I think I got what I needed from the other side of the spectrum.

Me: Thank you!

Autistic Reality's Public Comments for the 2016 Interagency Autism Coordinating Committee (IACC) Strategic Plan

In 2016, the US government's interagency autism coordinating committee (IACC) asked for public comment on formulating their new strategic plan. Here are my firm's comments.

Question 1: When should I be concerned? (Diagnosis and Screening)

Please identify what you consider the most important priorities and gaps in research, services, and policy for Question 1. Topics include: diagnosis and screening tools, early signs, symptoms, and biomarkers, identification of subgroups, disparities and diagnosis.

Autistic Reality firmly believes that being overly concerned about autism diagnosis and screening can be harmful to everyone involved. When diagnosing and screening, treating the individual who is being diagnosed and screened as a human being worthy of respect and dignity is paramount. Autistic individuals are not lab rats. Also very important during diagnosis and screening is not to treat autism as a problem or a defect. If you treat diagnosis and screening as if you are looking for a sickness or disease, then you are attaching unnecessary stigma to both the condition and the individual being screened and diagnosed. Autism is a form of diversity, not a sickness and not a disease. Autism does change the way that individuals act and think, but it is not a defect if properly accommodated and/or perceived. If you are a parent and/or a guardian suspect that autism must be an issue, then observe, check the sources, and check with a medical professional who will put your child's needs first. Please make sure that your child has input and understands what is going on. Please impress this upon your child even if your child is nonverbal. Nonverbal does not mean stupid. If you are an adult looking for diagnosis of yourself, then you may handle these matters on your own if you are capable. Please be sure to demand the respect you deserve from any professionals you encounter who treat you as if you are a lesser person. If you are an adult looking for the diagnosis of another adult, then the issue is more complicated. In the opinion of Autistic Reality, the individual for whom you are seeking a diagnosis must need assistance dealing with the process, and you must be assigned as a legal guardian, power of attorney, or proxy. If the adult is capable or you do not have these powers, then there diagnosis and screening is none of your business unless they let you into it. Please understand that autism is widely varied, and no two cases will be a like. It is important to note that no one source will be able to nail things down for you concretely, and researching from multiple sources is important. In addition, no one person, no matter how knowledgeable, knows everything. The only person able to make it concrete diagnosis should be a licensed medical and/or mental health professional.

Question 2: How can I understand what is happening? (Biology of ASD)

Please identify what you consider the most important research priorities, policy issues, and gaps for Question 2. Topics include: molecular biology and neuroscience, developmental biology, cognitive and behavioral biology, genetic syndromes related to ASD, sex differences, immune and metabolic aspects, and co-occurring conditions in ASD.

Autistic Reality believes that the biggest key is understanding that autism is not anyone's fault. It is not a preventable condition caused by someone's error, but rather a naturally occurring condition that has existed as long as has humanity. Education on natural forms of diversity including mental health issues is currently lacking, and simply must be improved. People must also learn how to shift the blame for disability away from a fault-based model. Understanding that mental health conditions occur naturally is extremely important. It is also very important to realize that males and females and old and young people can have autism, despite the common misconception that children are mostly affected by autism and that mostly males have autism. Autism may manifest itself slightly differently in females than it does in males. Autism often brings with it other conditions such as Obsessive-Compulsive Disorder (OCD), Bipolar Disorder, and

ADD. Once again, it is important to realize that these conditions are not sicknesses or problems, but rather forms of mental diversity, which is called neurodiversity.

Question 3: What Caused This to Happen and Can It Be Prevented? (Risk Factors)

Please identify what you consider the most important research priorities, policy issues, and gaps for Question 3. Topics include: genetic and environmental risk factors, gene-environment interactions, and the potential role of epigenetics and the microbiome.

Autistic Reality must emphasize that autism can happen in anyone, and is biological. It is not caused by vaccinations or the fault of any individual or group. Any evidence that vaccinations, pollution, or any other artificial factors cause autism has been proven to be falsified. Autistic Reality believes that there is genetic predilection for autism, and that although environmental factors do not cause autism, they may impact the manifestation or severity of the condition. By environmental factors in the previous sentence, we do not mean pollution or vaccinations or the like, but rather we mean the environment in which the autistic individual exists: the living environment, their schooling environment, their working environment, etc. Autism cannot be prevented, nor should it, since it is a natural form of diversity just like being African-American or gay. To prevent autism is eugenics and genetic warfare, and altering the genetic code to eliminate undesirable traits is illegal.

Question 4. How can I understand what is happening? (Treatments and Interventions)

Please identify when you consider the most important priorities and gaps in research, services and policy for Question 4. Topics include: behavioral, medical/pharmacologic, educational, technology-based, and complementary/integrative interventions.

Autistic Reality believes that the best way to understand what is happening is to communicate with autistic individuals about the condition. Autistic individuals may not always be verbal, but they always understand you. This is very important to understand, since there is a common misconception that nonverbal autistic individuals cannot understand the world around them. This is false. The second-best way to understand what is happening is to communicate with friends and peers of the autistic population whether or not they have autism. The third best way is to speak to the family members of those with autism, who often love their autistic family members, although they may have interests that cloud their judgments. The fourth best way is to talk to clinicians and doctors. It must be understood that clinicians and doctors are in a business, and it also must be understood that they most frequently view autism as a sickness, which it is not. The same priority ranking system goes when dealing with books, websites, and other resources. Please steer away from Autism Speaks, as they are a eugenic-minded apologist group that wants to see autism gone and does not believe that the opinions of autistic individuals hold valid weight in the world. Please also steer away from the Autistic Self Advocacy Network, as they often use radical methods such as cyber bullying and character assassination if their very specific, often incorrect mindset is not met. A good organization would be the Autism Society of America. Please also understand that medication can work for the autistic population. While it is harmful to over-medicate, some medication may help with autism or co-occurring conditions. Behavioral modification is generally a bad idea, and instead one should seek to accommodate the autistic individual with their autistic habits intact. Nonetheless, adopting more appropriate habits when necessary should also be taught, so that the autistic individual has a safe zone of time and space to be themselves, and also does not act untoward in social settings. Many autistic people have sensory difficulties that get in the way of enjoying social settings. Autistic Reality believes that with proper conditioning, autistic individuals have the potential to become accustomed to settings which may initially trigger their sensory difficulties. Therefore, autistic individuals should be encouraged and prompted to test their limits safely, and grow their potential.

Question 5. Where can I turn for services? (Services)
Please identify what you consider the most important services research, delivery, and policy priorities and gaps for Question 5. Topics include: service access and utilization, service systems, education, family well-being, efficacious and cost-effective service delivery, health and safety issues affecting children, and community inclusion.

Autistic Reality believes that for general advisement on services and benefits, one should seek benefits advisement. Benefits advisement can tell you what services are available for your needs, and help you get them. Every area in this country has a corresponding Center for Independent Living, or CIL. Your CIL frequently provides benefits advisement, free of charge. Similarly, if one is having an access issue and needs advocacy done for legal, educational, transportation, housing, and more your CIL will often have people to help with that, too. Another important service includes therapy. This may include talk therapy, art therapy, occupational therapy, or just about any kind of therapeutic practice. Please understand that there is no shame in getting any kind of reputable therapy. In fact, Autistic Reality believes that therapy can greatly improve the quality of one's life, and that it should be a point of pride, rather than shame. When one is seeking therapy, they are seeking to better their quality of life. That sounds like something of which to be proud! Therapy also often works for families and couples, and quality counseling may work for other groups as well. In general, Autistic Reality recommends public schooling. Children should have Individualized Education Programs (IEPs), and adults should have accommodation in the workplace. This means coordinating with special education, disability services offices, and human resources departments in order to get the proper accommodations and/ or services. Please understand that as the autistic individual ages out of childhood, there is a good chance that they will become competent enough to manage their own affairs. Parents and/or guardians should not only let them do this, but should provide guidance and enable them to make their own decisions, with proper training to do so. Autistic youths should sit in on many of the meetings that involve them, especially their educational planning meetings. Autistic individuals both young and old should continuously be asked for their input not only into their services, but into life in general.

Question 6. What does the future hold, particularly for adults? (Lifespan Issues)

Please identify what you consider the most important priorities and gaps in research, services, and policy issues, relevant to Question 6. Topics include: health and quality of life across the lifespan, aging, transition, and adult services, including education, vocational training, employment, housing, and financial planning and community integration.

It is important to realize that a huge population of autistic adults exists in today's society and has always existed since the beginning of time. One of the biggest problems with lifespan issues today is the common misconception that autism only affects children. This is just false. To better help of autistic adults, life skills training is essential. Autistic Reality is of the firm opinion that life skills should be required learning for every single high school student. Everyone, not just autistic individuals, needs to know how to manage finances, rent an apartment, find a job, and deal with professional interactions. In addition, specialized life skills services need to be available to the autistic population to help the autistic population better understand how to navigate the world around them. In addition, non-autistic individuals need to be better trained on accepting people who are not like themselves, and understanding how diversity of all kinds is only natural inhumanity. Vocational training, employment, and financial training should, in a perfect world, be available free of charge to those who request it, both autistic and non-autistic. Employers need to be much more willing to hire autistic individuals, whether or not they identify as autistic in their application or workplace. This includes both traditionally hired individuals, and individuals hired through various work forms for the disabled. Social clubs and common interest groups with bylaws need to include sections of procedure relating to those with disabilities, both visible and invisible. They also need to enforce these bylaws. Finally, organizations that exist to help the disabled need to streamline their services, and be easier to work with. Autistic Reality understands the absolute nightmare of bureaucracy governing these organizations. Nevertheless, this does not mean that these organizations do not have to do their jobs.

Question 7. What other infrastructure and surveillance needs must be met? (Lifespan Issues)

Please identify what you consider the most important research priorities, policy issues, and gaps for Question 7. Topics include: research infrastructure needs, AST surveillance research, research workforce development, dissemination of research information, and strengthening collaboration.

The most important priority is to understand that autism is not a problem, but a form of biological diversity. Organizations that are founded on the principle that autistic individuals are incompetent or lesser human beings need to be done away with, and have their public powers severely curtailed or even revoked. This includes organizations such as Autism Speaks. Similarly, other organizations such as the Autistic Self Advocacy Network (ASAN) which work on a principle of being incredibly narrow-minded and bullying anyone who isn't equally narrow-minded have absolutely no place in the advocacy world. People need to be more accepting of others. Autistic individuals do not meet a cookie-cutter mold, and should not have to conform to the unreasonable wishes of anyone, whether they be outside or within the disabled community. Workforce development must be researched, as must universal design with autistic individuals in mind. Research information must be available to the public. Asking the public to pay for research information which may help them is, in the eyes of Autistic Reality, completely unreasonable. Individuals wishing to do their own research should be able to do so, but must only be enabled providing that they have no unsafe biases. Autistic Reality also calls for the strengthening of inter-disability networks, and the strengthening of relationships between non-disability groups and disability related groups. Finally, Autistic Reality tends to frown on the electronic surveillance of autistic individuals. Autistic individuals are not incompetent, but rather sometimes have trouble expressing themselves. If there is surveillance, it should be completely voluntary.

A Review of
Lights! Camera! Access! 2.0

I am writing to inform you about the wonderful disability and media symposium that is Lights! Camera! Access! 2.0!

I got to know Tari Hartman Squire through a number of prior business dealings. She is the Founding CEO of EIN SOF Communications, Inc., a disability marketing firm. One thing that the firm does is promote disability inclusion in the media through its Lights! Camera! Access! Symposia.

I moved to the Washington, DC area on November 1 of 2016. I had not been there for three days yet when I received an invite to the main event for Lights! Camera! Access! 2.0, a key disability and media symposium. This event would be held at the White House, and proper permissions were needed. It was pretty amazing to get an official invite to the White House!

Almost all events held at the White House are actually held at the Eisenhower Executive Office Building (EEOB). I walked around the White House area taking photos of the beautiful architecture before I lined up for the conference. There was quite a bit of security to go through, but it was easy since we had the proper credentials.

The event started with introductions by those in charge, including Tari Hartman Squire, Obama Director of Public Engagement Maria Town, and others.

After this, there were few panel discussions. Some of the panelists were disability professionals, while other panelists were media professionals. A few people teleconferenced in from other places, including Los Angeles and New York City. The ability of people to teleconference into a meeting makes things much easier for all parties involved.

At its heart, Lights! Camera! Access! Is a mentoring event, so in the midst of all of this, there were sessions where we, the younger and/or more inexperienced attendees, most of whom have disabilities, met with mentors in the disability rights and media fields. I myself met with some interesting professionals from an advertising firm in New York City. Other mentees came from around the country.

In addition to all of this, there were many networking opportunities, and panels and workshops on mentoring and advocacy. Many professionals in both unique and general-purpose disability in media fields or present.

To follow up, I have had Skype conversations with some of my mentors, and other meetings with them in person. We have also exchanged contact information.

In addition to all of this, there was a second Lights! Camera! Access! 2.0 conference a couple months later. This one was also hosted by the White House, although it was not physically held at the White House, but was instead held at Gallaudet University, a remarkably relevant location given its disability rights history. I refer to this conference as Lights! Camera! Access! 2.5.

There were many people at this second conference who are not able to make it to the original conference. At the second conference, I was able to meet with not one, but five mentors in the disability/media fields.

A while after my second Lights! Camera! Access! Symposium, I was hired by my mentor, Jd Michaels as an editor at BBDO New York, and international advertising firm. Jd was able to help me publish this book, attend conferences and important meetings, and better pursue my dreams as a disability rights advocate. I have since attended another Lights! Camera! Access! symposium in New York City, at which I was a mentor, a speaker, and a co-sponsor. In addition, one of my own mentees was able to attend and receive guidance at the event.

I highly recommend attendance at a Lights! Camera! Access! event. Your perceptions of the world around you will change, and you will get wonderful ideas for promoting inclusion, not just in disability and media, but in many other cross disciplinary fields! In fact, you just may find an amazing, rewarding job.

Disability Pride Questions
and Answers

I sometimes do interviews to help further the disability cause. In this interview, questions were provided by disability rights advocate Kings Floyd.

Name: Alexander Fuld Frazier. Call me Alec.

Age: 31

Pronouns: He/Him/His

Disability (if comfortable sharing): autism, ADD, ADHD, bipolar disorder, obsessive-compulsive disorder, sensory processing disorder, digital atonia, dysgraphia, facial atonia, HHT, born without hip joints which were later grown, possibly also PTSD and dyscalcula

How did you learn about your disability? At what age?: I have always known that I was different. I never once thought that I was less because of these differences, although I sometimes felt sad about a lack of inclusion as a child. As soon as I became able to understand, which was around later elementary school and middle school, my parents taught me about my diagnoses, while being careful to impart the knowledge that I am different, and definitely not less. As my diagnosis took place in the early 1990s, I was the first person with a higher functioning autism diagnosis and most of the communities I lived in. As such, my self-identity as an autistic individual predates much of the current autism politicking. For example, I fail to see a reason to choose either identity-first or person-first terminology, and I do not see what the fuss is about between the two options. I believe that we have become overly obsessed with language and terminology, and that it hinders our ability to properly represent ourselves. As such, I also believe that usage of slang can be very healthy. We often talk about fitting in with the rest of the world, and we won't be able to fit in if we use cold, clinical terminology all the time.

How much are you involved in the disability community? When and how did you become involved?: I am extremely involved in the disability community, although not in the ways in which you may think. I first was involved in advocacy in third grade, when I gave a speech to the Lieutenant Governor of Colorado. In eighth grade, I helped get a state constitutional amendment passed in that state raising funds for special education. In high school, I supported my first political candidate. In 2011, I was an intern for the American Association of People with Disabilities. It was there that I learned more about the national disability community. Since then, I have been involved in a great many ways, including but not limited to peer advocacy, public speaking, writing and selling my book, lobbying, attending conferences, and a great deal of other activities. I have spoken to schools and independent living networks, I have worked with parents, educators, politicians, and individuals with disabilities. I believe that every single voice has a right to be heard, although the voice of those with disabilities ourselves is most important. I tend to shy away from both extremes in the disability rights movement. For example, I shy away from Autism Speaks because they tend to believe that those without disabilities should not have self-determination. On the other hand, I tend to shy away from the Autistic Self Advocacy Network because they are disability supremacists who believe in segregating themselves from the rest of society and bullying anyone who does not fit their myopic worldview. I believe in the work of the Autism Society, and of course the work of my own firm, Autistic Reality.

Do you have a sense of disability pride? Why or why not?

I definitely have a sense of disability pride. However, I do not believe in disability supremacy. I very involved in advocacy, but not activism. For the definitions of those two words, I use them as defined by the Google dictionary. An advocate is someone who campaigns for various causes. An activist is a protester, a demonstrator, a zealot. These are Google's words, not mine. I believe strongly in negotiation and peaceful means to end oppression. Although I see a valuable role to staging protests and demonstrations, I prefer not to do it myself. I believe that the best way to manifest my disability pride is to live a productive, happy life whether or not I have a disability. Disability should not get in the way of living such a life. For the past approximately five years, I have been an incredible optimist. As someone with bipolar disorder, I used to get quite unhappy, and often. Then one day, I made a decision not to get depressed or seriously sad or angry anymore. The amazing thing is that it worked! I have not been depressed or seriously sad or angry in five years.

What other identities are you proud of? Do they intersect?: I am proud to be disabled, and I am also proud to be a homosexual individual. Just as I attend disability pride events, I also sometimes attend gay pride events, although I find that they can be bogged down by showboating, rather than identity pride. For example, the pride celebrations in Buffalo, New York are more oriented towards causing a scene then fighting for equality. The ones in Washington, DC are awesome, though. In addition, I have many less life-altering identities. For example, I am a fan of James Cameron's Avatar, Twilight, Star Trek, comic books, and an aficionado of architecture, history, governmental theory, and many other disciplines. These have intersected into disability pride in many ways. For example, as a fan of James Cameron's avatar, I have lobbied the producers in person for disability inclusion in future films, and talked with them about disability and other identities in the arts. As a fan of Twilight, I have served as a consultant on the number of fan works, some of which have become original works and been published as books. I have also written some disability fanfiction myself. As a fan of comic books, I have written and copyrighted a literature review of a Marvel comics character who happens to be the first autistic superhero. The book is called <u>Without Fear: The First Autistic Superhero</u>, and I have sold it and spoken on it at several venues. I have also spoken with a few executives at Marvel comics, and am working on hopefully writing or consulting on a comic for them.

What does disability pride mean to you?: Disability pride means living your life to the best of your ability with proper accommodations and services to the point that you can be empowered, content, independent, and happy on a day-to-day basis. To me, any kind of pride involves living life in this way regardless or perhaps because of the identity in question. As far as I'm concerned, one does not need to march, protest, or raise any kind of ruckus to be proud. One must live their life with dignity, satisfaction, and fulfillment. I take this definition of pride very seriously. It comes from my grandfather, Arthur Jacob Fuld, who was a Holocaust survivor and liberator. He believed that the best way to both commemorate fallen populations and be proud of your life was productive acts and a satisfying life.

Are there any images/quotes that represent pride or disability pride to you? : There are several images that represent disability pride to me. One of them is some fan art of the autistic comic book character I cover in my literature review. Another one is a photo of me standing with the wheelchair used for the main character in James Cameron's avatar. Another one is a photo of me speaking in front of the US Capitol building. Another one is me with a group of friends before the Women's March earlier this year. Another image is my hand with the original Americans with Disabilities Act of 1990. These images are spread throughout this blog post.

Are there any disabled role models you look up to? : I have had many role models and mentors. Mathew McCullough, Director of the District of Columbia's Office on Disability, has been a mentor since I met him during my 2011 AAPD internship. I consult with him often about my future, and while he provides advice, I also tell him of what I am doing. In addition, he is an amazing friend. Somewhat more professional is my relationship with Joyce Bender, CEO and Founder of Bender Consulting, whom I also met during my 2011 internship. She is immensely successful professionally, and provides professional advice. I have also developed a friendly relationship with Andy Imperato, who has held many roles in the disability community over the years. I often bounce ideas off him, and ask him for his advice on disability-related matters. I appreciate these folks because they are moderates in the disability rights field, just like me. There are others I have looked up to, of course, but not to the extent that I look up to these folks. In addition, I have done some mentoring of my own in recent years. Due to my tendency to work with parents as well as individuals with disabilities, there are many parents of those with disabilities who also look to me for guidance. It is an absolute honor and a privilege to be a source of guidance for anyone, and it is a trust that I will never abuse.

My Mentors

This essay originally started as a blog entry of mine and was later rewritten for the National Disability Mentoring Coalition. I am sure that many of you will find it quite informative, as it also provides a key insight into professional development and disability rights work.

I would like to talk to you about mentors. Throughout my many business endeavors, I have gained a few mentors. The title of mentor is not something that I give away lightly. Out of my hundreds of professional contacts, I would say that I only have four mentors. They are Mat McCollough, Joyce Bender, Emil Novak, Sr., and Jd Michaels.

Mat McCollough was assigned to me as a mentor in 2011 by the American Association of People with Disabilities (AAPD), the nation's largest cross disability rights network. I was serving as an intern through them at the time. Mat was the Executive

Director of the Developmental Disabilities Council for the District of Columbia when I met him. He has since become the director of the District of Columbia's Office on Disability Rights. He is also a presidentially appointed member of the US ACCESS Board, the United States government agency which deals with physical access matters mandated by federal legislation. He met with me frequently during my internship, invited me to functions, spent some down time with me, and has met with me since then. When I was in Washington for the 25th anniversary of the ADA, I met with him to discuss an eventual move to the Washington, DC area. He was very forthcoming about tips for gaining employment, for which I am most thankful. Since I have moved to the Washington, DC area, Mat has continued being a professional contact, and also a very dear friend.

I met Joyce Bender on the very first day of my internship for the AAPD. She was just about to assume the role of board chair of that organization. I will admit that I did not know much about who she was until part way through the internship. I soon learned that she has done more for disability employment than almost anyone alive today. She runs a temp agency, Bender Consulting, out of Pittsburgh, Pennsylvania. She has helped develop policies that are now implemented on the federal level, and she frequently meets with delegations from overseas who are hoping to improve their disability employment measures. Joyce has always been willing to provide job recommendations, references, networking, and other opportunities. When I last met Joyce, she gave me a gigantic hug and repeatedly referred to me as "my son". I feel honored to have someone of her stature in my corner, and it is absolutely incredible how close we have become!

Emil Novak, Sr. is a successful independent businessman in Buffalo, New York. He approaches life with common sense, and always jumps at opportunity. He has been working at the biggest comic book store in town, Queen City Bookstore, since his father founded the business over forty years ago. He is now the owner of the business, which is the oldest bookstore in Erie County, New York. He also runs an independent film studio, two local comic book conventions, and manages Visions Comic Art Group, a local group that makes comic books and coordinates artists and writers. Emil has graciously allowed me to do publicity for him, honing my skills in photography, events management, and social networking. When I came out with a paper that I wanted published, I was told that there was no chance of that happening. Emil came forward and allowed me to get it published. He has also coordinated artwork for this publication, and allowed me to promote it at his conventions. Since moving away from Buffalo, New York, I have remained friends with Emil, while developing a new mentor-mentee relationship in Washington, DC.

That relationship is with Jd Michaels. In another blog post, I spoke of the benefits of the Lights, Camera, Access 2.0 seminar on disability and media. I have been invited to these seminars, both during the closing days of the Obama administration. At the first one, which actually took place at the White House Complex, I met Jd, who is the Executive Vice President of a large, prominent international advertising firm in New York City called BBDO Worldwide. Although we are not located in the same cities, we frequently meet over Skype. At one point, he proposed some rough deals to me. I later traveled to New York City to meet with him at his offices and discuss details. For one thing, I am being given a job at BBDO Worldwide as an editor. My job is to edit stories from authors in the Deaf and disability community for collection into an anthology. Editing includes work on flow and consistency of content, and monitoring disability-related themes. This job shall last at least one calendar year. In addition, based simply on the fact that Jd believes I am a good person, BBDO will be paying for the production of a book collecting a number of my essays. Amazingly, all profits will be mine. I am stoked! Finally, Jd will be working with me to find conferences and other events where I can be a guest speaker. It is clear to see that Jd Michaels is a terrific friend and mentor!

All of these wonderful people have contributed greatly to my success in my professional life. I thank them tremendously for all of the help and patience they have given me in helping to contribute to my professional growth. I would like to extend my heartfelt thanks to Mat McCollough, Joyce Bender, Emil Novak, Sr., and Jd Michaels!

Advice in Making Cell Phone Stores Autism-Friendly

I occasionally get questions from people doing academic studies on disability. In this case, an academic at Waterloo University asked me, in my capacity as Director of Autistic Reality, for advice in making cell phone stores more accessible to individuals with autism. Here is my advice, slightly edited for clarity.

As far as improving the experience of autistic individuals in cell phone stores, there are a few suggestions I could make. A number of us with autism have sensory disabilities. Cell phone stores can be difficult, because they are often filled with bright lights and crowded with people. One may often wish that they were dimmer, or included a dimmer area. A quieter area would also help the autistic population, and not just in cell phone stores, but in many different kinds of establishments.

In addition, cell phone stores often rely heavily on procedure. There is someone to greet you as you come through the door, and they immediately demand case information, before passing you on to their colleagues, who may also shirk politeness in favor of efficiency. This leads to one of the biggest changes that cell phone stores and many different types of businesses can make, to benefit all of humanity and not just the autistic population: they can be nice to you. The effect that a courteous staff person has on the customer cannot be overstated. Autistic people often spend their whole lives being treated as "other" by society, being socially ostracized or being tested by doctors and educators. Courteous staff may seem like a small step, but it is much appreciated. On an autism specific level, staff at cell phone stores and once again all stores should be educated that not all people fit the same social models. Social disability is incredibly prevalent in a large portion of the population. It is time that businesses start accommodating social disability the same way that they have been accommodating or attempting to accommodate physical disability. Social disability is, in fact, a civil rights issue.

Finally, not all autistic people are capable of speech, and that does not mean that they are stupid or uneducated. Autistic people who do not speak are just as capable of thinking as you and I, and often use tools such as iPads or cell phones to communicate, since they are not capable of or comfortable with speech. This provides cell phone stores and companies with a very unique opportunity to cater especially to and even higher autistic individuals who do not communicate using traditional methods. Cell phone companies can lead the way in a very unique form of diversity inclusion.

Interview on Employment
of Autistic People

Journalists sometimes seek my expertise on various issues. In this case, a journalist asked me for my viewpoints on improving the employment of autistic people.Please note that my answers are definitely not exhaustive, but are rather a combination of what is true to me, and what answers I find to be least given by other people.

What does inclusiveness and accessibility mean to you in the workplace?

Autism is a social and behavioral disability. Therefore, to me, inclusiveness and accessibility in the workplace means a kind, understanding staff. It also means office social situations that I can easily become acclimated to. I recognize that some autistic people have a harder time becoming acclimated than others, but I also understand that some are unwilling. In my opinion, being willing to acclimate to certain social situations as much is comfortably possible can help one in business tremendously. There are meetings to go to, presentations to give, and coworkers to get along with.

What are some of the challenges facing autistic people who are in traditional workplaces, particularly due to a lack of accommodations or accessibility?

Interestingly, the least accessible workplace I have ever been in was an independent living center in Buffalo, New York. This is highly ironic, given that independent living centers are disability-run, and are supposed to be the most accommodating workplaces in the country. This was definitely not true of this business. My immediate boss yelled at me and belittled me every single day—often until I cried, one of the receptionists repeatedly told me I did not work there, the IT staffer told me to "fuck off" repeatedly, and the entire place was run by three members of the same immediate family, in the most glaringly obvious ethics violation I have ever encountered. Sadly, the autistic community often encounters staff members with bad attitudes or lack of understanding.

What can employers, coworkers, hiring managers, HR departments, etc. do to better support autistic employees?

As a contrast, my current employer, the Executive Vice President of Diversity at BBDO Worldwide, a large advertising firm, recognizes that I have my own idiosyncrasies, odd behaviors, and needs for accommodation. In terms of the odd behaviors, he actually encourages them! He is the nicest boss I could ever imagine! He understands that a large part of inclusion is a good attitude and being tolerant of people who are mentally and emotionally different. He and I love to tell jokes, talk about our personal lives and our work experience, and get all geeky and nerdy together! HR departments need to recognize that not everybody is going to fit the same behavioral mold, and that just because someone is goofy, geeky, or "weird", does not mean that they are necessarily a bad employee or job candidate.

What stereotypes or myths have you come across about autistic people that affect how autistic people are treated in the workplace?

One stereotype is that we are all into things like math and computer science. That is absolute hogwash. While it is true that autistic people tend to fixate on specific issues, there is nothing about the autistic population that guarantees that we will all be mathematicians or scientists. I, for example, am interested in things like history, political science, and architecture. Another stereotype is that we are, by and large, completely socially inept. In reality, social experience can often lead to us being quite savvy to the moods and emotions of others. It has for me.

Can you give me a specific example of different things that help you succeed in the workplace? Have you ever been in a

situation where you've had to ask for your workplace to be made more accessible to you?

This plays into another stereotype, which says that sensory issues are inherently severe for the autistic population. First off, the sensory diagnosis is actually separate from autism, and has gone by various names such as Sensory Integration Disorder and Sensory Processing Disorder. This is often quite severe in many autistics, but that is not always the case. In addition, our tolerance for sensory overload can be grown and expanded with experience. As I mentioned earlier, many of us in the activism world are not interested in growing that tolerance. I respectfully disagree, as growing my tolerance for sensory exposure has allowed me to become a better worker, a better friend, a more integrated member of society, and a more independent adult. That said, I have asked that my workplaces be aware of my sensory issues and be more accommodating. The abusive workplace I was in earlier demanded medical documentation, when all I wanted was for the break room likes to be off for five minutes. My job for BBDO Worldwide actually has a dark study room/library built specifically so that the bright lights of the office do not overwhelm the workers all the time.

Are there any common workplace trends that you feel employers need to re-think in order to make the workplace/office more inclusive? (For example, Skype interviews or open office plans)

My biggest suggestion is actually not for the workplaces, but for the training of potential employees. Throughout school, throughout social skills classes, throw job training seminars (of which there were plenty), throughout vocational rehab, throughout job counseling (which was seemingly endless in my case), a clear majority of the training involved putting together a resume and filling out an application. Although it is sometimes a relatively recent development, workplaces no longer rely solely on resumes and applications when hiring people. Networking, networking, networking is the skill that gets at least half of America their jobs in today's society. This is actually not as new as it seems. Back in the day, giving your friend a job was not a big deal. The difference between then and now is that now employers are looking to hire qualified employees because they know them well, and they know that they are right for the job. In Buffalo, New York, I applied for at least one hundred and fifty jobs in a row without even hearing back. It's not like I was declined, but I never even heard back! Three days after I moved to Washington, DC, I was invited to the mother of all networking events at the Obama White House and met my current boss. We Skyped, talked by phone, and one day he offered me a job that I didn't even apply for. Not just that, but it is a well-paying job, with lots of benefits. And, it is terrifically fun to work at! This is a perfect example of how training those entering the workforce needs to stop focusing entirely on resumes and applications and start focusing on networking!

Have you ever worked remotely, or do you have anything to

say about the benefits of working remotely or flexible working hours for autistic employees?

In fact, I am working remotely right now. What I do is not like telework. Instead, I set aside some time to do my job, which involves creating written content, and editing other people's written content. A large part of my job also involves traveling and experiencing things so that I may write about them and attending conferences and meetings in various localities such as New York City and Boston. My hours are up to my discretion, and the location where I do my work—often at my laptop—is also up to my discretion. I do realize that not everybody can have a job this flexible, but it has proven extremely beneficial. Many of the experiences I have for my work are extremely fun, and I get compensated for writing about them. It also allows me to set my own leisure time.

Alec Frazier is an editor and disability rights advocate from Washington, DC.

My Dream Job:
On the Importance of Networking

What follows is an essay on my experience looking for and finding employment, and how I have learned about the importance of professional networking as a result.

Hello, I'm Alec Frazier. I'm autistic and have been a self-advocate and an advocate since I can remember, although definitely professionally since I gave my first speech in third grade in 1994. I am currently the director of Autistic Reality, by on advocacy and consultancy firm. Today, I wish to discuss employment, and the importance of networking.

Individuals with autism are often passed over for employment. In some cases, it is because we are not as socially adept as others. In other cases, it is because we may have unusual quirks which employers find less than desirable. As such, we can be completely capable of carrying out a job but get turned down time and time again. Eighteen is seen as the age of majority, but I did not get by first paying job until at least ten years afterwards, and it was for an agency run by the disability

More frequently, by applications were turned down, or even ignored. For six years while I was in university, I lived in a Rust Belt town, and that one point I submitted at least one hundred and fifty job applications in a row with no response. We are not talking about denials. We are talking about lack of response. Back in the day, people used to at least send you denial letters, but this practice is growing incredibly rare.

In addition, employment workshops operate on a very large misconception. In my life, I have been to at least two dozen employment trainings, some as standalone seminars, and some as ongoing sessions. Some of these have been disability centric, and some of them have been for more general purposes. At these training sessions, those in charge, whether they be vocational rehabilitation counselors or others have constantly stressed the resume and the application process. It seems to be all they ever talk about. At many of these sessions, I was told out right that if I applied enough, I would get a job, and a pretty decent one, too. In addition, every single one of these trainings and seminars had me rewrite my resume. It got to the point where I no longer allow most people to get me resume tips, as one person's advice is always conflicting with another's.

Over the years, I built up a very solid list of volunteer activities and other work. Some of my work, such as volunteer work for an independent living network, was actually more intense than some of the paid staff, and this was acknowledged by my superiors. However, they lacked the ability to pay me.

Finally, having obtained a bachelor's degree in political science and a master's degree in disability studies, I moved to the Washington, DC area to pursue a career and advocacy.

I was not disappointed. Three days after moving here, in late 2016, I got invited to the White House for a business conference on disability in the media called Lights! Camera! Access! 2.0. At this conference, I met Jd Michaels the Executive Vice President of BBDO Worldwide, and international advertising firm. Although I continue pursuing employment in other venues, Jd and I continued communicating regularly, sometimes emailing, sometimes talking by phone, and sometimes Skyping.

After a few months, Jd approached me with a job offer: he hired me as an editor for an anthology of writings by authors with disabilities. In addition, I told him that I had a number of writings that I wished to get published, and he agreed to help me with that at no cost to myself, and in such a way that I could receive all of the profits. These essays are varied in character, with some being pop-culture reviews, some being academic papers. In fact, this essay is going in that book, which is titled Veni! Vedi! Autism! and will be out within about a month.

Jd has been an amazing employer. He has provided me with all of the tools I need to succeed. I have writing disabilities, so he has provided me with Dragon NaturallySpeaking software for me to dictate my papers and even blog entries like this one. He has provided me with computer software and hardware. He has provided me with camera batteries so that I may better publicize my experiences, hotels, meals, and travel so that I may attend conferences, and even photo shoots to publicize our work.

I have finally found a job that provides me with stability and everything I need to succeed. Want to know how many times I applied? The answer is zero. Networking got me this position. It is my firm opinion that at least 50% of gaining employment is networking. It is time to train our workforce with that fact in mind.

Alec's Independent Living Tips:
A Home of Your Own

As you know by now, I have several disabilities. I am proud of the fact that I live on my own, and I have since at least 2008. What follows is my advice on Independent living in a safe, reliable home.

Please move to a safe, reliable, livable home. I know many people who suffer because they live in subpar apartments. This essay will assume that you will be renting, rather than owning. Ideally, you can live in a good apartment for years on end. In fact, in most of the world, people rent properties over the course of decades, and even generations. You need to know what to look for. That is where I come in.

It will never cease to amaze me how many people with options choose to live in slums or bad apartments. A number of these people have defended themselves by saying that this gives them the freedom to party. I know that I have never been one for much partying, but the freedom to party is, in my mind, not a proper excuse for lack of safety, comfort, financial security, and many other factors. Many of these slumlords are gougers. In one case, I knew people who were being charged over $2,000 a month to rent a house that was so bad that inspectors had appraised its sale value at $500.

Many, many slumlords run absolute disgraces, and rent them out to the public. I have seen some amazingly bad things. I have seen sinks which are made of materials that poison the water that comes out of them. I have seen doors made from cardboard and cheap plastics. I have seen houses where more windows are broken than intact. I have seen pipes made from what is supposed to be posts for chain-link fence. I have seen bullet holes, lack of insulation, lack of three-pronged wall outlets, lack of heating, lack of basic fixtures, and many, many other travesties. It is a shame that anyone would want to live in such disgusting conditions, but many people do not know what to look for. I am trying to help.

In addition, negotiating a lease agreement on time is incredibly important. Please negotiate your lease agreement approximately a month in advance of planned occupancy. You need to make sure that the place is ready for you to move in on time. In addition, not signing a lease in advance gives the landlord an opportunity to back out of the deal, and I have known of landlords who have done this at the last moment. It is far better to be prepared.

Please make sure that you have a kind, responsible landlord. A proper landlord will have maintenance take care of issues, and will, in fact, have much less issues to take care of, if they are constantly looking after the place properly. I tend to recommend apartment buildings above all other kinds of apartments, as they are much harder for both landlords and tenants to mismanage and abuse. Please try to move to a nicer neighborhood, nothing super fancy or expensive, but not a slum or unsafe area. I discourage moving into apartments divided out of pieces of houses, as there is less incentive for a landlord to be responsible, and because these units tend to be in bad neighborhoods more often than apartment buildings. The perfect landlord has a website for online payment and maintenance requests, although not everybody has this.

Even if you drive, please look for a place near public transportation. I do not advise moving to a place without it, especially if one has disabilities. If your town doesn't have public transit, then I wouldn't advise living there. Also, sign up for Uber or Lyft. Buses are useful, and subways are amazing, since they usually run on a preset schedule. If you have mobility impairments, please make sure that you move to an area with transit stations that are accessible. Please do not overuse Uber and Lyft. They should only be used when there is no other option. This will help save the bank. If there is a public transit card for your area, please get it.

In fact, please make sure that you have an easy or at least simplified way to get to the greater world outside of your city by public transit. For example, to get anywhere in the United States, all I must do is take the subway few stops to Union Station in Washington, DC, and I can take Amtrak or other train services virtually anywhere in the country. For those distances a longer way away, I take the subway to either one of the two local airports. Remember, it is best not to deal with long-term parking and your own vehicle when traveling out of town, whether by train or plane.

Please move somewhere close to a reasonable grocery store. In fact, the more food options, the better. There is something in geography called a food desert. A food desert is a place where you must travel a way to have access to proper nutrition and nourishment. Ideally, there should be a good grocery store within walking distance, even if it is a longer walk. The idea is to be able to access your food easily, even if you do not drive. Even if you do drive, please keep this fact in mind. In the modern technological age, it is good to sign up for a service like Instacart. Ideally, they will cover your local area. Instacart and other services like it allow you to order delivery of food from grocery stores online, or over a mobile app. This will help you shop when you are unable to leave the house. Be aware that services like Instacart do not accept food stamp benefits, though.

Please make sure that your apartment or home is also reasonably close to other shopping as well. It is good to be in close distance to clothing stores and places to get basic electronics, such as power cords for your devices, or Internet connection. It is also a great idea to make sure that you can easily get to a home supply store and a furniture store. Make sure to take note of your other needs, and to move to a place where they are within reach.

Don't forget about fun! The perfect place to live will have areas within access which have restaurants, at least one movie theater, hopefully a bookstore, and places to meet and hang out with friends.

These are my basic independent living tips regarding places to move into. I hope they are helpful! When people say home is where the heart is, they mean it. A wonderful, loving home gives you fulfillment and happiness.

For the Anti-Vaxers

One of the most dangerous and ill-informed trends today is the anti-vaccination movement. Here is my refutation of that movement.

Throughout history, people have feared what they don't understand. One of the fastest-growing diagnoses is autism. In my own personal opinion, autism kicks ass! Yes, my childhood was difficult, and learning to live on my own and finding employment was, at first, a chore. However, since then, autism has led to some truly remarkable advancements in my life. I have an amazing, high paying job where I get compensated to go to theme parks, write books, and meet celebrities. I have my own beautiful home, filled with wonderful belongings and original artwork that symbolize who I am today. I have far too many friends to count, from your general "friends next door" type of person to a United States senator, authors, and even a nuclear scientist. My life is fantastic.

In 1998, British scientist Andrew Wakefield published an article in the scientific journal, The Lancet stating that a vaccine for measles, mumps, and rubella caused autism. Wakefield was lying, of course, and later admitted that fact, and went to prison. Nonetheless, many people refuse to admit that he was lying, and seek external causes for autism. I have endlessly encountered people who say that there must be "something in the water", or something in vaccinations, or something else to be cured.

There is nothing to be cured. There is nothing wrong with us. There is nothing you can do to vaccines, "the water", or any other substance or factor on this planet to make us go away. And that's what you want to do, underneath it all. You want autistic people to disappear. Don't try to deny it. You are bigoted and hateful, no matter how much you wrap it up. I cannot convince all of you to stop thinking the way you do, but I can hopefully convince some of you.

One of the worst things about all of this is that those of you who believe that vaccines cause autism would clearly much rather that people have horrible conditions like measles, smallpox, polio, and many other deadly diseases. All of you who believe that vaccines cause autism clearly believe that these horrible conditions are much better than having autism. Think about that. That's extremely messed up. Thanks to you, there are now increased cases of all of these diseases and more, putting millions and risk of death, all because of your bigotry.

In fact, although its diagnosis was broadened by recent standards, autism has existed throughout history, including such individuals as Leonardo da Vinci, Thomas Jefferson, and Nikola

Tesla, all of whom would not have been able to contribute what they have to society without their autism. Imagine no Mona Lisa, no United States of America, and no use of electricity. You want that? Imagine the current people with autism who are changing the world for the better. People like Bill Gates and Elon Musk, amongst others. Want their achievements to go away?

But this isn't about them, is it? This is about your precious child. You are willing to take the word of someone who was a part-time nurse several years ago, or some doctor who lost his license, or even a porn star like Jenny McCarthy, so long as they reinforce your narrative that something is wrong with your child. I repeat, nothing is wrong with your child. May I suggest, that if you continue thinking so, something is very wrong with you. Even if you do not have children, if you think that there is some external factor such as "the water", vaccines, pollution, which causes autism, then you wish to disbelieve science and instead believe that something is wrong with people with autism.

There are studies on external factors which can be taken seriously, but they are few and far between. Almost every single time I see someone sharing one, it is a crackpot study shared simply to reinforce their own very incorrect viewpoints. The clear majority of the scientific community agrees that autism is a naturally occurring phenomenon, and that there is nothing external which causes it. I honestly don't care what your nurse friend has to say, when your discredited doctor friend has to say, or what a porn star you have never met has to say. They are very, very wrong.

But you don't care about that. You look for something that can hopefully "cure" us. I don't care if that "us" includes your child, or your student, or your brother, or whatever. The very notion of wanting to cure us insists that there is something wrong with us. Because if there is something wrong with us, then your fear of us or our condition is justified. Stop being afraid of us. You may not admit to being afraid, but you clearly are. Instead, try to understand us, accommodate us, and love us for the wonderful, unique individuals we are. There is nothing wrong with us. If you believe there is, then there is clearly something wrong with you. I suggest you try to cure yourself.

What I Do

I recently completed an interview about what I do for my advocacy and other work. I am glad to include that interview in this book.

Where are you currently employed? What do you do?

I am currently the director of my own firm, Autistic Reality. I do disability and human rights advocacy including but not limited to public speaking, lobbying, peer advocacy, and generating original creative content.

How would you describe your job to a complete stranger?

To elaborate on the previous question, I fight for the disability community and other people who are underprivileged or have had their rights infringed. This takes a variety of forms.

Traditionally, I have been speaking with legislators and their staff to push various agendas, giving speeches at various conferences and conventions, and serving as a mentor for various individuals. I have just been inducted into the National Disability Mentoring Hall of Fame. I work frequently with the National Council on Independent Living, As Well As My Local Independent Living Center, Independence Now. Independent living centers exist nationwide, and even internationally, to promote the disability branch of the civil rights movement. They focus on much more than just living, and cover other areas including employment, education, civil rights issues, and personal development. I also work with any number of task forces or other groups that I either agree with him which desire my services. For example, I am currently speaking at a writers' conference in Richmond, Virginia which I had been invited to after its organizer met me at another convention. Networking is important. I also am starting my own podcast soon, and have several episodes recorded.

While I am a disability rights advocate by trade, most of my recent work has involved writing and editing, and I have come out with a three-hundred-page book called Veni! Vidi! Autism! In addition to that, I have been compiling, editing, and curating a collection of original works by individuals with disabilities. This collection is called Stories About Us, and consists of short stories, poetry, novels, and entire series of books. This work has entailed me traveling to various pop-culture conventions to promote my own work, and speaking at those shows, as well as selling my book and various artwork. There will be further promotional events as new works in Stories About Us get published.

Any uncommon skills/ tasks your job requires of you?

Believe it or not, the writing load can be quite heavy. I write blog entries frequently with my points of view on everything from art exhibits to films to social decorum to disability policy to travel essays and just about anything. A number of these blog entries make their way into my published works. One of the benefits to the blogs is that I can include images, as well as reaching an audience that is in some respects wider. I include the writing as an unusual task because I have two writing disabilities and require computer software to get any real volume of writing done. In fact, I am using it to write these answers right now. By using this software and being patient with it and becoming an expert in its use, I have written my way to be a published author.

Another unusual skill required of me is the ability to experience pop-culture in depth, with an analytical mind. I do this for fun, too. A typical day off involves photographing the heck out of a museum. I then go home and caption the images thoroughly. I also do this with architecture and, of course, delicious food. There are huge benefits to my work in recording these experiences in such detail, because I can easily write about my experiences. As a result, I have written detailed and evocative chapters on things such as famed artist Yayoi Kusama, the Kennedy Space Center, and even theme parks! Of course, in addition to in-depth physical experiences, I also write about films, books, and other more traditional pop-culture experiences.

How do your personal experiences help or hinder you at work?

This keys into the last question. Another set of skills required for my work is social awareness. I know what you're thinking; autism doesn't usually lend itself to that. However, over the many years of my life, I have developed quite a knack for social skills. Don't get me wrong! I sometimes still goof up, and that has caused some of my biggest professional pitfalls. Fortunately, they seem to come further and further between, in addition to being more and more minor. In fact, they often help me get further in business. For example, one time I had a meeting with my Senator, and I spend my time ingratiating myself with him whilst also pushing agenda issues. At the end, I asked him if he would be on my podcast, and he surprised me by saying yes. There are other guests I have gotten on the podcast by using deft social skills. One of them is a civil rights pioneer and independent business owner in Washington, DC who is in her eighties. I realized that her family, which manages her business affairs, may be sensitive if I just outright asked for her to be a guest, so I spent time getting to know her while visiting her business. We chatted and became friends. This helped convince her daughter, who is also her publicist, to allow me to put her on my podcast.

What makes your job interesting?

For one thing, the people I meet are truly one-of-a-kind. Every one of them is noteworthy in their own way. Not all of them may be famous, but they all have an interesting story to tell. I work with politicians, artists, caseworkers, parents, and even children. Of course, meeting some famous people has become a given. One time, I met Senator Tammy Duckworth, and it didn't even enter my mind how impressive that meeting was, because such work is a given in my field. I am also somewhat expert at befriending noteworthy personalities. It is my policy that it can't hurt to try! If they have a personal Facebook profile, often, I send them a request. You'd be surprised who I have amongst my social media contacts!

The most rewarding part of my job, however, is when I make a noticeable difference in someone's life, whether it be one person or many people. I don't care about awards or official recognition. In my experience, those often goes to people who game the system. Instead, I the deepest impact upon me comes when someone tells me I have changed their life for the better. This means the world to me.

How does your job impact other professions/vocations?

As mentioned in the previous answer, I often hear people about the differences I have made upon their lives. My advice impacts several professionals and their various vocations, including but not limited to rehabilitation counseling, editing, writing, public speaking, healthcare, education, workforce inclusion, and much, much more. As for how my job impacts these professions and vocations, I provide an optimistic yet realism-based disabled point of view on all these various facets of life.

In one notable example, I was in a group of about ten people who lobbied Senator Chuck Schumer to help create a federal agency on Independent Living and disability civil rights. Our voices were very clearly articulated to him, because the next day, he walked into the Senate chamber and proposed legislation to do so. By the next summer, I was having a meeting with the head of the Administration on Community Living, the agency that I was in small part responsible for founding. I recognize that thousands of people over the years who have had roles in promoting the establishment of such an agency, however it was my group's talk to his staffer that provided the final impetus to get it created. In this way, I have had a small but vital role in the establishment of the current state of affairs in Independent Living.

Sometimes other people ask me about anything from healthcare benefits to housing options to employment choices and even about recreational activities. I recognize that my knowledge is not as in-depth as a specialist in each matter, but I help provide basic jumping off points for them to look for benefits. I cannot even begin to count the number of people I have helped in this way. Nonetheless, I am humbled when they come to me, and always put their own needs and wants first.

If you were trying to "sell" what you do to a potential collaborator/colleague, what would your elevator pitch be?

Hello, I'm Alec Frazier. I have autism and several other disabilities, and I run a human rights advocacy firm called Autistic Reality. I do public speaking, lobbying, benefits advisement, peer mentoring, policy consulting, and editing and writing. I work equally with people with disabilities as well as parents and other family members, caregivers, other professionals, and even politicians to make sure that the rights of the disability population are heard. I consider myself a compromiser, and I am willing to work with almost anyone in order to pursue these goals.

If you are a writer, and you have disabilities, I'd like to tell you about the Stories About Us anthology project. I am the Managing Editor on this project to get writings by disabled authors published. I will be happy and proud to provide you with the publication of your own copyrighted book. I will provide the necessary fees to copyright your works, as well as layout and some publicity materials. I strongly believe in the right of everyone to get their stories told, and publishing should not be restricted only to people with a great deal of time, money, and resources.

A note on the second paragraph: we are still working out the particulars of Stories About Us as a sustainable, long-term project.

Do you think we as a society are making progress when it comes to understanding and accepting autism?

I absolutely do think that we are making progress on the front. Family members, caregivers, other professionals, and peers are constantly learning about autism, and along with that learning comes understanding. When I was younger, many years ago, a peer of mine said that I couldn't be autistic because I can talk. That was the first and yet only time I have heard such gross misunderstanding. Today, everyone knows someone with autism, and everybody has a basic understanding of the inherent worth and dignity of the autistic individual. Whether or not they choose to act on that understanding is up to them, but I find that over 90% do.

It should be mentioned that, as a more moderate advocate, I do not see the world as pessimistically as many more radical autistic activists do. Those radical activists often harp on the negatives, and perceived lack of understanding. To them, lack of understanding is ammunition and business and perhaps even money in the pocket for them. I have asked several of them whether they want to be happy and more optimistic, and many of them have mentioned that they choose to be negative and combative. I work for an opposite standpoint, and choose to see the glass as half-full, and that everybody has a potential to work together toward a better future. I think that most of the people who are not understanding of autistic individuals want to learn and be more respectful.

What kind of stigmas do you face while doing your day-to-day work?

None! Maybe it has to do with my skill at socialization, but I almost never encounter negative stigma when doing my advocacy work.

In casual situations, I try to ingratiate myself, and often bring up advocacy after we have been talking a while. People's reactions in casual situations are always positive, and they frequently mention that they know someone or have a family member with autism. We build on that. These people often end up becoming proud supporters of my work, and even friends.

In more businesslike situations, people always seem to understand where I am coming from. One of the key things I do in the middle of conversation is let people know that I am not as radical as some of these autistic activist groups, and that I recognize that they are trying to help no matter how they do things. This immediately puts individuals and organizations at ease. Many of them have reiterated that they are used to hostile, militant, stubborn, and closed-minded groups of radicals who refuse to consider multiple viewpoints. I tend to win people over by being tolerant and accepting of diverse views.

Now, there are some organizations and individuals that I dislike more than others, but, if business were to have me work with them, I would do so on a professional basis. I am a compromiser, and I will not automatically hate you just because I disagree with you. There is only one way to make me hate you, and that is to treat me or countless others like garbage without a basis. More of the radical disability activists tend to do this then the people without disabilities. One needs to come at things with an open mind, not with hate in their heart.

You said in your initial email to me that you were pushing for legislative change on forced institutionalization, even planning on taking the case to Congress. What happened? What was the response?

We, the disability community, have been pushing to eliminate forced institutionalization for those with disabilities and in the aged community for quite some time now. In fact, ever since the

Americans with Disabilities Act (ADA) was passed in 1991, various groups have been pushing further to allow people in these populations to live in the world at large. Accessibility is very desirable indeed but cannot be had when a significant portion of the population is forced to live in situations without their consent, set apart from the rest of society.

I know you may be thinking that people in the disability community may not have it that bad but let me tell you a story. I was living in Buffalo, New York, where I was working for the independent living agency in town. One gentleman was being taken out to eat by the institution he lived in. It was a halfway house sort of environment. He had his own money and wanted to go to McDonald's. It would have been an easy stop for the drive through and would have cost about five bucks. However, the halfway house staff said that they had agreed that he could only have healthy food, so they did not allow him to eat what he wanted, even with his own money. I'm sorry, but I tend to view such a horrific lack of self-agency is nothing other than slavery. Most of the rest of the disability community agrees, which is why we are trying to pass this bill.

To this end, we have been pushing something called the Disability Integration Act (DIA), which would set up a rigorous system for people with disabilities and elders to live under our own self-determination and terms. This would use almost no additional funds than are currently in use by the federal government, and in fact, in the long run, it would save the government and society endless amounts of money. It costs a lot more to keep people locked up than it does to let us live on our own. This bill would allow for home care aides and would add sections to the Affordable Care Act to allow us to determine our own destinies.

This bill is currently being considered by Congress and has a much greater likelihood of passing now than it ever has before. It has been written by people in the disability community, and we will continue to push this bill until it passes. Luckily, we have some very powerful supporters in Congress.

A Grim Becoming

The area around Buffalo, New York has over forty independent film studios, and many of them make very high quality work. One day, I was scheduled to go out to lunch with a friend I had made on Facebook. One thing that often happens to autistic individuals is sudden, random termination of friendship. On that day, I found that the friend in question had cut off contact with me, clearly not wanting to meet up or even know each other. So, instead, I went to the premier of the locally produced film "A Grim Becoming". It is one of the best decisions I have ever made. In so doing, I made endless new friends and business contacts, and saw one of the best films of my life. Now, without further ado, I give you my review of that film.

Death has many faces. Death is often a frightening, intimidating concept. Death is the destroyer of worlds. And, in the film *A Grim Becoming*, Death is named Magoo. Of course, this is no laughing matter to Death, who is not familiar with earthly animation.

A *Grim Becoming* is a dark comedy set mostly in the fictional town of Metzburgh, New York, with some scenes set in Buffalo, New York. Overall, the premise for this film is so ingenious that one can't help but wonder why it hasn't been made already. The film explores how someone becomes a grim reaper, what their powers are, the politics of life after death, and how death manifests itself in our world. It follows a young architectural executive, Raphael Stockford (Brandyn T. Williams), as he is granted the powers of a Grim Reaper. This poses a great problem though, because he really doesn't want to kill anyone. In this film, the Grim Reapers are employees of Death (Michael Sciabarrasi). Death is a ghastly gentleman dressed in Victorian garb with an ever-present cigar. He takes his job quite seriously, and is not to be toyed with. Nonetheless, he often finds the oddities of everyday human life quite comical. Raphael is coming to Metzburgh from his hometown of Buffalo to take care of final affairs for his nephew, who has just passed away, leaving behind a scarred girlfriend and a saddened family. However, the family is quite out of its gourd with their own problems and quirks. Add to this ever-present mix Raphael's office life, which is an absolute nightmare, and the other guests at his hotel, who are just having a devil of a time trying to get laid. Throw in a zombie, the truth about the JFK assassination, and pot smoking Angels.

You may be asking at this point, "Isn't this too much for one film?" Absolutely not! The film is quite well-made by DefTone Pictures Studios, Inc., which is based in Hamburg, New York. In fact, the film, directed by Adam Steigert, is on the level of some of the smaller films made in Hollywood. The premier took place at the historic Hamburg Palace Theater in Hamburg, New York, and there was a question-and-answer period afterwards. The love that the filmmakers have for the film shows through in droves. All of the movie was filmed in Buffalo, New York, by local acting talent and a local production crew. With museums, historic landmarks, a vibrant comic book scene, and excellent independent filmmakers, Buffalo has great potential as an art town. The film clearly shows as an independent flick, but the quality is superb. The film manages to tackle the philosophy surrounding death as well as excellent humor at the same time. The film is terribly funny! The film manages to draw on the hip vibe of current day pop culture in a way that a bigger, Hollywood-made film is not able to genuinely capture. You feel like you are friends with the characters in this film. You don't just feel for them, but you feel like you could BE them! The acting is wonderful, the sets are spot on, and the character development is genius. A local community came together to create this masterpiece!

I will admit that when I went to see this film, I had had correspondence with Brandyn T. Williams, Michael Sciabarrasi, and Adam Steigert. However, attending the premier with them has cemented a friendship among local businessmen. Local businessmen who are, indeed, awesome people on the personal level. On a personal level, I, Alec Frazier, appreciated the film tremendously. My business is a disability rights firm called Autistic Reality. Autistic Reality has also come out with a book, a literature review called <u>Without Fear: The First Autistic Superhero</u>. A big part of our firm's business is appreciating realistic standards, as opposed to irrational expectations or setting the bar too low, or too high. We also have a healthy ideal of what fun should be. Fun should not be afraid to be politically incorrect, and should play to the human element in us all. In our mind, fun should be awesome, enjoyable, intelligent, and worthwhile. It should be awesome in that it fills you with wonder. It should be enjoyable in that it fills you with joy. It should be intelligent in that it makes you think. It should be worthwhile in that it should be worth having. My firm, Autistic Reality, would full heartedly like to endorse *A Grim Becoming* as meeting our criteria of awesome, enjoyable, intelligent, and worthwhile fun! We give this film our highest recommendations! We also would like to give the best of endorsements to Brandyn T. Williams, DefTone Pictures Studios Inc., and the Hamburg Palace Theater. This movie has just become an annual Halloween tradition in my house. Buy a copy! You will be glad you did!

Scope of Practice

"I first met Brandyn T. Williams when he starred in the film "A Grim Becoming". Soon afterwards, he came out with the film "Scope of Practice". Brandyn was in my circle of friends when I lived in Buffalo, New York, so I decided to do him a favor and review his film. Here is that review.

Criminals often get what they are due: punishment by the penal system and condemnation by their community. However, as real-life events can tell us, there are still many criminals who do not get what they deserve. For example, in 1992, Nicole Brown Simpson was murdered and the person responsible, her husband OJ Simpson, was let off by the courts. Why is this? Why do these horrible people get away with horrible things? The answer in most of the cases is favoritism. In OJ Simpson's case, he was a famous football player with fantastic lawyers. Other crimes by people of privilege throughout the country and the world, both past and present, may come to mind at this moment.

Enter onto the scene the film *Scope of Practice*, produced by BeWILderedMedia Productions, and directed and written by Brandyn T. Williams. In this film, a rookie EMT named Derek Reynolds (Chris Barbis), is called to the scene when Emma Phillips (Arlynn Knauff) apparently falls down the stairs at the home where she lives with her husband, Buffalo football player Donnie Phillips (Matt Fleck). Derek notices a footprint on Emma's back, and suspects spousal abuse. He reports the fact, and waits for a result. I won't try to ruin the film for you, but I can summarize the rest by mentioning that it is about the lengths to which Derek will go to see Donnie held responsible for his crimes.

For you see, Donnie Phillips holds a great deal of favoritism within the local community. He is a celebrity. Not just that, but he is a football player. To digress on this for a moment, America has what I believe is an unhealthy fixation with every little minute detail of American football. It is a gladiatorial sport, where we see people beat each other up on a field, and we encourage bad behavior from many of the players, because we believe that it shows that they are more of a man. These are unhealthy values to have. A real man would not beat the person he says he loves. A real man would admit to wrongdoings for which he is responsible. However, just like OJ Simpson, Donnie Phillips' prestige in the community tends to keep him out of trouble.

Unfortunately, Derek Reynolds realizes that overcoming the favoritism held by Donnie Phillips will probably risk him his job and his safety. Are those risks worth the effort to ensure Emma's safety? That is the key question that *Scope of Practice* addresses.

At the end of the day, the film teaches us that favoritism can be overcome, a good lesson for anyone and any community.

When it comes to rating this film, I choose four out of five stars. It is a very good film, but it doesn't call to me the way a five-star film like *A Grim Becoming* does.

Of Immorality and Immortality,
A Film Review of
Frankenstein's Patchwork Monster

As I have mentioned, the City of Buffalo, New York and the surrounding areas are home to over forty independent film studios. The amount of arts proliferation in this area is truly amazing. One of the most creative individuals in the Buffalo area is Emil Novak, Senior, who is also a dear friend and mentor mine. Mr. Novak is the owner and operator of the oldest bookstore in Buffalo, New York, Queen City Comic Book Store. Mr. Novak is the owner and operator of Buffalo Comicon, the biggest independent comic book convention in Western New York. Mr. Novak is the founder and coordinating proprietor for Visions Comic Art Group, a group in Buffalo, New York that makes local comics. Another thing that Mr. Novak does is run an independent film production studio, Buffalo Nickel Productions. In this blog entry, I wish to discuss Mr. Novak's latest film, "Frankenstein's Patchwork Monster".

Frankenstein's Patchwork Monster is a mix between thriller, intellectual, steam punk, romance, and historical fiction. One early storyline in the film follows Mary Wollstonecraft Shelley (Tara Rosado) at that fateful party where she decided to author the book Frankenstein, or, a Modern Prometheus. There is a great unease amongst the rest of the party over the topic of alchemy. In this case, alchemy implies the reanimation of the dead into living. Pay attention to Lord Byron (Jason John Beebe), as he pops up later in the story.

Victor Frankenstein (Bill Kennedy) is an immoral man, aided by his almost equally immoral assistant, Herman (Patrick Mallette), and their strange companion, Proteus from the Erie Lagoon (Sean Sanders), a strange amphibious creature. Victor Frankenstein thinks nothing of endless experimentation upon both the dead and the living. He commissions two famous grave robbers, Burke and Hare (Bob Bozek, Mike Schiabarrasi), who were real life figures, and have gone down in British legend. Burke and Hare serve as comic relief in the film. Although to a great deal immoral, Herman's love for his wife (Melantha Blackthorne) knows no bounds. Victor, however, is jealous of Herman's relationship with his wife, and desires her for himself. It soon becomes clear that Victor is willing to murder and rape to get what he wants.

Arguably the best part of the film comes as Victor has finally created a successful monster. He spends a great deal of time with the creature (Daniel James), watching with fascination as the creature discovers the world. However, the creature starts reading through Victor's journals and discovers the horrible truth, the truth that Victor is completely immoral and has practically sold his soul whilst pursuing his ultimate goal, immortality. The showdown that commences in Victor's laboratory is an epic match of words. The creature accuses Victor of being completely immoral in his search for immortality. Victor argues that immortality is worth the great sacrifice that he has made. The creature leaves Victor, who is left with only Proteus as a sympathetic companion. Victor then performs the final procedure to grant himself immortality, and sets Proteus free. Victor soon learns that rumors of his dastardly deeds have led to the creation of Shelley's book. He spends the rest of his thankless existence cursing the immortal fame that he has been granted, because others are reaping the rewards.

Frankenstein's Patchwork Monster is an original take on a greatly repeated tale. This alone makes it worth watching. Another factor that makes the film highly commendable is the fact that it kept itself completely local to the Buffalo area. Local actors, local sets, local locations. Mr. Novak takes great pains to make sure that things are appropriate to their era. Victor Frankenstein's lab in this film is much more contextually accurate than any other representation I have seen of the same lab. Amazingly, the set for the laboratory was completely constructed in Mr. Novak's basement. The film is highly intellectualized, which leads to occasional slow pacing, and the effects are low-budget. There are some editing errors in the film as well. Nonetheless, this is a story worth seeing for many reasons, including those philosophical, romantic, and terrific. We at Autistic Reality give this film eight out of ten stars. Is immortality truly worth the immorality? See the film, and decide for yourself!

Truly the Worst Film
I Have Ever Seen.
Popstar: Never Stop Never Stopping

This piece of garbage does not deserve an introduction.

There are many films in this world. Millions. Billions, maybe. I cannot profess to have seen all of them, but I have seen at least 1,000, and probably more. Furthermore, I do not pretend to be hypersensitive to the fine arts. I am a viewer, not a trained film-maker. Nevertheless, I have seen some really awful films. Now, granted, the definition of awful changes from person to person. However, *Popstar: Never Stop Never Stopping* (2016) is the single worst film I have ever laid eyes on.

I have been cooped up in my apartment for the last few days and was in the mood for something fun. I heard this film was a comedy. Ha! The joke's on me! The reviews looked pretty good, and I have not seen the previews, so I read some of the reviews. Those couldn't possibly have been reviews for this film. They said that although this film missed some of its mark, it remained smart, entertaining pop culture satire. Pardon me, I am laughing as I write this.

One minute into Popstar, my reaction was, "Seriously?" Three minutes in, my reaction was, "My God, this is horrible! I wonder if I should leave..." Five minutes in, I thought, "This is in no way entertaining. I hope this is just a joke that ends soon." Seven minutes in, it dawned upon me, "Holy cow, they are completely serious." This is how they wanted to make the film. Finally, nine minutes in, I decided to stay for the entire damn movie, because I was going to watch them destroy pop culture, rape my mind, and ruin America. Sorry if I seem overwrought, but the film really is that bad.

It's not that *Popstar* doesn't try; it tries very hard. It tries to be the worst, most tasteless film ever produced by humanity. The film follows a popstar, Connor4Real, played by Andy Samberg, as he comes out with his second solo album. He used to belong to a group called Style Boyz, whose members are played by Samberg's real-life "comedy" troupe, "The Lonely Island". Connor's second solo album starts to tank, and he makes music videos, goes on tour, and interacts with people in his life and business, who are played by a veritable Who's Who of D-List celebrities, except for his publicist, who is played by comedienne Sarah Silverman, who definitely does not give her all for this film. This film insults a number of A-List celebrities by using stock footage of them to associate them with the goings on in the film. A number of other celebrities appear throughout the film to talk about turns of events, and you get the feeling that most or all of them had no clue what they were signing up for.

The film contains many songs authored by The Lonely Island. The songs have the most artificial, forced, intentionally offensive lyrics that one can contemplate. It is stretching it too much to call them music. There are a number of jokes, but they either have no punchlines, or the punchlines do not meet up with the setup. There are only a couple of jokes that actually make you laugh, and you get the distinct impression that those were mistakes on the parts of the writers. The writers, of course, are also The Lonely Island. There is gratuitous nudity, including director Judd Apatow's penis shoved brazenly in your face. He of course directs this film. Popstar is meant to scandalize, and does not shy away from alienating many populations when possible. This film is also extremely gross, involving turtle vomit and fecal pancakes among other things.

This film will have you cringing, sighing, gasping, groaning, and hiding behind anything and anyone just to catch some peace. This could have been an incredibly successful satire of the modern pop culture phenomenon. Instead, it is absolute, unmitigated trash. At the end of my viewing, I laughed and clapped for several minutes straight. I truly did not know that such a horrible film was possible. Hats off to the cast and crew for lowering the bar of film by several degrees. This film is endemic of a huge problem with this country, and to some degree the world. America is constantly dumbing down, but that assumes that some vestigial amount of intellect is left. This film has no intellect. Common sense has been murdered with a butter knife, and shoved down the port-a-potty.

Conclusion

Popstar: Never Stop Never Stopping is, to my knowledge, the worst film ever made. On a 1 to 10 rating scale I give it 1. On a 1 to 5 rating scale I give it 1.

Good God, this is horrible.

Attack Of The Killer Shrews

In my time living in Buffalo, New York, I made many friends. One of them is Bill Kennedy, a local of Niagara Falls, New York who currently serves on their City Council. Over the years, he has done a great deal of acting in the local scene, including "Frankenstein's Patchwork Monster". After I moved to Washington, DC, I decided to do him a solid and review his latest film! Here we go!

I just finished watching a wonderful and exciting movie! *Attack of the Killer Shrews* is a remake of the 1950s B horror film of the same name. The original film is extremely cheesy, and, by today's standards, very poorly made.

The remake was locally made in Western New York, using regional and local talent, settings, supplies, financing, and other resources. I have spoken before about the wonder of the Western New York film scene. Western New York has almost fifty studios, all made locally by local people and local resources. I cannot speak highly enough of the Western New York film scene.

My friend Bill Kennedy is the star of this film, playing a small-town sheriff whose motley crew happens upon the titular killer shrews, which are result of what else but a scientist's evil plan gone awry. Our crew includes at various times the Sheriff, his deputy who, in true small-town fashion is also his cousin, an eccentric genius professor, his agent, the agent's wife, a movie star, and any number of soldiers and/or small towns people.

As mentioned, the original film from the 1950s is very cheesy, and does not have the best production values. This film, made in Buffalo, New York and the surrounding area, was made with limited financing and resources, and it shows. However! That is not a bad thing! In fact, the exact opposite is true. The fact that the film was made on a shoestring budget with shoestring resources amplifies its fulfillment of its goal.

What is the goal of this film? The goal of this film is to serve as satire and homage to the original film and its genre. In this goal, a small-town film made out of Western New York can truly shine and succeed! The film has plenty of cheesy effects, jokes, corny exposition, and breaking of the fourth wall.

The film starts out slow, and although it was initially difficult to figure out, it developed into a fun, exciting effort to rid the small town of what else, but killer shrews! I recommend this film full heartedly for several reasons:

· this film is an awesome example of how a great film can be made on a budget

· this film is a true throwback to cheapen cheesy horror films of the 1950s

· a local community did a wonderful job putting on this film

· this is proof that anybody can make a good film if they put their minds and hearts to it.

With those reasons in mind, I give this film a 9 out of 10 rating, or a five out of five rating! Please enjoy *Attack of the Killer Shrews!*

Autism Can Make You
A Better Superhero

When I was young, I was a huge fan of the Power Rangers. When the 2017 film came out, I heard rumors that one of the Rangers was supposed to be autistic. Naturally, I was curious, and decided to see and review the film. Here's my review!

Yesterday, I went to see *Power Rangers*, directed by Dean Israelite, and based off the fan favorite TV show from the 1990s. I was somewhat skeptical of how successful the movie would be, given the reviews and my own experience with the franchise. The original show was somewhat poorly written, with very cheesy effects. However, it is the whole concept behind the story that makes said story so appealing.

We began with Jason Scott, a star football player for a high school in the fictional Angel Grove, a small town with both fishing and a gold mine, both of which play important roles to the plot. Jason is fond of engaging in hijinks, and winds up off the team with detention for the rest of the year. (This prank involves a cow. Please don't ask me why. It is darn funny, though!) In detention, we meet with much of the rest of the cast. This review would like to focus on Billy Cranston, played by RJ Cyler.

The very first thing we see Billy doing is arranging colored pencils quite meticulously. I immediately thought, "Ooh, I used to do that!" And in fact, it is very true. I used to be absolutely obsessed with coloring in floor plans with Crayola colored pencils. In fact, my theft of two colored pencils wound me up doing juvenile community service once. Unfortunately, Billy is being bullied at the time that Jason meets him. Jason tells the guy off, and then gives him a humorous slapping. "Did you just slap him?" Billy asks. "Yes, yes I did," Jason replies.

Jason is on house arrest due to said hijinks earlier in the film, and is unable to play sports due to injury. However, Billy mentions that he can reset Jason's ankle bracelet, so that they can chill later and that he has found something out by the gold mine. He also mentions that he is on the autism spectrum, to which I in the audience said, "DUH!! Of course you are!" We are treated to a view of Billy's sanctuary in the basement of his house. It looks like a dream come true for an intellectual individual. There are tons of gadgets, often cobbled together by Billy's own invention from items that he has salvaged from various locations. The thing is that in real life, as opposed to the stereotype, autistic individuals do not tend to be absolute wunderkind savants. This results in a number of hilarious moments throughout the film when Billy accidentally makes things blow up, slip, trip, sproing, fladap, shtoink, and just about every other word invented by

Don Martin. (Look him up. One of the greatest cartoonists of all time!)

The something that Billy has found by the gold mine ends up being the whole Power Ranger deal, which comes complete with magic coins, a humorously talkative robot, an alien spaceship, a magic portal, superstrength, speed, and agility, and their own personal Brian Cranston. It also comes with sci-fi armor and giant robots called Zords, but those enter the story later. Billy and Jason encounter three other individuals from detention at the site of this mysterious discovery: Kimberly, Zach, and Trini.

A word about Trini. There is a wonderful scene where they are all getting to know each other better, and someone mentions boyfriend troubles, and she hesitates a bit. The person then mentions girlfriend troubles, and she also hesitates about that. You see, Trini identifies as a female in terms of pronouns, but she makes it clear that she does not let conventional definitions apply to her. Trini is queer, and may be the first big-budget superhero in the Hollywood film to definitively have that identity. Her new friends warmly accept her for who she is.

One major criticism of the characters from the original TV show is that we never saw them living their family lives at home. In this film, we spend some time at home with the Rangers. Zach has a loving but sick mother. Trini has parents who don't understand her too well and younger siblings who look up to her. Jason has a father who tries his very best to be proud of him. In fact, Jason even saves his father's life during the climactic battle.

All of the five are somewhat hesitant to explore their new discoveries, except for Billy. He is extremely excited about the entire thing. During the whole film, he talks a lot, and he sometimes divulges inappropriate information. That is par for the course with autistic individuals, including myself. Luckily, Jason will sometimes politely remind him that his cup runneth over. I would like to reiterate at this point that friends are amazing, and that autistic individuals should never be afraid of socializing. Billy is also sometimes hesitant to engage in physical stunts, and in real life many autistic people are more involved in the intellectual than in physical activity.

As it turns out, the team's Brian Cranston is an ancient alien named Zordon, who had been the Red Ranger 65 million years ago. At this moment, someone must be thinking, did the Power Rangers kill the dinosaurs? Yes, actually. You see, Zordon was fighting the former Green Ranger, who had turned into an evil being known as Rita Repulsa. As Zordon's Ranger team lies dying, he summons a meteor weapon to attempt to destroy Rita. The problem is, however, that bad guys (and girls) don't tend to stay dead very long. Fortunately, Rita stays dead for an entire 65 million years, before fishermen from Angel Grove discover her corpse at the bottom of the sea. Naturally, chaos ensues.

Now, back to our team. They have been busy practicing. However, they have been unable to generate their armor. Suddenly, one of them does. Billy becomes the first one able to do so. They later discovered that, because the unit is a team, their ability to generate armor depends on their ability to know each other. This is actually tremendous news for Billy, and the autistic community. It is frequently said that we autistics do not get the rest of humanity. However, Billy clearly gets the others better than they get each other. Many autistic individuals are incredibly observant of everything and anything, including other people.

Rita instigates a fight, and the team gets thoroughly thrashed. In fact, Billy ends up getting killed. They take him to Zordon, who was planning on using the Rangers' power to regenerate his life. Before he plans to do so, the rest of the Rangers speak of how they would all give their life for Billy. For autistic people to find real, tangible friendship, the kind which involves self-sacrifice, is a gigantic triumph. As mentioned before, autistic people are not always the best at interpersonal relations. However, with proper time and effort, we can form wonderful friendships. In the end of this scene, Zordon decides to regenerate Billy's life instead of his own, and they go off to fight Rita.

Rita's goal is to destroy the Zeo Crystal. In this movie's cannon, a Zeo Crystal can be found on each planet that supports life. Indeed, the Crystal provides that life force on each of those worlds. Naturally, the Zeo Crystal in this film is located right under a Krispy Kreme. In fact, Rita stops to enjoy some of their doughnuts as she tries to destroy the world. Wouldn't you?

Rita builds a gigantic monster out of gold from the mine outside of town, and said monster starts destroying said town. The Rangers use their Zords to protect the town and tried to stop the golden monster, which is named Goldar, after a henchman of Rita's from the original TV series. Goldar is nearly destroyed, until Rita joins with it and is nearly successful. She tosses the Zords into a pit of lava, but they arise, combined into the mighty Mechazord, which Billy has named. Goldar is finally destroyed, and the Rangers demand Rita's surrender before Zordon. She refuses, which angers Jason, the Red Ranger and leader of the team. I could hardly believe what I saw next, and neither could Billy. "Did you just slap Rita?" Billy asks. "Yes, yes I did," Jason replies. In fact, Jason has slapped her into outer space. As her frozen body heads towards the moon, we see a smile spread upon her face. I smell sequel!

The town is absolutely overjoyed, and Billy makes the Mechazord dance to country music, which is his guilty pleasure. Two townspeople are played by Amy Jo Johnson, who played the original Pink Ranger, and Jason David Frank, who played Tommy Oliver, the original green Ranger. There are many moments in the film that throw back to the original TV show. In fact, it even gives off the same feel. Near the end of the film, there are more scenes depicting the successful Rangers interacting with their families.

There is one scene during the credits, during which reference is made to Tommy Oliver. There is also a massive explosion in the bathroom of the school, to which Billy says "Oops! My bad!"

Billy is the first definitively autistic superhero in an A-list Hollywood film. Based on criticism of *The Accountant*, various members of the autistic activist community may point out that it is not realistic to portray an autistic person as a superhero because we autistics are not special, but rather a naturally occurring subset of society. To this I say, "WTF!?" This film has dinosaurs, ancient aliens, giant robots, a humongous golden monster, and a woman who comes back to life after 65 million years at the bottom of the sea! I think we can learn to suspend our disbelief a little bit.

In addition, it is noteworthy that the Blue Ranger is autistic, as the color blue is symbolic of autism awareness. Although many autism activists do not like the color blue standing for autism, they should recall that use of the color to symbolize the autistic movement predates any of the harmful efforts by Autism Speaks. The autism activists would point out that the color blue was chosen because it was initially thought that was prevalent mostly in males. Once again, may I point out that perceptions and symbols can change and adapt. What was once thought of as mostly male is now known to be spread more or less evenly between genders, although autism sometimes manifests slightly differently in each gender. Although the blue color was initially meant to reflect the male gender, the intent was not sexist, and the color can be perceived as applying to both genders.

As an autistic person with autistic friends and acquaintances all across the autism spectrum, I do not think I have seen a more accurate depiction of autism in popular culture, except for possibly the character I review in my first book, Without Fear: The FirstAutistic Superhero. Both myself and my firm, Autistic Reality, would like to fully endorse this film. We will attempt to get in touch with Lionsgate Entertainment and Saban, to make that endorsement official. Both myself and my firm give this amazing wonderful film ten out of ten stars, or five out of five. It is very rare to see a good, high profile film that so flawlessly embodies diversity. SEE THIS FILM!

Autism Can Make You A Better Artist

A few months after I moved to Washington, DC, I heard rumblings of an amazingly famous artist whose display had taken over a whole floor of the Hirshhorn Museum on the National Mall. Admission was free, but tickets were only available the week of admission, and usually ran out within five minutes, or so I heard. In fact, tickets usually ran out within a few seconds of the opening of that week's queue. It seemed like I would miss the exhibit. Later on, I was informed that the artist was autistic, and also considered the most famous artist alive today. Her name is Yayoi Kusama. Thankfully, I was able to get a press pass, and see the exhibit so that I could convey its wonder to you. Here we go!

I had the extreme pleasure of seeing the exhibit *Infinity Mirrors*, by Yayoi Kusama at the Smithsonian's Hirshhorn Museum and Sculpture Garden. Yayoi was born in Matsumoto, Nagano, Japan. She is 88 years old. At the time, Japan was still a very buttoned-down imperialist society. Etiquette and honor governed society to the extreme. Yayoi entered into this world on March 22, 1929. Her childhood was traumatic. Her father was incredibly lecherous, and Yayoi's mother used her to spy on his affairs, including multiple sexual acts.

During her life, Yayoi has engaged in a great deal of outlandish work. At the height of 1960s counterculture, she composed a great number of performance pieces called Happenings. A great deal of them involved public nudity. One of them in the early 1970s was a highly illegal gay wedding en masse. She also at one point ran a gay bar as an art installation. On another occasion, she offered to have vigorous sexual intercourse with United States President Richard Nixon if he would end the Vietnam conflict. Yayoi's disciples have included many individuals who have been influential in their own right, such as Andy Warhol and Yoko Ono.

Since she was a child, Yayoi has had vivid hallucinations which have reflected themselves in her art. She is also documented as having a number of other mental health issues, including but not limited to obsessive-compulsive disorder, bipolar disorder, and a number of other conditions. Due to these conditions, Yayoi voluntarily checked herself into a psychiatric hospital in the late 1970s. She has been a self-admitted guest of that facility ever since. It is practically an open secret that Yayoi has autism. Her moods, social tendencies, and other diagnoses lend incredible credence to this fact. This blog shall attempt to highlight Yayoi's autistic dependence on order and her obsessions in her artwork as seen in her infinity rooms in Infinity Mirrors.

Yayoi has gone out of her way to make the entire exhibit disability accessible. She realizes that her infinity rooms are not accessible to some with mobility impairments, so she has worked with the Smithsonian's Hirshhorn Gallery to provide complete 360° virtual reality tours of all spaces in the exhibit.

The first large-scale artwork we encountered was a dark, black room. In one end was a rowboat made out of phallic shapes, all in violet. The black walls, floor, and ceiling were covered with a pattern depicting this artwork. When one has autism, they often feel alone adrift in a sea of humanity, which they often feel passes them by. Yayoi grew up as a girl in Imperial Japan, which was absolutely stifling by today's standards. She is an extreme feminist, and those burgeoning feelings would have made her feel even more alone at the time. As a girl and as a feminist, the phalluses and multiple pieces of her artwork represent the forest of masculinity she perceived to surround her. This boat travels through dark and dangerous waters, searching for a safe port of call. This artwork was made in 1994, at which time Yayoi was already an older woman. This signifies the fact that people may feel uncertain or lost at any time in their life. Yayoi once said, "If it weren't for the art, I would have killed myself long ago."

Completed in 1965 when the artist was 36 and re-rendered in 2016, Phalli's Field is the original infinity room. The 1960s were a great time of sexual awakening, and Yayoi, always in the spirit to provoke, envisioned an endless field of phalluses, made from stuffed cotton and reflected in board covered with mirrors.

The phalluses are white, covered in red polka dots, which the artist has always adored. The need to provoke or cause a scene is often felt by autistic individuals. It often serves to give us a feeling of legitimacy in society which we may otherwise lack. If it can be done in a novel and risqué form, then even better. The artist would often pose in this room, as if riding a sea of male genitalia. Yayoi certainly knew how to harness the sexual energy and thoughts of her artwork, as well as society's perceptions of sexuality.

This particular room, "Love Forever", has been rendered in metal and lightbulbs reflected in mirrors on wood. It was first completed the year after Phalli's Field, 1966, and re-rendered in 1994. The reflected light bulbs and metallic patterns form geometric shapes that constantly change color and pattern, endlessly radiating, aggregating, blinking, and spreading throughout the infinity room. One would think that an autistic person with a sensory disorder would find this room alarming and jarring. On the contrary, it is actually quite calming. Autistic individuals often find comfort in dim, soothing lights and geometric patterns. Yayoi is not a psychologist, but as an artist, she realizes which forms will please people. It is my firm suspicion that she worked on this room with a particular amount of personal satisfaction, as it most likely helped calm her always temperamental moods.

A rather recent addition to the infinity rooms is "The Souls of Millions of Light Years Away", made in 2013. As usual, the mirrors are mounted on wood with metal details. From the ceiling hang endless ropes of colored LED lighting strands made of plastic, acrylic, and rubber. While all small, the lights vary in intensity and are of many different colors including white light, blue light, red light, and even green light. Just like Love Forever, the effect is immediately calming. However, instead of being pulsing and rhythmic, the effect is serene and wonderful. It gives the feeling of traveling in a jungle of magical plants and creatures. This infinity room provides great calm to me as an autistic individual, and the effect on other autistic individuals would be the same. The lights sometimes dim, and sometimes go dark altogether before lighting up again. The patterns in which they dim are at random, but the effect is still completely pleasing. Once again, one may suspect that Yayoi used personal experience to achieve the calming, therapeutic qualities of this room.

The largest display in *Infinity Mirrors* is "Love Transformed into Dots". Yayoi, who has a lifelong love of polkadots, conceived of this detailed exhibit in 2007. It was finally installed in the Hirshhorn in 2017. It consists of a large room filled with deep pink vinyl balloons covered in black polka dots. Inside the biggest balloon is an infinity room lined as usual with mirrors on the walls, floor, and ceiling, and filled with spherical lanterns, also in deep pink with black polka dots. There is a peep-in infinity space inside a round kiosk that is made to look like another polkadot balloon. Inside this peep-in mirror dome is a dreamlike scene of mirrored spheres and polkadots all placed in front of a miniature infinity room made out of mirrors. The entire display inside the mirror dome is tinted deep pink by the light that glows within. Yayoi has stated that, to her, polkadots have always been incredibly calming and happy. It has been theorized that her love of polkadots originates from light reflecting off of the pebbles in the stream in her parents' garden. For autistic individuals, many patterns can prove soothing. The perfectly round nature of polkadots, and the random playfulness with which they are dispersed, gives a feeling of peace to the mind. A deep, calming pink, rather than a bright, hot pink also serves to ease one's mood. As an unequaled artist, Yayoi realizes the therapeutic qualities of her polkadots, and a projection of her, in a longer, light purple wig, ruffled red shirt with black polka dots, and black smock, seems to float in midair near the entrance to this installation, in which she sings a calming song to the crowd that passes by. There is no way that Yayoi does not know the psychological effects of her artwork, and the presence of this video proves it.

The infinity room Aftermath of Obliteration of Eternity once again has mirror covered wood with aluminum fastenings. It is somewhat recent, having been conceived of in 2009. It is filled with hanging lanterns made of plastic and acrylic and filled with LED lights. These lanterns give the room the feeling of being filled with floating candles much akin to fireflies. Much like "The Souls of Millions of Light Years Away", the lanterns randomly dim and go out, and also like "The Souls of Millions of Light Years Away", the overall effect is quite calming. It leaves you a serene feeling of peace in what might be a chaotic world. It is easy to have much reflection in the brief time spent in this room. Yayoi has had a great deal of chaos in her life, and she wishes to impart the gifts of peace and well-being.

Yayoi has a great love of pumpkins. When she was a child, her family was well-to-do, and owned a plant nursery and seed farm.

She finds the round shape and often large size of pumpkins to be happy and joyful. In this recent infinity room conceived in 2016, pumpkins are made of plastic and acrylic and filled with LED lights against the usual mirrors covering the wooden space. Each pumpkin glows orange with rows of black polka dots. The title, "All the Eternal Love I Have for the Pumpkins", signifies the never-ending love Yayoi has for these gourds. Naturally, the field of pumpkins which have brought her such joy appears to be endless, a bountiful harvest for one's positive emotions. Yayoi is fond of pointing out that her art is born of her obsessions, which are clinical. When one has obsessions, it is a very good idea to turn them into something useful. For example, I have an obsession with taking photos of things I see as noteworthy. I have used this obsession to further my career, and even to make this blog post. Yayoi wants to share her delightfully joyful pumpkins with the world.

The exhibit ends with "The Obliteration Room", a fully furnished room completely in white covered with polkadots. Yayoi has taken us on a grand journey. Her journey starts out unsure and perilous, and surrounded by dangerous elements of society such as toxic masculinity. Through this journey, she asserts herself, and engages in self-therapy by art. She finds means of bringing order to her life and calming herself, as well as making herself happy, and shares them with us as art installations. It is only fitting, then, that in this last installation, she asks us to share in the joy with her. The exhibition opened on February 23. It closes on May 14. By the time I saw the exhibition on April 24, it was mostly over. By that time, an endless sea of visitors had completely covered this once white room in simply wonderful, fun polkadots. I proudly covered it, and myself, in even more dots. In almost 90 years, this artist has seen the emotional condition of the world. She has had an endless journey trying to stay happy. As I, Alec Frazier realized about six years ago, so has she: happiness lies in our unique insanity. Be proud of who you are. Be proud of the world you belong to. Live life. Have fun. Enjoy!

He Belongs To The City
Good Time

I'm a big fan of Robert Pattinson, and many of the independent films in which he stars. In 2017, I saw the film Good Time, and was blown away. Here is my review.

The film *Good Time*, directed by the brothers Benny and Josh Safdie, is an absolute thrill ride and it epitomizes how a very good film can be made on a small budget.

Robert Pattinson stars as Connie Nikas, a Resident of Queens of Greek descent. He cares a great deal about his brother, Nick, played by Benny Safdie, and does try very hard to do right by him. Connie shows up at the beginning of the film to take his brother out of a counseling session. You see, Nick has developmental disabilities, and Connie just wants to do right by him. Of course, the counselor also wants to do right by him. The views of family members versus the views of "the system" often conflict.

Often there is not a clear answer of who is in the right. On the one hand, the questions during the counseling session are making Nick cry, on the other hand, Connie does not have the best of intentions either.

The main thrust of the film starts when Connie manipulates his brother Nick into attempting a bank robbery with him. A chase ensues, and Nick gets arrested. Connie tries to use the stolen money to get Nick out on bail, but since the money is dirty, he ends up having to go to his girlfriend, the significantly older Corey Ellman, who is played flawlessly by Jennifer Jason Leigh. Ellman has quite a fickle personality, and this obviously means that she has a great deal of trouble making decisions. This is further evidenced by the fact that she lives with her mother, with whom she has a bad relationship; they bicker and argue frequently. Connie lies to Corey about the reason why his brother is in jail, but it is all for naught as when Corey tries to use her bank card to bail Nick out, she finds that her mother has canceled it. The night spirals downward even further from here.

Nick had gotten into a fight with another inmate, and was placed in a hospital under guarded supervision. Connie finds out which hospital, finds the police guarding a room, and breaks out the heavily bandaged man handcuffed in that room. He proceeds to further manipulate his way to a very bad neighborhood in residential Queens, and into an old lady's house, where he attempts to distract her 16-year-old granddaughter, Crystal, played by newcomer Taliah Lennice Webster, with sex. Keep in mind that Robert Pattison is 31, and we are to assume that Connie is of a similar age. The inmate Connie broke out of the hospital wakes up, and pries off his bandages, only to reveal that he is a stranger, Ray, played by Buddy Duress. Connie manages to calm him down with painkillers, and they trick Crystal into accompanying them on a trip in her grandmother's car.

References on the television throughout the film infer that law enforcement is getting closer to finding Connie, we also see police talking to people seen previously in the film. We learned that Ray had a wild ride of his own the previous day, and left a bottle full of acid and a bag of cash in an amusement park ride a few streets down from where he, Connie, and Crystal are currently laying low. Ray and Connie break into the amusement park, leaving Crystal in the car. They are cornered by Dash the security guard, played by Barkhad Abdi. Dash calls the police, but Ray and Connie managed to overwhelm him. Connie then impersonates the security guard, and the paramedics and police take away Dash, who has been force-fed some of the acid. At the same time, Crystal is also taken in for questioning. Connie and Ray escape to Dash's apartment in his security vehicle. Upon arriving at the apartment, it is becomes apparent that Dash engages in illicit activity as he is living well above his means. Connie has Ray call his dealer and demands the cash he needs to bail out his brother Nick. The dealer leaves, ostensibly to get the cash, but in actuality to get a gun with which to kill Connie. It is at this point that the police close in on them. Ray accidentally kills himself when trying to escape the apartment, and Connie is taken away by the police.

In the final scene, the therapist from the first scene in the film takes Nick Nikas to a boring, monotonous group activity for those with developmental disabilities, while remarking that Connie is now in the right place, and that Nick is in the right place, too.

This film is incredibly thought-provoking. It goes beyond questions of right and wrong, and into degrees of personal accountability. One thing that should be noted is that this entire film after the bank robbery and before the final scene takes place over the course of just one night. During that night, we get to delve deep into the psyche of Connie Nikas. It is extremely clear that he loves his brother a great deal. At one point, he tells Nick that it is just the two of them against the world. It is true that they both have a very aged grandmother, but she is incapable of looking after them. Connie obviously believes that the bank robbery will be simple and easy. He lacks foresight, and this makes him a poor planner.

After the robbery, Connie's dive into further crime is gradual. It all starts with a lie he tells Corey as to why his brother has been incarcerated; he tells her that Nick lashed out against his therapist. Connie clearly does not like the idea of Nick going to therapy, and this is consistent with toxic masculinity as well as some Greek-American cultural norms, which believe that asking for help is a sign of weakness. Throughout the film, Connie consistently believes that things are either out of his control or most definitely not his fault, or both. For example, Crystal mentions that her last boyfriend was her drug dealer, who was significantly older than herself. This makes it a non-issue to Connie when he starts to force himself upon her a while later. Ironically, Connie later attempts dealing drugs himself with the bottle of acid.

It is as if Connie does not notice how deep he is slipping. He quite willingly suggests drugging the security guard and posing in his place. Breaking and entering into the amusement park is nothing to him. Given that Connie's first significant act in this film is a bank robbery, we can only hazard a guess into his past, although we are made aware at one point during the film that he has a record; we see a past mug shot of Connie on the news.

Connie shows a great deal of willingness to manipulate others. He is aware that Corey has psychological issues that give her weakness and malleability, as well as a willingness to help with finances. It is hinted that before the events of this film, they were planning a trip to the Caribbean, perhaps to be assisted with the money from the bank robbery. Nick is also incredibly malleable, doing whatever others tell him to do. Connie uses this to his advantage in getting Nick to assist him with his various nefarious schemes. The therapist is equally able to convince Nick to do his bidding. It is not in Nick's best interest to spend his days in monotonous, clinical group activities. However, Nick does not have an in-built group of friends, and the clinical system is still often ill-versed in the social needs of those with disabilities.

The amazing thing about Connie is that he probably believes that everything he has done, including the bank robbery and the actions of this fateful night are without question and in the right. Connie is extremely well-intentioned, but he has shown himself to be addicted to bad behavior, and even deeply sociopathic. The fact that he thinks nothing of kidnapping a 16-year-old girl or having sexual relations with her is proof of this. At one point,

Ray asks him about his intentions. Connie makes it clear that he is focused on the here and now, and not the consequences of his actions. There is something deeply flawed about Connie Nikas, but he is portrayed in such a way that we can still have a tremendous amount of empathy for him.

This portrayal, of course, comes courtesy of Robert Pattinson. Pattinson was thrust into the film world by the *Harry Potter* and *Twilight* films. He jokes that if he had his way, he would be a nobody in a British dive bar playing guitar and singing for a living. Pattinson is absolutely stunned and surprised by his fame, but not unhappy with it. He has spent his time since the *Twilight* franchise becoming a fixture in the independent film community. Pattinson is definitely a more artistic type, as is shown in his quite recent photo shoot for Wonderland magazine, in which he pays tribute to Yayoi Kusama, who is arguably the greatest artist alive today. In the photo shoot, Pattinson pays homage to Kusama by wearing gender-ambiguous costumes similar to hers, and posing amongst backgrounds evocative of her art. An artist is truly fearless when they are willing to deny social constructs such as gender, and Pattinson is clearly that brave.

In addition to acting, *Good Time* is also noteworthy for its locations. The film shies away from the glitzy and famous locations in New York City, instead placing itself amongst bad neighborhoods, mostly in Queens. There have been far too many films exploiting the New York City of tourists, and far too few focusing on the city of everyday people. The Safdie brothers are to be praised for their realism.

Good Time defies one specific genre. It is incredibly philosophical, action-packed, and dramatic all at once. It is clear that none of the characters in the film are actually having a *Good Time*, but this is a very, very good film, and you, the audience, will.

Five out of five stars, or 10 out of 10. Absolutely flawless.

The Customers Can Go To Hell
A Review of the Ithaca Dispatch

I have been many places in my life, but the place I like to call my hometown is Ithaca, New York. Like many people, indeed, a great majority of people on earth, I do not drive. And, until the advent of Uber and Lyft, those who do not drive have been royally screwed by the cab companies in upstate New York. This piece shall attempt to review the primary taxicab company in Tompkins County, New York, Ithaca Dispatch. I shall recount a number of individual experiences, as well as some general traits of said company. Corporate identities have not been changed, but personal names have been.

Uber and Lyft came late to upstate New York. In part, the disability community is to blame, for refusing to allow them until various accessibility standards were met. I have been a disability rights advocate since at least 1994, and I have at least a dozen. While I greatly respect a number of people in the disability community who have tried to prevent Uber and Lyft from coming to the area, I respectfully disagree. In upstate New York, many of the towns do not have public transportation, and even in those that do, taxicabs are often the only option to fall back upon. And, given these facts, one would expect taxicab companies to be reliable, courteous, professional, and very good to customers.

They are not. They don't even try to be. As mentioned, this review shall focus on Ithaca Dispatch, which holds an extreme monopoly on all taxicab services in Tompkins County, New York. There are a couple of other companies, but they each have only a couple of cars. In name, there are a number of cab companies in town, but almost all of them are owned by Ithaca Dispatch. In all but name, they are one company. You are stuck with them. And, until Uber and Lyft came to town, they knew that they were the only game in town and proceeded to make the customer's life a living hell. In fact, they still do, but the difference is that now there is an alternative.

Ithaca Dispatch is corrupt to the core. One way in which they are corrupt is their fare system. They have flat rates dividing the region they cover into zones. This may seem like a good idea, but they have pulled one over on us. Each zone is always measured from the center of downtown Ithaca. For example, if you live in the town of Lansing, and want to go to the supermarket in the town of Lansing, you will be charged the same fare as if you were going from downtown Ithaca to the town of Lansing. This ends up being $13-$15, without tip. The actual amount is somewhat flexible, as drivers like to stiff you for cash, and Ithaca Dispatch lets them get away with it. Uber charges around six dollars for the same trip.

The cabs are often very unclean, and absolutely falling apart. The company prides themselves on passing inspection, but the inspections they pass are subject to just as much corruption as anything else the company does. There is bribery, inside manipulation, and the fact that the company de facto regulates its own inspections. The company often does have some wheelchair accessible vehicles, but they do not keep them in reserve for wheelchair users. Instead, they assign them like any other cabs. One time, we said we needed a cab with a lot of room, so we got a wheelchair cab when we would have been fine with a van. We then proceeded to take it all the way from Ithaca, New York to Syracuse, New York, thus potentially depriving someone with a disability of a necessary ride for absolutely no reason.

Dispatch itself is absolutely rude, and brags about that fact. As has been noted by a seemingly endless number of other reviewers, they hang up on you without telling you the estimated arrival time for your cab. If you do ask them for an estimated arrival time, they will say "a few minutes", or "on its way". Sometimes you will have to call back to ask for an estimated arrival time. Sometimes, in fact, frequently, they will refuse to give you one. If they do, in fact, give you an actual number of minutes, it will, without fail, be incorrect. I say all this as someone who has over ten years' experience using this company frequently because there was no other alternative. At one point, I took the dispatcher to task and told him it was his job to know where his cabs are and what time they would arrive. He actually said to me, verbatim, "Yeah, it is, but I'm not in the habit of being convenient." Other times, they will actually yell at you and swear at you.

The drivers for the cab company do not care about customers, or, if they do, they absolutely hate you. A great number of the drivers to not live in town. One particular driver who has been driving for over ten years likes to brag about the fact that he does not care where things are in town. At one point I told him I wanted to go to Viva! Taqueria in the center of town. He pulled up to the main intersection in town and asking where it was. I asked him how long he had been driving in the town, and then asked him why he didn't know where things were in town, to which he said he just didn't care. I told him to look out his right-hand window, and there was Viva! Taqueria. This very same driver has had disgusting toilet issues every single time I've taken a ride with him, at one point farting all over the customers in the cab.

There have been endless other times of cab drivers bragging about not knowing where things are in the town where they work. Not a single cab driver knows where the County Chamber of Commerce is, despite the fact that it is the official visitor center for the county. Other drivers intentionally get in political arguments with you. One started by saying, "You know, the Constitution doesn't guarantee us safe drinking water." Unfortunately, he picked the wrong person to argue with, as I have known every word of the Constitution verbatim since fifth grade and now have a college degree in the matter. Another time, when I had gotten out to use the ATM, the cabdriver started to drive around with his taxi doors open and my things falling out. When I got back to the car, he denied ever doing that, and then admitted it a few minutes later. Drivers will often include other parties in your cab without consulting you, often drawing out your trip significantly. Initially, I thought that this was just incredibly inconvenient. It turns out that it is actually against state law to include other parties in a taxicab without the consent of all parties. Unfortunately, very few people know that, and it is one of the more minor infractions perpetrated by Ithaca Dispatch.

I wanted to devote a paragraph to the lovely Miss Sue*. Sue hates her job, hates her boss, hates the law, and you can damn well bet that she hates you. I have been in her cab a number of times over more than ten years. She has never had her legally required paperwork on her. At one point, a fellow passenger asked her why it wasn't present, and she laughed and said that breaking the law was fun. Another time, she refused to accept my credit card, even though company policy required that she accept it. I had to call her boss to make sure she would take it, but only after she had given me a lot of grief. A few times, I have had misfortune when in her cab. The last time, in fact, I have accidentally hit my head on the trunk door of her cab. She thought this was hilarious and laughed profusely. Sue hates me. Sue hates you. Sue hates all customers. One time, she picked me up and I started to say, "Hello. How are you today?" only to be confronted by her yelling at me for no reason whatsoever. If Ithaca Dispatch were not run by absolutely corrupt individuals, she would have been fired years ago.

It should be mentioned that there is absolutely no grievance process. There is a number for complaints, but it just goes to one of the dispatchers. As mentioned, the dispatchers do not want to do their job, and brag about the fact, and make no secret of the fact that they hate you. One time, the dispatchers left me sitting in three feet of snow for over an hour and a half. When my cab finally arrived, he said the call had only just gone out five minutes earlier. In other words, the dispatchers just wanted me to suffer. I can assure you, from reading other reviews, that they have wanted other customers to suffer as well.

Do not place a timed call with Ithaca Dispatch. A number of drivers have confirmed to me that timed calls are not noted. They have said that in almost all cases, dispatch waits for the impatient or angry customer to call asking for their cab, and then dispatches it. Also, if drivers do not care about the layout of their town, then dispatch has actual disdain for the facts of where places are located. A number of times, I have asked to be picked up at the Tops supermarket on Southside. Dispatch has told me that they do not know what Southside is, but that there is a Tops downtown and a Tops in Lansing. As any local can tell you, the Tops in Ithaca proper is quite far from downtown. In fact, I used to work at the town zoning commission, and there are at least three neighborhoods between downtown and South-side. Heck, the entire reason why Southside was established was to take various businesses out of downtown. Dispatch doesn't care. They will yell at you and curse at you some more. It's what they love doing.

Uber and Lyft have finally come to upstate New York. The managers of Ithaca Dispatch wrote a lengthy editorial in the local papers, riddled with spelling and grammatical mistakes, demanding that these new services be subject to the same legal requirements that they are. May I ask why? Ithaca Dispatch doesn't even follow its own self-imposed rules, let alone the law. In fact, a number of drivers and dispatchers have bragged to me about breaking these rules and the law. Some of the managers of Ithaca Dispatch went on Facebook to plead their case, and by "plead their case", I mean insult people and make bigoted statements littered with profanity. For many, many, many years nobody has liked Ithaca Dispatch. Nobody has wanted them. And now, let us hope that we are finally rid of them.

If I were to give a star-system based rating to this cab company, I would give them one out of ten stars, or one out of five.

We Are All in This Together: Lessons in Advocacy from Marvel's Black Panther

Last night some friends of mine and I went to see Marvel's "Black Panther". We were completely blown away by the storyline, and by the leadership of the African-American community in making this film. It is, on that front, a tremendous civil-rights landmark.

The film stars Chadwick Boseman as T'Challa, King of the fictional African nation of Wakanda, and its protector as the Black Panther. This nation is the most technologically advanced civilization on earth, and is far, far ahead of the rest of the world. This raises an interesting quandary, as the King is encouraged by various others to share his kingdom's knowledge and technology with the rest of the world.

Let us not kid ourselves: even the best-off nations in the world can use some help. The United States is rife with gun violence, poverty, and corrupt politics. Those are just a few of our problems. However, no one society on earth should have the right to claim superiority above the rest. This is part of what motivates T'Challa not to meddle in global affairs, in addition to a long-standing tradition of noninterference from his ancestors.

Enter N'Jadaka also known as Erik "Killmonger" Stevens, played by Michael B. Jordan, a rival to the throne, who has grown up amongst the urban poor African population in the United States. He is feeling hurt, betrayed, and angry at the way the African ethnic group has been routinely abused and mistreated around the world. He seizes control of Wakanda, and attempts to use their advanced resources, and more importantly, their more advanced weapons, to arm the marginalized African community around the world. He wishes to start a global revolution.

Nevertheless, by the end of the film, T'Challa defeats Killmonger, and offers Wakanda's aid, science, and technology to the rest of the world.

At the end of the film, T'Challa gives a speech at the United Nations in which he says, "We have spent far too long focusing on what sets us apart, when we share so much in common." At this point, in the audience, we at Autistic Reality shouted, "Thank you! That's what we have been saying for years!" and the audience clapped.

There are obvious parallels between T'Challa and Killmonger and today's society. Believe it or not, there are parallels between these two and the autistic advocacy community.

The traditional Wakandan point of view about the world has some parallels with the view of Autism Speaks, an advocacy organization run by parents and caregivers. The traditional Wakandan point of view states that other nations are naturally inferior, and that Wakanda should not get involved in world affairs. Meanwhile, Autism Speaks believes that the autistic population is naturally inferior, and that autistic people do not have a right to equal involvement in the world.

Killmonger's point of view is that Africans in general, and Wakandans in specific, are superior to the rest of the world, and that they should overtake it by means of a violent revolution and rule it. Various groups such as the Autistic Self Advocacy Network (ASAN) draw parallels to Killmonger. Whether or not it is their stated policy, members of organizations such as ASAN repeatedly voice their own superiority to the rest of the world, and even threaten violence against people with whom they disagree. Even when they are not threatening violence, they are needlessly combative, focusing more and more on identity politics then the commonalities which draw us altogether. In fact, the same feelings felt by Killmonger, hurt, betrayal, and anger, are often turned into emotions and actions of hostility, superiority, and separatism by organizations such as ASAN and their members.

Meanwhile, at our firm, Autistic Reality, we feel a strong parallel with T'Challa's policies at the end of the film. T'Challa has decided to use the unique resources available to him and his kingdom to help the world become a better place. As an autistic individual, I feel that I have a unique worldview, and experiences from which I can gain knowledge to better help the world. In addition, I have other resources at my disposal, thanks in large part to networking, befriending people, and overall getting along with individuals and organizations whether they are autism-centric or not. I could care less if you are fat, thin, gay, straight, black, white, transgender, cisgender, old, young, disabled, or nondisabled. Are you a good person? Do you seek to better yourself and those around you? If you do, then I believe in your potential.

T'Challa's speech at the United Nations plays into a philosophy I have had of the world for years, long before the release of the film Black Panther: we are all human, and are common, shared identity is the most important attribute we have. Too many people play identity politics, squabbling amongst each other, instead of focusing on the fact that any benefits we make should serve society. When we are separate, we are small minority groups. When we are together, we are humanity; we are one!

Wakanda forever!

Together forever!

A Landmark in Civil Rights: "Love, Simon" (2018) is Real Gay Life

When I saw "Love, Simon" at the movie theaters, I expected a cute teen romantic comedy. It was not. It was a profound piece of civil rights history: the first mainstream gay romance film about the high school generation.

I saw a great deal of myself in the film. Like Simon, I am not an extremely effeminate gay guy. Like Simon, my family was ridiculously accepting of my coming out. Like Simon, I had some trouble with peers in school bullying me for being gay. Like Simon, I have an amazingly tolerant group of friends.

It's funny, because this film portrays gay romance as a mostly run-of-the-mill thing, and, in today's society, it is increasingly becoming so. I have seen reactions on Facebook from people who say it is not, but they are from places like Billings, Montana where viewpoints on the issue is hardly moderate. I came out at age 19 in 2005. In my years as an openly gay man, I have, for the most part, encountered people who are incredibly tolerant of homosexuality. In fact, I would say at least 80% of the individuals I have encountered think of it as a nonissue. I will admit that I travel and mostly liberal circles, but I do not shy away from conservative areas of the country and the world, either.

Family acceptance is also becoming more and more common, and Simon's family is indicative of that. When I came out of the closet, my mother said she had known since I was six months old. Simon's mother tells him that she had suspected for quite some time. My father was extremely tolerant, and even asked me extremely technical questions about gay relationships. Simon's father makes awkward jokes and also gets out of his depth about gay culture; he thinks Grindr is like Facebook for gay people! Simon's sister has no issues whatsoever, and neither did my brother. In fact, not a single family member of mine raised an issue.

This isn't just a trend with myself and my family: I have even met people from the middle of rural Iowa whose families are ridiculously accepting. I will admit that I encountered members in my university's LGBTQ alliance who had a tough time coming out, but I also met many people on the LGBTQ spectrum who did not have a tough time of it. It is curious, because most of those people did not belong to the alliance and were often not actively involved in LGBTQ matters at the school. I would hazard a guess that people in my college joined LGBTQ causes and groups exactly because they found little acceptance at home.

There are a few dream sequences in the film, and in one of them, Simon is in a college that is so gay-friendly that the entire sequence is a musical bedecked in rainbows. As a matter of fact,

I actually went to such a university. While tolerance of the gay population was absolutely amazing, tolerance of other groups such as the disability population lagged significantly. In addition, since I am not a very visibly gay person, there was incredible pressure upon me to become so, but that is just not me. It's not Simon, either. There is a moment the film when he googles "how to dress like a gay guy", but he decides that it is not for him.

Simon navigates a series of common high school interactions with friends, all of whom are tolerant of him being gay. For the record, my friends are all completely tolerant of that facet of my life, some even brag about it. Many of girls and I appraise guys together, there is a scene where Simon does that with his friend Abby. There is a moment he is outed by a guy, but the guy in question isn't homophobic; he's just being a jerk, and even apologizes profusely.

There are a couple of bullies in the school who make fun of him and the school's only other openly homosexual male student. They are dealt with swiftly by those in charge. Like Simon, I was bullied and even gay bashed by students in school, in this case, roommates at my community college. Unlike Simon, the students never apologized, and the staff of the school all the way up to the vice president aided and abetted the gay bashers. I made a much, much better place now.

Simon's relationship with his online boyfriend, Blue, parallels many relationships that I have had. Like Simon, I tend to look for romance, and not casual hookups. In real life, gay couples often chat extensively online before meeting in person. There are many dating apps where this happens, in addition to more traditional platforms such as email. In the end, it is revealed that Blue is Simon's acquaintance Bram, an African-American jock from school. In gay relationships, interracial dating is widely accepted. The idea is that our whole population has had to go through an entire civil rights movement to gain the right to have open relationships, so it really isn't a big deal if someone you date doesn't look like you. There are many more important factors. I myself have dated a number of different kinds of guys, African Americans included.

At the end of the film, Simon and Bram start their relationship together. It doesn't happen with a bang, or with overwhelming drama. It just happens. This has been true for straight couples for generations. There is no reason why it shouldn't hold true for us.

Love, Simon is an absolutely sweet, cute, accurate portrayal of romance amongst many gay teenagers in today's world. For that simple fact, it is a landmark film unlike any before. Gay youth having trouble with acceptance should see this film. Others having trouble accepting people who are gay should see this film. People who are friendly or family to the gay cause should see this film. Not to mention, on its own, it is a wonderful film. We give it five out of five stars, or ten out of ten.

In Defense of the *Twilight* Saga

I am an honest fan of the Twilight Saga by Stephenie Meyer. My-self and others have been horribly bullied for liking this story, this is my response to those bullies and any individuals who see problems with series. I know there are people who will disagree with me, but I'm hoping that this essay helps get rid of some of the rampant hatred for this literature and its fans.

This is my response to criticism of the Twilight Saga. It's a book, people. You're not supposed to hate on a book like you hate on the Nazi party, genocide, and racism. You know what? I'd like to amend that. People have often shown much greater hatred for Twilight then they have for any of those three things. The hatred does not make sense and is almost comical in its intensity. What is not comical, however, is that people often resort to violence, emotional and otherwise, out of their hatred for the Saga. In terms of emotional violence, someone once waited until

I was depressed for an unrelated reason, and then suggested that I kill myself because I like Twilight. Normally, I would have laughed that off. But since I was already quite sad, I almost took their suggestion to heart. One time, hooligans tried to beat the hell out of indie actor Bronson Pelletier, because he is involved with the Twilight movies. This amount of hatred is not easily explained.

It is my own personal belief that many, although not all, of the people who dislike Twilight beyond regular amounts of dislike have a hidden motive in hating it so much. I am not one of these people, so I cannot point these motives out concretely. One possibility why some people may hate it is because they are jealous of the ideal view of romance that the story promotes. They know that this view of romance is basically unattainable, and therefore they will not have it themselves. Another common motive is that people often hate what they fear. And throughout history, people have feared what they can't understand.

Let me explain. The mythology laid out in Twilight vastly changes previous conceptions about the nature of vampires, werewolves, shape-shifters, etc. Many people who hate Twilight try to nitpick with the official explanations given in the illustrated guide in saying that they do not make logical sense. I know of a very good reason why they should not nitpick with this: It's a book! It's a book! It creates an alternate universe in which its own logic makes sense. To deny this is to deny the logic of other books, or for that matter of other creations, such as TV series, movies, plays, songs, etc. According to my own personal opinion, I can nitpick the Bible into a state where Christianity no longer makes sense. But the reason why the Bible has survived is because it is a system of general guidelines and not a blow-by-blow sportscast. Similarly, Twilight is a book that tells a great story, but is not made to be analyzed to the point of nausea.

Other people, especially people who, like me are members of the LGBTQ community, have told me that they will not have anything to do with the Twilight Saga because the author, Stephenie Meyer is a Mormon, or Member of the Church of Jesus Christ of Latter Day Saints. And? And what? At no time whatsoever has she stated that she believes in bigotry. In one interview, she has actually come out and said that a gay person will become a gay vampire, because being gay is not an imperfection. As a member of the LDS church, Ms. Meyer is obligated by her vows to give 10% of her income to the Mormon Church. There are very few faiths that do not include a monetary obligation of some kind in order to be officially considered a member. I am a Unitarian Universalist Humanist, so I have to pay two dues: one as a member of the First Unitarian Society of Ithaca, New York, and one as a member of the HUUmanists, the society of Unitarian Universalist Humanists. In addition, I had to pay a one-time entry fee into the Unitarian Universalist Association of Congregations (UUA). Does the Mormon Church get some of the money that Stephenie Meyer makes off of Twilight? A little. She is probably exempt from paying most of it due to the massive amounts that she gives to charity. In addition, Mormonism is very patrilineal, and the dues in her family are most likely paid by her husband. May I just take this moment to say that if the Mormon Church were not so institutionally homophobic, I would totally rock that faith. I would not necessarily join but might take part in some of their efforts. It is a very good group of people that unfortunately let a few petty bigotries balloon to a point where they govern their whole policy. And may I also say that it is very hypocritical of the LGBTQ community to throw discrimination the way of a member of the Church of Jesus Christ of Latter Day Saints who is not involved in discrimination themselves. No one wants to be a victim of discrimination.

Another accusation that fans of the Twilight Saga face is that the books are very conservative. The books do not go into politics, but they are very socially conservative. While I agree personally that this is not how I would live my life, I believe that in this society which is grown very socially radicalized, it is wonderful to have a constructed, socially conservative foil to idealize, with imitation optional, although in my opinion not completely possible. Take the relationship between Edward and Bella. Even the way Edward treats Bella is conservative. Her father is a police chief and is frequently out. Edward sneaks in, and when Bella is done with dinner, he carries her, yes, carries her, to her bedroom. You will ask me, "Alec, why do you like these books—and Edward—so much if he acts this way?" The answer, my friends, is why so many "secular" people love the Twilight Saga. Like thousands, I see the truth: that Edward does not treat Bella with condescension, but with reverence. And that is what makes him the ultimate ideal of a lover to women—and men—everywhere. It is this kind of romance that distinguished the great works of Brontë and Austin from the lesser works beneath them, and many of Twilight's detractors do not like the fact that this romance means that Twilight is on a higher emotional plane than many other books. It has also been said that the character of Bella Swan is a Mary Sue. Once again, I must ask, and? Yes, she may be a Mary Sue, but that does not mean that she is a horrible character. It simply means that she falls into a trope, and she must work her way out of that trope to distinguish herself. And you bet your life she does!

Another thing that many people hate is that Twilight has introduced many talented actors to the world. Actors who are not that hard on the eyes either! The cast consists of gorgeous men and women who make beautiful vampires and werewolves. Many people immediately write off the actors and creators behind the Twilight Saga because of the hatred mentioned above. Many of the creators involved with the Saga are the kindest most gentle-hearted people you will meet. Yes, some of them have done embarrassing things on camera. And yes, one or two of them has been drunk and disorderly in public. But as celebrities, they get news coverage when that happens to them. Not a single one of them is a genuinely bad person. Not a single one of them is a genuinely bad person like Mel Gibson or Tom Cruise. Indeed, the degree to which they are involved in charitable endeavors will put almost anyone to shame. And not a single one of them has ambitions of being the next Brad Pitt or Tom Hanks. They know and are content with the fact that most of them are relatively small potatoes in the Hollywood world. Perhaps this is why so many of them get so much hatred. Many people have tried to point out to me that they are not the greatest actors or creators in the world. I know that, they know that. Their detractors know that, too. And they are angry that the actors and creators are fine with that fact. Because it shows that the actors and creators are content with being less than someone else. This is something that the detractors would never be content with.

Let us delve into the accusation that Twilight glorifies abuse of women and is rampantly sexist. This is definitely not the case, and stems from a gross misunderstanding of the literature at hand. Twilight is not about a human courtship. It is about a vampire courtship and adheres to vampire rules. Bella consents to this, acknowledging in the final book, Breaking Dawn, that she was always meant to be a vampire. Repeatedly throughout the franchise, the dynamics of vampire mating are emphasized, and it is pointed out that these interactions are quite different from human courtship. Does it seem unusual and even invasive? Yes, but Meyer is an extremely talented writer, and makes it clear that in Edward and Bella's relationship, regular dating rules do not apply. Those who accuse Edward of being abusive are losing sight of the fact that he is not human; he is a vampire. The alternate biological instincts of the vampire race have been a facet of the genre since the beginning.

Finally, Twilight has been accused of showing weak female characters. Yes, it does, at the starting part of their story arcs. Throughout every female character's development, she becomes immensely self-empowered, and even physically powerful. If this is not feminist, then I do not know what is. Bella, for example, starts out as the only human in a family of vampires, and winds up being the most powerful being on the planet, a vampire with an incredibly powerful shield capability. Over the course of the

Twilight Saga, the human Bella saves the vampire Edward several times, despite the fact that she is physically much weaker than him. What does Bella want? She wants to court the vampire, and be a vampire, and she succeeds on both counts.

So, what is the overall point behind this? The overall point is that twilight is a book. Books are powerful, I know. But they are only imbued in the power which we give them through our perceptions. And by less than a year after the first Twilight novel was published, the perceptional appeal of Twilight was so powerful that Stephenie Meyer was named one of the Library of Congress's authors of the year and got to speak at the young adult tent of the National Book Fair on the National Mall in Washington, D.C. I have heard accusations that she bought this success with some massive fortune. There was none. Any money she had at the time was her husband's earnings from his job. At the time of the National Book Fair, she had yet to see a single paycheck from the Twilight Saga franchise. Dreams are powerful things. And Twilight had come to Stephenie Meyer in a dream. It is very hard to destroy dreams. And people who dislike Twilight are fine. But people who wantonly disparage it by making Twilighters feel terrible will have to destroy a dream. That, my friends, is impossible.

Rantings on Technology by an Elderly 32-Year-Old

What follows is my opinion on today's technology fixation. Please bear with me! My views are nowhere near conservative, and I absolutely understand the need for technology in today's society.

I am old. I am so old, in fact, that when I was born, we thought there were only nine planets in the entire universe, all of them are in this solar system, and one of them was Pluto. Now we know there are thousands, millions, or even billions across the entire universe. How old am I? I am thirty-two years old. I have used the previous example to illustrate a point: that great amounts of change can take place over short amounts of time.

Yesterday, I went to see Bo Burnham's film Eighth Grade. The film is being regarded as a highly realistic depiction of life in that absolute hell hole of a year in one's existence. There is bullying. There are the beginnings of a sexual awakening. There are mean people. There are misunderstanding parents. There is low self-esteem, and so much acne. Apparently though, all any eighth-grader does anymore is look at their smart phone and their computer.

As I mentioned, I am thirty-two years old. I graduated high school in 2004. I started three years of undergraduate experience in 2010. I switched to graduate school in 2013. I graduated with my master's degree, very heavy in social theory, in 2016. I got my first "dumb" cell phone in junior year of high school. I got my first smart phone in 2011. I got my first laptop that I actually owned in senior year of high school.

Throughout the film, we are treated to teenagers who focus on their electronics to the excess of all else. They don't pay attention in class, they don't pay attention to friends, and they don't even pay attention to family during meals. At one point, there is a moment when the main character is that dinner with her father, and he doesn't even see anything wrong with her being on her cell phone with headphones in all throughout the family meal. True, there is some bonding between some of the kids over electronics: the main character uses her cell phone as an excuse to flirt with a guy, and later on makes a friend who watches her YouTube videos. But don't get me wrong, this film actively tells you that it is better for you to endlessly hang out online instead of making actual friends.

I must be particularly old and senile, and cranky, too, because my reaction is extremely stereotypical. Get a life! Yes, it is true that I hang out on my computer a lot, but it is never turned on before 9 AM, and is always turned off by 4 PM. In addition, I routinely go out on the town, seeing architecture, tourist sites, museums, and hanging out with friends. I hunger for the world around me. I make excuses to travel.

In fact, in senior year of high school, I liked to hang out on the computer a lot. So much so, in fact, that I did that instead of hanging out with my family. This ended up really hurting me, and contributing to massive depression. It is not a coincidence, in my opinion, that the most depressed people I know are also the most solitary.

Look, I got by in school just fine without endless technology. I am now horrified to learn that everyone is being handed iPads by their schools. Don't! Teach the kids yourselves! Go on a field trip! Do a class activity! I am asking the kids not to hang out on technology during class, but I am also asking the adults not to enable the destruction of our educational fabric by making yourselves dependent upon technology in order to teach.

I definitely understand that technology has a role in life. I am frequently looking at my smart phone for Facebook posts, and I sometimes spend hours a day on my computer. However, the key is to do this in moderation, and not all the time.

What could you do instead? You could read a book! You could see a museum! You could visit a historic site! You could see nature! You could enjoy good food! There are endless amounts of wonderful things to do and a whole wide world in which to do them!

Don't obsess over technology! Live your life! It can be amazing, and you'll be glad you did!

My First *Twilight* Fan Meet Up

As you should already know by now, I am a big fan of Stephenie Meyer's <u>Twilight</u>. Like any fan group, we have periodic meetings, all over the place. Here is my account of my first such meeting. Please note that it overlaps with my chapter on the Ruderman Family Foundation and Special Olympics Massachusetts.

I have had two wonderful experiences with the Twilight Fan Meet Up. The first was in Boston, Massachusetts. I took Amtrak from Buffalo, New York to the Meet Up. I stayed with a friend in North Haverhill whom I had met when he was my teacher's aide in middle school. Each day, I commuted by train into Boston.

The first night, we had an excellent dinner at the Union Oyster House. Up until then, I thought that I hated shellfish. But, the Union Oyster House is the oldest restaurant in North America, so I simply had to try their signature food, and I fell in love with shellfish on the spot! I also took plenty of photos, and had a fun time educating myself about the profound history of that location. Did you know that the Union Oyster House building was a pay station for the Continental Army during the revolution? George Washington certainly was there! Abigail Adams held a feminist women's club there. After the restaurant opened, abolitionist legislator Daniel Webster ate there every single day, having no less than six platters of raw, freshly shucked, naturally raised oysters for lunch. Many presidents have eaten at this restaurant, including my favorite, Franklin Delano Roosevelt. John F. Kennedy turned it into a hotspot for his presidential campaign, and you can still sit at his booth today.

The next day, I headed out on a whale watch. I had tried to host a get together for the whale watch, but the others were pretty busy with other group activities. It is sometimes difficult coordinating with such big groups. Now, normally when you see whales, you see one or maybe a couple on an outing, and you can consider yourself lucky. However, on this particular day, the sea was boiling with whales. They were doing everything, from showing their tails, to feeding right in front of us, and even lying on their backs and flipping their fins in the air, which is no small feat when each fan is fifteen feet long! Afterwards, I went to Legal Seafood, and continued my seafood kick by having some delicious softshell crab!

From there, I walked to the site of the meet up, while seeing the sights on the way. I took photos of the exterior of the customhouse. The customhouse, now a hotel, is pretty far in land by now, but when it was first built it was right on the shore. It consists of an old, Greek temple style building with a much later Gilded Age tower rising out of it. Many years after that, a professional restoration artist shook Boston by demanding why the tower clock had not been working for years, and volunteered his services to fix and restore this neglected landmark.

After that, I went to Faneuil Hall, a wonderful old building that has served as Boston's common meetinghouse since the mid-1700s. It was greatly expanded by one of my favorite architects, Charles Bulfinch, the first professional architect to be born in the United States of America. Bulfinch has a number of wonderful projects to his name, including the Massachusetts State House, the Maine State House, and the Old Connecticut State House. He was a public servant as well as an architect, and also built the very first memorial to the American Revolution, which you can still see on the Massachusetts State House Grounds. The highlight of his work is his completion of the United States Capitol Building under its original design. There is some push to rename Faneuil Hall, since its donor and namesake was a slaveholder. It is ironic, then, that the building was the site of some of the most fervently abolitionist meetings of all time. The main focal point of the interior is a massive painting called Webster's Reply to Hayne, depicting Daniel Webster when he was a senator in Washington, DC defending the Union against "states rights" secessionists who were in favor of slavery.

After this, I met with my Aunt Betti Gefecht and our friend Born on Halloween. Aunt Betti Gefecht is an absolutely insane German fanfiction author whom I have informally adopted. We share our insanity in common, and I have gone to visit her multiple times. We love each other very dearly, and I was thrilled to learn that she was coming to the Meet Up in Boston. I had never met Born in person up to that point, although I love her dearly as well. Together we went to Quincy Market, and also chatted at a nearby hotel.

That night was the highlight of the Meet Up. There were at least fifty women from around the world, and I was the only male, but I do not care. We had drinks and dinner and wonderful discussion of writing, editing, publishing, and fandom. I was absolutely thrilled to be there!

The next morning, we went out to breakfast, and had a wonderful time. The highlight was when I got the author nicknamed Punchy to pretend to punch me! After that, we went on our way.

However, this was not the end of the road for me. I am a disability rights advocate by trade, and the next day, I went to Newton, Massachusetts and had a very productive meeting with the leaders of the Ruderman Family Foundation, a group that donates much time, money, and effort to disability-related causes.

The next day, I went to Special Olympics Massachusetts in the town of Marlborough with the friend who was hosting me who was, at the time, the vice president of Special Olympics Massachusetts for public engagement. I am a former Special Olympics athlete, with a number of medals in state-level competitions. I gave a speech to their staff, recorded a podcast, and guest lectured at a college class via video. I also got to tour their facilities, which are noteworthy because Massachusetts is the only state with its own purpose-built Special Olympics headquarters.

The next day, I went home, content with my wonderful new friends and business prospects. This one Twilight Fan Meet Up definitely changed my life for the better!

I Get Interviewed by
The Movie Mom

I was interviewed by a quite reputable film critic, The Movie Mom, Nell Minow, on my book, Veni! Vidi! Autism! Without further ado, here is the interview..

As I looked at your table of contents, of course the first chapter I turned to was called "Truly the Worst Film I Have Ever Seen." Tell me what that film is, why it is the worst, and, if you could have given them advice about how to make it better, what you would have told them. Was there anything in the movie that wasn't terrible?

The film was an MTV production starring Andy Samberg called "Popstar: Never Stop Never Stopping". It is a mockumentary based on the various documentaries following musical talents of their journeys of creativity. Andy Samberg's character is the popstar in question, and his comedy troupe serves as the writers. I would say that the film is in bad taste, but there seems to be absolutely no taste in the film. It is horrifying and humiliating to watch. I am quite ashamed that they would think of putting it on screen. How do we make it better? Well, we can turn it into actual satire of modern-day pop musicians and our fixation with them. I seem to recall other mockumentaries like "Best in Show" and "A Mighty Wind" which seem to do that quite well. There is even a very entertaining humorous documentary on Tammy Faye Bakker called "The Eyes of Tammy Faye" which could have been used as a more realistic template. From another angle, Penn and Teller used to have a show called "Bullshit" where they satirized idiotic concepts by interviewing those involved in them and catching them in their stupidity. All of these ways of making documentaries or mockumentaries would be preferable to the absolutely tasteless drivel that we got instead. There are a few acting talents in the film that had the potential to be good but suffered from tremendously poor writing or their own lack of interest. In my opinion, the film is utterly unredeemable.

I was very touched by your essay about the Power Rangers. Why did you like them as a kid and what did it mean to you to have an autistic character in the recent film? What did you think about the portrayal of autism in the film?

To be honest, I am not even sure why I liked Power Rangers so much as a kid, other than liking the action and explosions! I stopped watching after a few years, but I grew up with the original cast. I am very thrilled with the new movie, because it is not just adventure, but there is plot development and character evolution as well. I have been around pop culture long enough to know about and critique disability portrayal. After all, a great amount of my book deals with it! I was already at the point where I knew of autistic characters in pop culture; my chapters on Tim Urich, the first autistic superhero from Marvel comics, deal with this major revelation to myself and my desire to share it with others. However, I had not seen a realistic autistic hero or more importantly, a superhero, portrayed in film until I saw Billy in the new Power Rangers film. In many ways, it was like watching myself! Billy displays many behaviors that I have had myself, even his counting of colored pencils, which I used to do in high school. Most importantly, it shows Billy with a group of friends from among his peers. It took me many years to develop friends amongst my peers.

Is there a movie or television show that you think portrays autism accurately?

Aside from Power Rangers, there are a few others. Alan Turing, the World War II code breaker who invented the computer, was homosexual but he was also autistic. The film "The Imitation Game" does not mention the latter but portrays it quite well. "Loving Vincent" is a wonderful film about Vincent van Gogh as told by those who cared for him most. It is also most noteworthy for being the first-ever completely oil painted film. When you listen to the accounts of van Gogh's friends and family, it is quite clear that he has autism. As I mention in my Without Fear essay, autism doesn't need to be mentioned in order to be present in a narrative. Of course, people were not aware of autism until the late 1940s, so it shouldn't be mentioned in most historical narratives. As for television, Sylvia Tilly in Star Trek: Discovery often comes across as quite autistic, but that has not been officially revealed...as of yet. I have yet to watch The Good Doctor, which is about an autistic young man who becomes a physician. I have watched the television series Westworld, and the characters of Dr. Ford and Bernard come across as quite autistic. Forgive me for spoiling the show, but Bernard is actually a robotic host who is patterned after Dr. Ford's deceased business partner, Arnold. It would make sense if Arnold also had autism. In the case of Dr. Ford, the portrayal is only natural, as he is played by Sir Anthony Hopkins, who is autistic himself, and was diagnosed as such at age 70. One of the best portrayals of autism so far in pop culture has been the character of Tim Urich in the Daredevil comics. I cover this portrayal heavily in my book and have talked to some major players at Marvel about it. They brought up my talking points about autism, disability, and comics at their annual planning meeting this year.

What do you wish people understood about autism?

There are many, many things that I wish people understood. I wish that people understood the great variety of people with autism. Some of us are nonspeaking, and some of us speak a lot. There are autistic conservatives and liberals, optimists and pessimists, and people of every race and gender identity. I find myself between extremes. I am not fundamentally conservative, and yet I believe in realism over hyper-politically correct culture. I consider myself an optimist, but I also temper my expectations with past and theoretical experience. Many of the more visible autistic activists are often busy waving placards and getting arrested for political change. Then again, on the other end of the spectrum, some of us stay home frequently. You will find me out and about trying to achieve political and social change by negotiating, meeting, and using diplomacy. I want people to know that autistic individuals are capable of all that I have previously mentioned, that we use a wide variety of methods for being in touch with the world around us.

On a more basic level, I want people to listen to us when making decisions about our lives. In 1505, the Polish Parliament passed constitutional legislation saying that they would have to be consulted in any decision about the public, thus taking the power away from the monarch. The bill was called Nihil novi, and included the Latin phrase, "Nihil de nobis, sine nobis". Roughly translated, this means "Nothing about Us, without Us". This has since become a motto for many groups and individuals in advocacy and activism. In fact, it is the URL for my website. As a rule of thumb, any individual or group of people deserves input into any decisions made about them. This includes autistic groups and individuals. Don't get me wrong! Loving parents should be able to voice their concerns, but autistic individuals should always have power to decide our own destiny.

You seem to have a special affinity for low budget films. What is it about those films that appeals to you?

These films do not usually appeal to me any more than Hollywood films. However, for six years, I lived in Buffalo, New York, which has approximately fifty independent film studios. I was an active member of the creative culture in that town, which is absolutely booming. As such, I became very interested in independent films being made there. There were several screenings that I attended, often in support of friends of mine who made or were in the films. It was phenomenal to see such a tangible product of local arts and ingenuity. I have always been in favor of supporting local, independently made products. As such, I wanted to support these films, and I found that the best way of supporting them was by giving honest reviews on my blog and on film review sites. These reviews have since made their way to my book.

You're a fan of the Twilight series. People seem very intensely pro and con the series. What is it that provokes such strong reactions? Which do you like better, the books or the movies?

You are right. Some people are incredibly appreciative of the Twilight Saga. In fact, I am friends with a great number of them. We hold meetups, attend films together, and interact online quite frequently. These people, who are mostly women, are my dear friends. Some of them are almost as close as family, and I have adopted one in Germany as my aunt and we have visited each other. Our strong feelings for Twilight come from the inescapable romance of the Saga, as well as the characters, plot, and feelings of empathy we have for the said characters. Twilight was never intended to be primarily about vampires. It is primarily a great romance story, with vampirism as a major plot element. Twilight fans, who are called Twilighters or Twihards, understand that. We also understand the great underlying feminism of the plot.

Bella, the main character, is very determined to be with her love interest, Edward, and to become a vampire, and she gets what she wants. She even saves his life several times during the Saga. Many of the facets of romance with a vampire are quite different than romance with a human, leading to a different dynamic and different actions, and Twilighters understand that.

However, a great deal of people have an irrational aversion to the series, even going so far as to insult and harass Twilighters. One time when I was quite emotionally distressed, I was told to kill myself because I like Twilight. If I may be brutally honest, in my opinion, many people, including women and people who may identify as feminists, are actually extremely afraid of the Saga because of how brazenly it depicts a powerful, self-determined female character, and because of the great, wondrous romance depicted in the Saga. Many people have an aversion to romance, especially idealized romance, because theirs can never measure up. I would even be as bold as to say that some hate the Saga because they believe that their love is inferior to that shown in Twilight. Furthermore, many people are disappointed that Twilight is not more action-oriented. Action was never the point of the Saga. Many are also disappointed that the mythology in Twilight, particularly the vampire mythology, is not consistent with a great deal of formerly established mythology. Do these people know that the modern concept of the vampire only dates back to Brahm Stoker's 1897 book Dracula? Do they know that many more established concepts of vampire mythology only date back as far as the 1922 film Nosferatu? Mythologies evolve over time, and Twilight even includes explanations for why its mythology is different. Nevertheless, the most hateful detractors of Twilight seem to be irrational and make it their goal to insult and even threaten those who do like the Saga. These threats, this hatred, this harassment and bullying will not stand. I know that my defense of the Saga is coming on strong, but we fans have been unjustly attacked over the years just for liking a good love story.

I have seen and loved the movies very much. I appreciate the casting choices and the camaraderie between the actors and the filmmakers. As for the books, I have read great portions of the books, but not the entire set of novels, because I have ADD, and my attention can't hold that long. However, with the advent of the smartphone, I find myself pulled into the world of fanfiction, and I read that frequently. I appreciate the great many possibilities that the Saga allows, and how easy it is for fans to show their love for it by inventing new stories around it.

What is AvatarMeet? What do you like best about it? What are you hoping for in the next movie?

AvatarMeet is a group of people including myself who meet up each year to celebrate James Cameron's film Avatar. We have a thriving online community, and I have been to two of the meetups. One year, we met up in South California and went to Lightstorm Entertainment, where we were given a tour of the studio, and got to interview the filmmakers. The next time I went, last year, 2017, we went to the theme park in Florida, where we were given a tour by the head of public relations for Disney Imagineering. While there, we also went to the Kennedy

Space Center, where I had a truly moving experience. You can read more about both experiences in my book. What I like best about AvatarMeet is the wonderful group of friends all over the world who love this film universe, and the ideals that it promotes. I have met truly kindred spirits through AvatarMeet. In the future films, I hope that we continue experiencing the messages of diversity that were in the first film. In the that film, the main character had a disability. While I was at Lightstorm, I got to personally question producer Jon Landau about diversity and the messages of the film, and he assured me that these facets of storytelling would be promoted in the narrative going forward, and we have already seen results. I include my interview with Jon in my book.

Why was Love, Simon especially meaningful to you?

Love, Simon was especially meaningful to me and to millions of others because it mainstreams LGBTQ romance. It is the first mainstream teen romantic comedy about a gay person falling in love. There is absolute love for this film and endless positive feeling amongst those who have watched it. There is a Facebook page dedicated to fans of the film which has optimistic followers around the globe. Many people in the world do not yet have the freedom to love who they wish in public. This helps give them hope. In addition, watching the film with one's family members and friends helps open the dialogue about coming out, and I have heard that hundreds of people have come out to their families while watching this film. This is truly feel-good way to start conversation about a very important topic. The motto of the film is, "Everyone Deserves a Good Love Story," and finally it is out in the open for everyone to see.

I should mention that my family and friends have all been extremely accepting of my coming out, and I realize that I am lucky in this way. In the film, Simon has many moments with his family that remind me of moments with my own. In addition, despite initial bumps, his friends are very accepting of him, as mine have been. Heck, my friends have been known to introduce me with the following sentence: "Yeah, this is our gay, autistic friend Alec. He's weird, and very smart! Once you get to know him, he'll be your dear friend, too! He'll never betray you." Yes, someone once actually said that. Actually, multiple people have said some variation of that sentence. As an autistic person who did not have authentic friends for much of his life, I treasure my friends' opinions of me greatly!

What is Autistic Reality? What are your priorities? What are you proudest of?

Autistic Reality is my advocacy firm. Through it, I focus on advocacy via public speaking, peer mentoring, lobbying, and other consulting services. Soon, Autistic Reality will have a podcast as well. In it, I will be interviewing people from many walks of life, including disability advocates, actors, artists, and others, about their points of view on the disability cause. In addition, we are getting set up as a publishing imprint, with the goal of getting works by authors with disabilities into the world at large, something we, the disabled population, have usually struggled with. Currently, I am working on this last point with BBDO New

York, the world's largest and most prestigious advertising agency. As part of that job, I am the managing editor of Stories About Us, which is beginning the work of publishing disabled authors, so that I may continue it afterwards. In addition to all this, I promote my book in meetings, such as with Marvel editorial, and at various pop-culture conventions. Soon, I will be giving a talk at a creative writing conference on turning disability into a creative asset. I am always looking for wonderful new opportunities to present and share disability advocacy and information.

I consider myself and my firm's work to be quite liberal, but still relatively moderate compared to some disability rights activists. For myself, I actually prefer the term "advocate" instead of "activist". Although I can sometimes support more radical work, I am not one of the people who tends to get arrested or make a lot of public noise for our cause. Sometimes making a spectacle of yourself can decrease your credibility with certain parties. I prefer negotiation, diplomacy, and a sharing of ideas. Even with the people I disagree with most, I try to understand them, and how they think. In this way, we can better promote the disability agenda.

On a side note, I do not believe in posting politics or much religion on Facebook. I post relevant politics on my firm's Facebook page, or on my book's Facebook page, but the lack of politics on my page has made my relationships more cordial and my discourse much more civil for years.

These factors help inform my firm's priorities, by approaching disability advocacy and advocacy in general with a realistic yet optimistic eye towards what can be achieved, and how to achieve it. For example, I do not get hung up on whether people say, "disabled person" or "person with disability". This is not a huge priority for me. Solving problems like transportation access, access to benefits, education, workforce reform, and representation in the arts are much more important to me.

What am I proudest of? I really do not like to toot my own horn very much. Every time someone tells me I have improved the conditions of their life, I feel like I am achieving my goal. Awards do not mean much to me. Making a noticeable difference does.

Everyone Is Human:
Prosthetics in *Alita: Battle Angel*

After my interview with Nell Minow, which you may have read in the last chapter, she put me in touch with an autistic film critic. He put me in touch with some of the sites he writes for, and this chapter contains my first ever professional film review, which resulted from those efforts.

The new film Alita: Battle Angel has done quite well at the box office, and many have praised its feminist ideals. However, the film is also quite a boon to the disabled community. It can be argued that it is a two-hour, $200 million treatise on prosthetics. During an interview with disability rights firm Autistic Reality at Lightstorm Entertainment in 2014, Alita co-producer Jon Landau came out with a novel position when asked about diversity in film. "We work on stuff creatively," he says. "When you push something to the forefront, I think it has much less of an impact than when you play it in the background." As such, the pro-prosthetic agenda of Alita: Battle Angel does not slap you in the face but is instead an inbuilt part of the film.

In the world in which the film exists, a future community called Iron City, prosthetic limbs and bodies are par for the course. In fact, it is rarer to come upon someone who doesn't have a prosthetic body part than it is to see someone with one. This is typified by a scene early in the film when Dr. Dyson Ido (Christoph Waltz) takes Alita (Rosa Salazar) around Iron City, and we see many people living their everyday lives with prosthetics. Some of these people work their prosthetic limbs to their advantage, such as a guitarist, who has two extra hands on his left arm, allowing him to play a double-necked guitar flawlessly. Ido's nurse, Gerhad (Idara Victor), is kind and compassionate, and has a prosthetic left arm that is finely tuned to better allow her to assist in surgeries. Some people use prosthetic body parts for sports, such as the much-favored sport of Motorball. In fact, at one point during the film, Dr. Ido fits Alita with prosthetic skates for the sport. Other athletes have prosthetic weapons that they use to gain an advantage in the game. There are even animals with prosthetic parts, and one bounty hunter named McTeague (Jeff Fahey) has an entire pack of dogs that are either robotic or cybernetic with prosthetics.

There are multiple amputees in Iron City, and Dr. Ido treats many of them. In fact, Alita's first body in the film was originally meant for his daughter, who was paralyzed from the waist down. Some in the modern disability rights movement would view the trait of a prosthetic body for someone affected by paralysis as unnecessary, and believe that person should probably live with their paralysis. Then again, the film takes place several hundred years in the future, and in a completely different world. One would expect that, as prosthetics became more readily available and more lifelike, people would take to them kindlier. In fact, Alita's love interest, Hugo (Keean Johnson), is given an almost entirely prosthetic body towards the end of the film, and, all things considered, it has relatively little effect on him psychologically since he grew up knowing that it would always be a possibility.

Of course, some characters take the prosthetic surgery to extremes. Merciless bounty Hunter Zapan (Ed Skrein) has heavily invested his earnings on a sleek, pretty-boy body and face, all the while engaging in insidious plots to defeat the protagonists of the film. He is cold and manipulative, and undeserving of his beautiful body, and gets his just desserts near the end of the film when Alita destroys his face, leaving him as ugly as his emotional bankruptcy would indicate. An even further example of extreme prosthetic modification is Grewishka (Jackie Earle Haley), one of the main villains of the film. He starts out just barely human, with a human brain with a modified human head, and over the course of the film, his cybernetic body is further and further "upgraded". By the time of his death at the end of the film, it is impossible to empathize with Grewishka, and it is more like seeing a machine terminated than it is seeing a person die.

As Landau mentioned, "...at the end, as we talked about, we want to make movies that affect people, and have an impact on their lives, and how they see the world, as they move forward." Therefore, through it all, Alita remains the most human character in the entire film, even though her brain is the only originally human part of her. She is compassionate, loving, empathetic, loyal, and sweet. The question thus becomes, "What makes us human?" If Alita can be human, then it does not matter how many prosthetic parts someone has. Just because one has prosthetics does not mean they are broken. Everyone is human.

You can find the full interview with Jon Landau on page 294, A Hollywood Titan.

Avatar - Navigating Public Transportation: A SoCal Case Study

One of the groups I belong to is AvatarMeet, the official fan group for James Cameron's Avatar. As a person with multiple disabilities, I am proud of being able to get my way around on my own. I decided to do a blog post on my methods of getting around Southern California before, during, and after AvatarMeet 2014. There is actually a whole discipline on ease of transportation access for those with disabilities. In fact, the reading that follows was made required learning in an accessible design class at my university. Happy reading!

Hello! In this entry I shall give insight into transportation during my major vacation this year, to San Diego and Los Angeles. It should be noted that I do not drive due to a number of sensory and motor disabilities that impact how external stimuli affect me. The simple fact is that public transportation is the way I get around. I encourage everybody to use public transportation when convenient! It is a good way of decreasing traffic congestion, environmental impact, and reliance on fossil fuels! I will not be covering every journey I took during my trip, because many of them used the same kind of transit that I will have already detailed. It should also be noted that a number of my rides during AvatarMeet 2014 were in people's personal vehicles. I will not detail those trips, but I will mention that it is very important to socialize with people you meet at functions, as they can be your ride back and forth!

I live right at the border of Amherst and Buffalo in New York State. I took a cab from my apartment to Buffalo Niagara International Airport. My first flight of the day was quite early, and I knew I had a long day ahead of me. I had some time to wait before my flight was to depart, so I got some breakfast. I flew from Buffalo to Minneapolis-St. Paul, with only about ten minutes between the time that my flight arrived there and the time that the next flight started boarding. Further complicating matters was the fact that my next flight was in a different terminal. However, the terminals were adjacent and within walking distance of one another. Once I got to my gate, boarding was just about to start. The gate was right next to the cafeteria, so I quickly got a sandwich and a soda to take on the plane with me. I then boarded my plane heading to LAX in Los Angeles.

From LAX, I took a cheap shuttle to the train and bus station in Los Angeles, Union Station. Once I got to Union Station, I had to pay for the shuttle, something that was not possible at the airport. Thankfully, there is a convenient ticketing counter at Union Station, and the driver waits for everybody to pay before leaving. Airport shuttles are very convenient, and one should not underestimate the flexibility that they allow you.

I arrived at Union Station earlier than I thought I would. When I went to the ticket counter, the line was taking forever. Train and bus tickets are something that I dread standing in line for. Most of the time, all I need to do is obtain a ticket I have bought previously, yet I am often held up by people with much more complicated questions. In my opinion, there should be at least one station for obtaining previously ordered tickets, and at least one station for all other concerns. Another thing that I take issue with is the fact that many ticket counters have multiple stations, yet only one of them is usually occupied. Therefore, when a gentleman opened up an accessible window for those with disability issues, I went to see him to obtain my ticket. I justified going to that desk because I have at least eight diagnoses, and receive assistance from the federal government due to my disabilities. The gentleman at the desk informed me that I could still get on an earlier train to San Diego that was still at the platform.

So I switched to an earlier train, and boarded it heading to San Diego. I took Amtrak's Pacific Surf Liner, which travels along the Pacific coast of California. It should be noted that people need to use the train much more often in this country. If one has an option between taking the train and taking the bus, always take the train. It is quicker and cheaper by far. I parked my bags on the train, and plugged in my cell phone to recharge. By this time I had been up for nine or ten hours, and the phone was running low on battery. It turns out that my charger was broken, a fact that I did not know, and I had to physically hold onto it the entire time that it was charging. At one point I got up and went to the café car. We passed by a number of towns in SoCal, each one getting a humorous announcement from the conductor. I eventually got off at Old Town in San Diego.

From the Old Town Station, I took the bus to my hostel, the International Traveler's House (ITH) Zoo Hostel. San Diego's transportation is dealt with by the San Diego Metropolitan Transit System (MTS). The buses I took tend to run at least once every half an hour, and at most once every fifteen minutes. A few days later, I went to the famous mission where California was founded, Mission Basilica San Diego de Alcala. I took the bus north to a transit center, where I got out and waited for the light rail. I soon discovered that I would need a ticket for the light rail, and got one, an all-day ticket to cover both my journey to the Mission, and the return trip. However, I missed the train while I was getting my ticket. While I was waiting for the next train, I went to the snack stand at the transit center and got lunch. A few minutes later, the next train came. Unfortunately, I got off a few stops too early. Quite fortunately, the train seems to run very frequently, so I got on the next one to the Mission stop. However, the door open mechanism was broken, so I got off one stop too late. I simply crossed to the other side of the platform, waited a couple minutes for the next train to come, and got off at the proper stop. On the way back, there were no errors in my travel plan, as I had learned from my past mistakes.

Earlier, I mentioned how important airport shuttles can be. It should be noted that you can easily use them to get between places near airports. For example, after I took the train back to Union Station in Los Angeles, I then took the cheap airport shuttle I had taken earlier back to LAX. From there, I took a completely free airport shuttle to the hotel where AvatarMeet 2014 was taking place. Another time, I took the free shuttle from my hostel in Los Angeles to LAX, where I once again took the free shuttle to the hotel where AvatarMeet 2014 was taking place. The only downside to taking free airport shuttles is that waiting for them can take a bit of time, and they often have a number of stops to make. Therefore, I would only recommend using them either when you were going one way to or from the airport, or if you have a significant amount of time to devote to your trip.

I hope that the lessons I have discussed in this entry have been informative, and it is my most fervent wish that somebody learn something about future travel from this text. I hope you all have a great rest of the summer, and a happy return to work, school, or whatever you do best!

A Hollywood Titan Alec Frazier of Autistic Reality Quizzes Jon Landau of Lightstorm Entertainment

In 2014, AvatarMeet visited Lightstorm Entertainment, the studio responsible for production of the film. One of our activities was a question-and-answer session with a number of the filmmakers and other people involved in the making of the Avatar franchise. What follows is my exchange with producer Jon Landau, one of the smartest, most successful people in Hollywood, after I asked him about involving disability and other forms of diversity in film. I am quite encouraged by his answers.

Me: I'm interested in that uh, you have this great environmental message but another message that I've liked a whole lot about Avatar is the message of tolerance and so I'm wondering about uh, I have a general part of this question and then specifically... I'm wondering how you're willing to in general enforce tolerance, will not enforce but address tolerance in the movies and specifically things like sexual orientation, religion, race, and disability, things like that. So I'm wondering if any of the future movies will deal with that, or will feature that in any way, and uh, and my general question is if they will go further to promote tolerance.

Jon Landau: Well look, I think that, a general answer? Yes. When you say feature something, it always makes me nervous.

Me: No I don't...

Jon Landau: No, no, no. I'm just saying, cause we work on stuff creatively. When you push something to the forefront, I think it has much less of an impact than one you play it in the...

Me: I agree.

Jon Landau: ...background. So, featuring things I don't think, you know will continue to exist. But, that sense, I mean I really see the future movies again, not about Na'vi versus human, but is about the choices we make. It's about good versus evil. It's about are you a good Na'vi, are you a bad Na'vi. Are you a good human, are you a bad human. How do you become accepting of other people and their differences. So I think those things, those thematic themes are going to play out and it's important for us, because those are universal themes. They are not American jingoistic themes. And as we make movies in today's world, we have to do it for a global audience and we have to, you know, attract people in and let them discover the types of things we're talking about, and not be beating them over the head Of discovery for them, and we're really looking at this, and while each movie will complete itself as a story arc, and I say that Jim [Cameron] twice has done sequels, I argue that both times they have at least lived up to if not been better than the first movies, but they were complete movies, so we have to do that and some of our themes that remain in the end are themes that are really gonna take the full story arc to play out, but I think that's okay um, andwith them, let it be a journey, a journey...

Me: That's what I believe, too.

Jon Landau: ...at the end, as we talked about we want to make movies that, that affect people, and have an impact on their lives, and how they see the world, as they move forward.

Me: Just in the interest of full disclosure, I don't like being labeled. People exist, that's what I think that they...

Jon Landau: Look, I'm going to use the movie "An Inconvenient Truth". I went through it, I enjoyed it, but their preaching to the people they already converted. What you have to do is you have to, like the first Avatar does, people have heard me say this before, it begins and ends with Jake opening his eyes. So what we need to do is get people to come in, and they may think that their eyes are open, but they're really not. Because if through our films we can get people to open their eyes and see things differently, then we've been successful.

My *Avatar* Story

One of my connections in the Avatar fan business made me aware of an interview being done about the Avatar fan experience. I gladly participated.

> What is your *Avatar* story' from when you first saw it?

When *Avatar* first came out, I heard the mumblings and then rumors of what a fantastic, world-changing film it was. Then, late in December, I saw a bit on the Daily Show with Jon Stewart where correspondent John Oliver reported from Pandora. I was intrigued, to say the least, but still not sure that *Avatar* deserves all the praise it was getting. However, the rumor mill was working full-time, and I finally saw the film on January 6, 2010. My life was forever changed. I have always been a consummate geek, and this film was, to me, the best of geekery, as well as having many messages that were completely in line with my worldview.

> What struck you the most about *Avatar?*

Identity has always been incredibly important to me. Fiction involving identity and revelations about identity have always struck me extremely potently. Jake finding his identity and finally becoming it moved me to my core. The way that the identity message figures in with messages about tolerance and acceptance only makes it more vital. Nevertheless, we should not let identity politics drive us apart, and I am extremely thankful that the Na'vi teach this lesson in the film.

> What did it mean to you?

I live my life every day with more than ten disabilities including autism, bipolar, and sensory integration issues. The fact that the main character has a disability himself, and that he can save an entire world while living with those disabilities has, in my mind, done a tremendous amount for disability civil rights. I am aware that the actor himself does not have those disabilities, but the fact that he was required to play a nondisabled role as well would have made it difficult for someone without use of their legs to play the role. I know for a fact that there will be disabled actors in the sequels.

> How did it affect you?

Because the film perfectly encapsulated how I felt about the world and where it should go, I was able to refer to it when voicing my philosophical, political, and even religious ideals. I believe in cooperation and was able to join a fandom that cooperated to bring reality to the values which I hold most dear. As a disability rights advocate, I teach of how honest work and good intent can change the world for the better. This film is absolute confirmation of those facts.

> What themes in the film/story/world resonated with you the most?

My entire life's philosophy is based upon optimism and a positive worldview. This film showed a world where you could live in harmony with the planet—in this case, literally—and triumph over many adversities. As mentioned before, I have many disabilities, and I am also gay. Nevertheless, I believe that we are all human, and that we all have the right and ability to work together for a better future.

> What connections did you make with other fans?

At first, I was vaguely aware of fan efforts to show some love for this phenomenal franchise. This all became abundantly clear when I learned about AvatarMeet 2014, when the group was set to visit Lightstorm Entertainment. I messaged them, and emailed those in charge, which got the ball rolling.

> How did you connect with other fans?

Initially, it was difficult, as there was no official Facebook page for the Meetup. I joined some of the *Avatar* web forums, but due to ADD and writing disabilities, among other reasons, forms are not a natural virtual space for me to inhabit, so there was quite a bit of emailing. We also used the resources that the AvatarMeet homepage keeps to help us keep in touch and appraised of each other's situations.

> What was the easiest way to connect?

At some point after the first Meetup I attended in 2014, a Facebook group page was created for all of us to interact. This has been incredibly useful, both in arranging Meetups, and in keeping in touch day to day. AvatarMeet has dozens of attendees from around the world, and Facebook really is the easiest and most convenient way to keep in touch. For example, I take a great deal of photos as a hobby and can share them on the page. My career also involves me generating a lot of content based on my experiences, and the Facebook page has become a place where I can share that content.

> What were some of the best things that happened to you because of *Avatar*?

As an autistic person, it has always been much more difficult to make friends. AvatarMeet and fandom of *Avatar* in general has allowed me to make many, many, many wonderful friends. As mentioned, some of these friends are from all over the globe. I laugh with them, I cry with them, I eat them, and their several whom I love dearly as compatriots in the fandom.

In addition, the organized fandom of AvatarMeet has allowed me to meet many wonderful people who are involved in the creation of Avatar itself. I have gotten to meet many the filmmakers at the 2014 Meetup and have met many the circus performers from the Cirque du Soleil show online. Heck, Dr. Paul Frommer, the inventor of the Na'vi language, is a very, very dear friend, and he and his partner have even invited us to their house in the Hollywood Hills for a party during the 2014 Meetup.

> Were there any bad things that happened as a result of your *Avatar* experience?

No, not really. There have been a two or three people I've met in the fandom who have turned out to kind of be jerks, or one or two who are not always too nice, but otherwise, my Avatar experience has been phenomenally good.

> How long did your interest in *Avatar* last?

I am still incredibly interested in *Avatar*. In November of last year, just three months ago, I went to the last AvatarMeet in Florida to visit the theme park and the Kennedy Space Center, both of which had tremendous impacts on me. In my apartment,

I have several memorabilia items displayed, and they include my Na'vi knife, my avatar, and my Ikran. I also have several *Avatar* books, some of which have been signed by people involved in the franchise, including Paul Frommer and John Landau.

> What keeps you interested in *Avatar?*

Forgive me, but at the risk of sounding like a broken record, the friends, positive message, and compatibility with my own opinions and beliefs sustains my interest in *Avatar.*

> How would you like to see the fandom evolve?

I would like to see the *Avatar* fandom grow and become even bigger, even more global, and even more diverse. I am noticing that the fandom is mostly white, and it would be great to expand that to all racial identities. One positive thing about the fandom as of right now is that there is a large LGBTQ population within the fandom. In addition to its growth, I would like to see the fandom stay progressive, fun-loving, environmentally friendly, and tolerant and accepting of fans from all different walks of life. It is amazing that at a Meetup, I can be talking to an IT professional from Germany, a lab technician from Virginia, a barista from Seattle, and the man who takes care of big cats in Nevada.

> What is missing?

In my opinion, it would be great to show Na'vi with developmental disabilities. Jake Sully was an awesome role model as a character with physical disabilities, and as a veteran, but many people today, myself included, are living full and productive lives with conditions such as autism, cerebral palsy, depression, and other developmental disabilities. In my case, for example, I have at least ten developmental disabilities including autism, and I work as an editor at a major advertising firm, and as a disability rights advocate, doing public speaking, lobbying, and even meeting with national legislators. If avatar has shown us anything, it is that we can decide what our limits are, instead of letting them define us.

In addition, it would be totally amazing to show some Na'vi living in homosexual or even polyamorous relationships. A scientist named Christopher Ryan has proven that monogamy is not natural for human beings, having only developed as recently as we started holding property. In addition, homosexuality is incredibly natural, just as natural as it is to breathe or hydrate. I can completely understand if the former tendency may be too radical to show in the sequels, or at least early in the sequels, but the Na'vi live in harmony with their world, which should include sexual identity.

I have had a discussion on these matters with Jon Landau, and he says he is incredibly in favor of showing diversity and teaching lessons in diversity by using the characters in the films. But he did say was that we must be careful not to beat people over the head with these ideas. I agree completely, as people exist with their identities, instead of the other way around.

> And here's a biggy, how do you think you will feel if/when there is a large influx of returning and new Avatar fans, when the next *Avatar* films hits the cinemas?

I will say, "Kaltxì", and welcome them with open arms! I would like them to acknowledge that there is already a thriving fan community, including an official get-together, AvatarMeet, and I want them to feel free to join, as well as ask questions if they have them. Our clan is always growing and is welcoming towards others! They should also know that there is no official litmus test to be an *Avatar* fan, and that everyone is welcome, so long as they respect others, and the world around them!

Of Alec and Älek: A Journey to Pandora – The World of *Avatar*

Kaltxì! That means "Hello!" in Na'vi, the language of the people of the same name in James Cameron's film, Avatar! I am a massive fan of said movie, and am very proud to share a special experience with you. You see, I belong to the official fan group, called AvatarMeet! Earlier this month, November, 2017, a number of us gathered in Florida and went to Pandora – The World of Avatar at Walt Disney World's Animal Kingdom.

The day we first went, it was foggy in the morning. We got to the park, and met with our guide, Diego Parras, the Communications Manager at Walt Disney Imagineering. Imagineering is a job that is very specific to Disney properties. It involves creating entire new worlds to explore through architecture, engineering, landscaping, and other forms of creativity. From the front area of the park, called the Oasis, we saw the gigantic floating mountains of Pandora through the dense fog.

One heads into Pandora via a bridge from the central area of the Animal Kingdom, which is called Discovery Island. It is at this point that you leave Earth, and travel to the moon of Pandora orbiting gas giant Polyphemus in the Alpha Centauri system.

In the film, Col. Miles Quaritch reminds you, "You're not in Kansas anymore. You're on Pandora!" This is immediately apparent as you see a ginormous plant that resembles a massive pod that glows from within. It is called a baja tickler by humans, although the Na'vi name is txumtsä'wll, which means "poison-squirting plant". It squirts moisture and glows when people interact with it

Then, as if in the film itself, the fog lifted, and we saw the floating mountains of the Valley of Mo'ara, the area of Pandora which you visit in this park. The science behind the floating mountains says that they formed when Pandora was in the molten state, with geological deposits rich in the magnetically repulsive mineral Unobtainium repelling themselves from the ground and dragging the rest of the mountains with them. These mountains are absolutely awe-inspiring, and are covered with plants and waterfalls.

We rode the Flight of Passage ride with Diego and Dr. Paul Frommer, our good friend who invented the Na'vi language. More on that later. We then went to Satu'li Canteen, where we were treated to a Na'vi lesson over an alien inspired brunch. I also got Diego to sign my copy of the Activist Survival Guide, an in-universe guide to Pandora that was created and sold when the movie initially came out. Diego said that, more than any engineering manual, this book was his and the other Imagineeers' guide in creating Pandora.

At another point, I had lunch at Satu'li Canteen. The idea is that it provides alien-inspired foods that humans can eat. They make these delicious bowls of food combining salad, meat protein, and sauce. Everything, including the meat at this location is organically grown. There are a number of vegetarian options. You can actually see them cooking the meat in the location. There is also an exhibition of Na'vi cookware in the canteen.

We also went to the gift shop, Windtraders, where they have a number of really awesome products. The highlight is a banshee rookery where you can select a banshee, or ikran, as the Na'vi call them—or it just might select you! These ikrans are robotic, and come with sound effects, and can be mounted to your shoulder or to a perch that you may purchase. I have named mine Tìronsrel, which means Imagination in Na'vi. I have also purchased an avatar, which I have named Älexänter te Frayzer Txawnält'itan, or Älek, for short. My personal mythology says that it has been turned into Na'vi by passing through the Eye of Eywa, much as Jake Sully did in the film. They actually scan your face and let you choose a number of the characteristics of your avatar, including stripe pattern, age, gender, hairstyle, eye color, and other facets. It takes at least half an hour to render your face into the Na'vi form. A note about Na'vi naming: The first name is the given name. The "te" comes from the word "ta", which means "from". The second name is the family name. The third name means "son or daughter of..." Males have their father's name mentioned in the third name, while females have their mother's name. I would imagine that intersex children may choose or have both. Dr. Frommer is very friendly to LGBTQ causes.

There is also a refreshment stand called Pongu Pongu, which sells exotic alien-inspired drinks! My favorite is the Night Blossom. A number of my friends and I also posed in front of Pongu Pongu, where they have an old AMP suit, or military exoskeleton, from the time when humans and Na'vi were enemies on Pandora. Pongu Pongu is also decorated with other old artifacts from the former military times on Pandora such as dog tags and various drinking vessels.

Please note that the Valley of Mo'ara and Pandora as you see it at Disney World take place several generations after the events of the films, when humans and Na'vi are at peace. A number of the plants are artificial alien plants, but the Imagineeers also took advantage of the rich abundance of Central Florida and the plethora of plants that grow there. One of the big draws of the film Avatar is the feeling of serenity you have after seeing it. This feeling of serenity exists in the theme park, as well.

One of the theme park rides is the Na'vi River Journey, in which you journey along a bioluminescent river as it glows in the dark, and creatures move around you. The amazing thing is that, although some of the creatures and all the plants are three-dimensional, most of the creatures and the Na'vi are actually on screens embedded in the foliage. At the end, the Na'vi tribes also gather around you, and you are greeted by the Shaman of Songs, easily the most advanced robotic ever built by man, who looks like she is actually real. Following the greeting from the Shaman, you see a number of totemic artifacts left by the Na'vi.

A Totem in the Valley of Mo'ara

Throughout the ride, you will hear the Shaman Song, at first sung by faceless Na'vi, and later sung by the Shaman herself. Here it is below, first in Na'vi, and then in English.

The Shaman Song

Na'vi
Ma Na'rìng alor, mì Na'rìng lu tsngawpay.
Atokirina'
Awnga leym, lereym san...
Ma Eywa, Ma Eywa, Ma Eywa.

'Awstengyawnem, Ma Sa'nok aNawm
Atokirina'
Awnga leym, lereym san...
Ma Eywa, Ma Eywa, Ma Eywa.

Tìnewfa leNa'vi, Na'rìng tìng lawr
Atokirina'
Awnga leym, lereym san...
Ma Eywa, Ma Eywa, Ma Eywa.

English

Oh beautiful Forest, there are tears in the Forest

Woodsprites
We call out, calling out...
Oh Eywa, oh Eywa, oh Eywa.

Connected as one,
oh Great Mother
Woodsprites
We call out, calling out...
Oh Eywa, oh Eywa, oh Eywa.

By the People's will,
The Forest is singing
Woodsprites
We call out, calling out
Oh Eywa, oh Eywa, oh Eywa.

Another highlight is the Swotu Wayä Na'vi Drum Ceremony, where human drummers who have assimilated to Na'vi culture sing, dance, and play drums, inviting you to join them and the clans on this magical world. The lyrics of their songs are as follows, first in Na'vi, and then in English.

Song 1: Spaw Eywati (Believe Eywa)

Na'vi
Spaw! Rol! Rey!

Swotu!
Eywa ngahu!
Rol! Srew! Spaw!
Wou!
O-ey-o!

English
Believe! Sing! Live!
Sacred Place!
Eywa be with you!
Sing! Dance! Believe!
It's awesome!
Oay-oh!

Song 2: Leym Ayolo'ru (Call the clans)

Na'vi
Leym san ma Tipani! Za'u! Za'u!
Leym san ma Kekunan! Za'u! Za'u!
Leym san ma Tawkami! Za'u! Za'u!
Leym san ma Anurai! Za'u! Za'u!
Leym san ma Omatikaya! Za'u! Za'u!

English
Calling the Tipani: Join us! Join us!
Calling the Kekunan: Join us! Join us!
Calling the Tawkami: Join us! Join us!
Calling the Anurai: Join us! Join us!

Calling the Omaticaya: Join us! Join us!

Song 3: Slu Na'viyä Hapxì (Become one of the people)

Na'vi
Eywa! Lawnol! Kato! Toruk Makto! Omatikaya!
Ma Sa'nok aNawm! Tìnew leNa'vi!

English
Eywa! Great joy! Rhythm! Toruk rider! Omaticaya!
Oh Great Mother! The People's will!

During this last song, the drummers invite a member of the audience to come up and join the clans. I was absolutely thrilled to see my friend Linda, who is quite possibly the most loving person I've ever met, join in and drum in this celebration of life.

The single greatest attraction on Pandora is Flight of Passage, a ride in which you actually get to fly with the Na'vi through the rich landscape of Pandora. The ride actually starts with the beginning of the line, at which there are totemic figures made out of sticks and reeds by the Na'vi.

After that, you enter a cave system containing a number of cave paintings left by the Na'vi. One noteworthy illustration depicts a triumphant Na'vi rising above a blue avatar handprint superimposed on a red human handprint. Could this be a representation of Jake Sully, the Toruk Makto from the original film? In another part of the cave, the Toruk soars above all.

Further on, you come across a human lab with a number of

experiments going on, and a number of materials paying reference to parts of the film and the ride introduction sequences. There is also an actual avatar floating in its tank in suspended animation. The quality of Disney workmanship is absolutely superb. Most of the time, Disney rides and attractions are above and beyond any other entertainment experience. In this case, Pandora at the Animal Kingdom is above and beyond anything else that Disney has ever done. You eventually go through and are matched to an avatar, as well as being decontaminated of parasites, educated about conservation, and about various aspects of Na'vi culture there are, in fact, three different levels of the ride, each with different intro sequences. You are then mounted on a link chair, and transported onto the back of a banshee. The sights, sounds, feelings, smells, and everything else will convince you that you're really there. You even feel the creature breathing beneath you, smell the plants of the forest, and get sprayed by the water beneath you. The ride also adds new elements to the Avatar mythology, with new plants and wildlife making appearances for the first time.

The first time I rode Flight of Passage, I was between Diego Parras, the head of communications for Disney Imagineering, and Dr. Paul Frommer, inventor of the Na'vi language. A number of times during my first couple times on the ride, I broke into tears with how wonderful the experience was for me. At other times I was hooting and hollering in the exhilaration. I told Diego after we got off the ride that, according to my five senses, I was actually party to riding on a banshee. It is by far the best ride I've ever been on. Diego told me, "Here at Disney, we do not build roller coasters or Ferris wheels. Instead, we strive to build emotional connections." It clearly worked. At the exit of the ride are the handprints of *Avatar* producer and director James Cameron, *Avatar* producer Jon Landau, and the chief Imagineer on the project, Joe Rohde. For those who are interested in the lines said by your guide during the ride, I include them below, first in Na'vi, and then in English.

Alaksi srak? Nong oet!	Ready? Follow me!
Fìfya'o!	This way!
Nìler.	[Fly] steadily!
Nari si.	Careful.
Tam. Var kiva.	Okay. Keep going.
Tsun tivam.	Not bad.
May' fikem sivi.	Try this.
Eywa ftxoley.	Eywa has chosen.
Alaksi lu nga. Tsun fikem sivi.	You're ready. You can do this.
Siva ko!	Rise to the challenge!
Soleia!	You rose to the challenge!
Makto ko.	Let's ride.
May' fikem sivi.	Try this!
Eywa'eveng. Oey kelku.	Pandora. My home.
Nìn tsat, sätaron.	Look, a hunt.
'Ä' ... Ke li!	Whoops ... not yet!
Oel ngati kameie.	I See you. (singular)

There are a few living creatures depicted in the Valley of Mo'ara as well. One is the Sagittaria, a squirting aquatic creature that resembles a cross between a mollusk and a crustacean.

At night, everything lights up, including these creatures, resembling the bioluminescence of the plants and animals in the film. Some of the plants that light up only light up on the tips of their blooms, whereas other plants light up in total.

Pandora is absolutely amazing, and I am so glad that I have got to share just a small portion of my wonderful visit with you. As they say on Pandora, "Oel ayngati kameie," or "I see you."

Dare to Dream:
An Autistic Advocate's Visit to
the Kennedy Space Center

I was in Florida for the AvatarMeet. We don't just do things directly related to Avatar during these meetups, so on one day during our meetup, we went to the John F. Kennedy Space Center (KSC), our nation's port in our adventure towards the stars.

I started the day by hearing a briefing about our nation's state of affairs in space. We have several programs taking place at the current moment, as well as partnership with several other nations. One of these greatest programs is the International Space Station (ISS), arguably the grandest symbol of international peace and cooperation ever produced by humanity, in which individuals from several nations and materials from several regions of the globe are used to work in unison for the betterment of mankind. We also learned that within a year and a half, Americans will continue launching into space from the Kennedy Space Center.

After this briefing, we in the audience got to hear from Mike Foreman, an actual astronaut who had been on two missions. His first mission was as a general-purpose specialist on the Space Shuttle. On his second mission, he helped several others restock and resupply the ISS, and he even did two spacewalks. Resupply missions are vitally important, and maintain our continued presence in space. After giving his talk, people were given the opportunity to meet and have photos taken with Foreman. I met him, and he saw my Ithaca Is Gorges T-shirt, and asked if I had gone to Cornell. I told him I had gone to the State University of New York at Buffalo, but that Ithaca is my hometown. I told him that I do disability rights advocacy, and we each told the other how proud we are of each other's work.

After this, I had lunch with people from the fan meetup, followed by a tour of the Rocket Garden. The Rocket Garden chronicles our mission to perfect the ideal space going vehicle. In the beginning, we were literally using missiles intended for weapons to shoot people into space. These missiles were relatively small, and also gave a really rough ride, not at all intended for human beings. Our tour guide talked about the first few satellites, and the first manned space programs, Mercury and Gemini. We saw the rockets use to launch each satellite and program. Mercury was meant to see ourselves into space. There were no scientific goals, and no way to actually live in space. There were intended to be seven astronauts, but we wound up with six. The first two were sub-orbital flights launched by the Redstone missile. Unfortunately, the Redstone lacked the thrust to get us into orbit, but thanks to computers like Katherine Johnson, we learned that the Atlas rocket could. The Gemini program was meant to actually test how we could live in space. In Gemini, we ate, slept, spacewalked, did detailed tasks, and even celebrated Christmas. We also learned how to dock with other vehicles, how to manipulate the course and direction of our spacecraft, how to rendezvous with other spacecraft, and achieved other significant goals. The Gemini spacecraft were launched aboard the Titan II missile, which gave an incredibly rough ride. Finally, it was time to launch the Apollo program, and get ourselves to the moon. The first few Apollo launchers took place on the Saturn IB rocket, which launched us to Earth orbit in the Apollo capsules. The Saturn IB was also launched to get us to the Skylab space station. We saw all of these rockets, and more, and also tried out basic versions of the Mercury, Gemini, and Apollo space capsules.

After this, I went to the gift shop, of course, and then waited for my friends. You see, we had booked the opportunity of a lifetime. We were going to be shown the headquarters facilities and launch facilities for the American space program. We started out being shown the Industrial Area Facilities of the Kennedy Space Center. It is here where the American space program and its missions are administered. A lot of activity is currently taking place! They are currently demolishing the old computer building, after building a new one. We saw both. Computers have gotten smaller and smaller, and so the space needed to contain them has as well. In addition, it is not a bad idea to have an updated building for such sensitive materials. There are also two headquarters buildings: the old one, which is being phased out, and the new one, which is just being finished. There is another building dedicated specifically to operations on the ISS. There are other buildings dedicated towards the development of outer space missions, as well as a communication center, a gas station, and a fire station.

Next, we got to see the Launch Pad 39 Complex. For the longest time, American rockets and space vehicles have been constructed inside the massive Vehicle Assembly Building (VAB). The VAB is the sixth largest building in the world by volume. The volume of the Empire State Building could fit inside it five times. It is 526 feet in height. The American flag painted on its side is 21 stories tall, and each star is 6 feet across. Rockets and other space vehicles are built inside it on top of mobile launch platforms, and then wheeled out to one of the launch pads in the complex. Because of the massive weight that the mobile launch platforms must transport, they move incredibly slowly. Much more slowly than the walking human being. There is a joke that if someone sees a turtle walking the same direction in front of the mobile launch platform, they should let it be, because it will get to its destination more quickly than the launch platform will! There are also several buildings surrounding the VAB, including buildings formerly used to outfit the Space Shuttle, which are currently used for outfitting other vehicles. The military is also using one of these buildings for a top-secret project. In addition, there is a launch control Center next to the VAB, and the nearby area for the press.

We next went to see Launch Pad 39A. Over half of the Space Shuttle missions launched from this launch pad. More importantly, every single mission that humanity launched to the moon launched from here as well. The fact that we have gone to the moon is the realization of an incredible dream, the journey of mankind. At the next stop, we got to see that journey up close and personal.

As you enter the Apollo/Saturn V Center, you learn about the absolute failures of the early American space program, and how achieving any real progress in space seemed like a pipe dream at the beginning. You are shown the failure of rocket after rocket, failures so horrible that they look like a bad blooper reel. Then you learn about the launch of the Mercury program, and the challenge a few days later by President John F. Kennedy to land a man on the moon and get him safely home by the end of the decade. That was a truly Herculean task to live up to. They talk about the progress of the early Apollo program, and the tragic loss of the crew of Apollo 1. Then, you are led into the Firing Room. The Firing Room is the exact same launch control room that was used during Apollo 8, the first manned launch of a Saturn V rocket. This is the biggest and most complex machine ever produced by mankind. In the Firing Room, you are on pins and needles as you witness the successful launch of Apollo 8. Then, as if in a dream, you are led to see the stunning achievement of humanity.

Here, laid on its side before you, is the massive Saturn V rocket. It is the biggest, most complicated machine ever created by man. There is only one that has been maintained intact into the current day, and it stretches out before you, seemingly endlessly. Alongside it are the mission patches of the various Apollo missions, hanging from the ceiling. There are also various artifacts, including a bona fide Command and Service Module (CSM), as well as a Lunar Module (LM). There is also a mockup of the cockpit of the LM so that you feel like you're actually there on the moon.

There are other artifacts as well. There is the command module of the Apollo 14 mission, which was given the callsign Kitty Hawk, after the location of the first heavier than air flight. There is a moon rock for you to touch, and an equipment wagon and a lunar Rover made for lunar operation.

There are space suits, various lunar artifacts, and Snoopy... Wait a second... Did I just say Snoopy!? Well, you see, several the Apollo program engineers started informally drawing Snoopy, so they asked peanuts cartoonist Charles Schultz whether they would be allowed to make the famous beagle's likeness. He said no, absolutely not, but that he would make it for them. As such, Snoopy became sort of the mascot of the Apollo program, and there is a statue of him in a spacesuit. However, try as they might, NASA physicists cannot figure out how his nose would have fit into the helmet. An intractable problem for the ages!

There is also a monument and a gallery dedicated to memorializing the astronauts lost in the Apollo 1 mission. At the time, American spacecraft used a pure oxygen atmosphere. If one remembers the Hindenburg disaster, they will recall that hydrogen is combustible. Oxygen is not combustible, but it is incredibly flammable. Some electric equipment sparked while the Apollo 1 crew was having a test on the launchpad. The triple-layer door was too difficult to open, and they all completely cooked in the capsule. Those doors are on display in the gallery. Because of this terrible accident, over 38,000 changes were made to the engineering of American space technology, many of which still last to this day. These changes have saved many, many lives. The door now takes a fraction of the time to open, and the atmosphere aboard all American spacecraft now has mixed content just like Earth's atmosphere instead of being pure oxygen. Some people will die in our quest for space, that is a given. The quest for the stars is too great a dream, though, and we should never lose sight of our goal.

Finally, you head into the Lunar Theater, where the landing of the Apollo 11 Lunar Module, Eagle, is actually reenacted on stage in front of you. You see video of astronauts both playing and studying on the moon. The American flag is planted, and there is more video of those same astronauts talking about the terrific wonders that we have achieved. The ascent module then lifts off to join the command module Columbia and head home. There is then video of the dreams of children, many of whom wish to go into space. Finally, the late Neil Armstrong appears on video. He talks about how, when he was born, we had just managed to cross the Atlantic by airplane. He says that when he was a kid, he thought that landing on the moon would take place centuries into the future, and certainly had no clue that he would be the first person to do so. He states that we came not from one country, but in peace for all mankind. He says that you should never be afraid to dream. The vision of Mars appears on stage. Our guide at the Kennedy Space Center confirmed to us that NASA plans to get us to Mars and back safely by 2035. That is within my lifetime. What once was considered impossible is now attainable.

Now for a personal story. When I was in early elementary school, the authorities behind the school tried to have me locked up for the rest of my life. They said that I would never amount to anything, and that there was no use in trying. My loving family fought tooth and nail, and parents and professionals, as well as friends, raised me into who I am today. I have since made endless friends, graduated from college with a master's degree, gotten an excellent job, and helped change the lives of millions, especially those of us with disabilities. Never, ever be afraid to dream. Dreams are attainable. The impossible is possible.

The late Carl Sagan was fond of saying that we are all made of star dust. In our journey to the stars, we are simply going home. Thank you, for joining me on this tour.

When I Die

My religious views are quite unconventional. In terms of organized religion, I belong to the Unitarian Universalist Association of Congregations, or UUA. In terms of actual beliefs, I believe in the dictates of reason, and then therefore a humanist. In addition, I have a live and let live philosophy, and I am a right reverend minister in the Church of the Latter-Day Dude, a genuine, federally recognized faith based on the live and let live philosophy of the Jeff Bridges's character The Dude from the Coen Brothers Comedy, "The Big Lebowski". Furthermore, I believe that if there is any divine presence, then it is the wherewithal of everything in this universe together. The best interpretation of this presence is the goddess Eywa from James Cameron's Avatar. She is a very humanist goddess. What follows is my wishes for my funeral in celebration of life.

When I die, I wish to be buried in the Frazier burial plot outside of Bondad/Elco, Colorado. I would prefer to be buried in earth, without a casket. If law requires a casket, a simple wooden one will suffice. I wish to be naked. I wish for a simple marker, to say:

Alexander Fuld Frazier
June 22, 1986 - [Date of Death]

With my body should be my Fraser of Lovat Coat of Arms, images of my family including my mother, father, brother and any significant others and children, the United Nations Declaration of Human Rights, and icons of the Unitarian Universalist Chalice, the Humanist Happy Human, and a copy of The Big Lebowski. Any other keepsakes my friends and family wish to place with me are acceptable.

Before the burial, the assembled should recite the Tree Song (Funeral Song) in Na'vi, the lyrics of which are thus:

[Utralä (a)Nawm   We are all seeds
ayrina'l(u) ayoeng,   Of the Great Tree,
A peyä tìtxur mì hinam awngeyä   Whose strength is in our legs
N(a) aysangek afkeu,   Like the mighty trunks,
Mì pun   In our arms
N(a) ayvul ahusawnu,   As sheltering branches,
M(ì) aynar   In our eyes
Na seze   The blue-flower
A 'ong ne tsawke.   Which unfolds to the sun.

Utralä (a)Nawm   We are all seeds
ayrina' l(u) ayoeng,   Of the Great Tree
A peyä tìrol m(ì) awnga.]   Whose song is within us.

Anyone present should feel free to say what they wish.

After my body is committed, the assembled should recite, in Na'vi: [Oel ngati kameie, ma tsmukan, ulte ngaru seiyi irayo. Ngari hu Eywa salew tirea, tokx 'ì'awn slu Na'viyä hapxì.]

The translation follows: [I see you, brother, and I thank you. Your spirit will run with Eywa, while your body will remain and become part of the People.]

My friends and family should, at some point, have the mother of all parties to honor my life.

Thank you.

Autistic Reality is a charitable organization,
and this publication of Veni! Vidi! Autism! and our previous publication of
Without Fear: The First Autistic Superhero are both educational.

As such, all sales of both of these two publications are exempt from New York State sales tax. This has been independently verified with officers of the New York State Department of Taxation and Finance. For your own reference, we recommend you look up New York State publication 750, A Guide to Sales Tax in New York State.

Any and all organizations or individuals who have in the past, are currently, or in the future require Autistic Reality to present a New York State sales tax Certificate of Authority are violating New York State law. Autistic Reality reserves the right to terminate business relations with any of the said parties.

50303904R00205

Made in the USA
Middletown, DE
25 June 2019